UNDER THE SHADOW OF THE RISING SUN

JAPAN AND THE JEWS DURING THE HOLOCAUST ERA

Series Editor: Roberta Rosenberg Farber (Yeshiva University)

Editorial Board

Sara Abosch (University of Memphis)

Geoffrey Alderman (University of Buckingham)

Yoram Bilu (Hebrew University)

Steven M. Cohen (Hebrew Union College – Jewish Institute of Religion)

Bryan Daves (Yeshiva University)

Sergio Della Pergola (Hebrew University)

Simcha Fishbane (Touro College)

Deborah Dash Moore (University of Michigan)

Uzi Rebhun (Hebrew University)

Reeva Simon (Yeshiva University)

Chaim I. Waxman (Rutgers University)

UNDER THE SHADOW OF THE RISING SUN

JAPAN AND THE JEWS DURING THE HOLOCAUST ERA

Meron Medzini

BOSTON
2016

Library of Congress Cataloging-in-Publication Data

Names: Medzini, Meron, author.

Title: Under the shadow of the rising sun : Japan and the Jews during the Holocaust era / Meron Medzini.

Other titles: Be-tsel ha-shemesh ha-°olah. English

Description: Boston : Academic Studies Press, 2016.

Series: Jewish identities in post-modern society

Identifiers: LCCN 2016037874 (print) | LCCN 2016038066 (ebook) | ISBN 9781618115225 (hardback) | ISBN 9781618115232 (e-book)

Subjects: LCSH: Jews—Japan—History—20th century. | Jewish refugees—Japan. | Jewish refugees—China. | Antisemitism—Japan. | Japan—Politics and government—1926-1945. | Japan—Ethnic relations. |

BISAC: SOCIAL SCIENCE / Jewish Studies. | HISTORY / Asia / Japan. | HISTORY / Asia / General.

Classification: LCC DS135.J3 M4313 2016 (print) | LCC DS135.J3 (ebook) | DDC 940.53089/924052—dc23 LC record available at https://lccn.loc.gov/2016037874

ISBN 978-1-644690-31-4
ISBN 978-1-61811-523-2 (electronic)
©Academic Studies Press, 2016

Book design by Kryon Publishing, www.kryonpublishing.com
Cover design by Ivan Grave

Published by Academic Studies Press
28 Montfern Avenue
Brighton, MA 02135, USA
press@academicstudiespress.com
www.academicstudiespress.com

Contents

Preface	vi
Introduction	ix
Chapter 1: Early Jewish Settlers in Japan	1
Chapter 2: Jewish Settlers in Japan at the Beginning of the Twentieth Century	9
Chapter 3: Japanese Images of the Jews: Myths, Canards and Fears	13
Chapter 4: Nazi Antisemitism and its Influence on Japan in the 1920's and 1930's	29
Chapter 5: Japanese Experts on Jews, Judaism, and Zionism	39
Chapter 6: Japan and the Jews of Manchuria Beginning in 1931	49
Chapter 7: Passports, Entry Visas, and Transit Visas: Japan's policy toward Jewish Refugees (1935-1941)	64
Chapter 8: The Jews of Shanghai under Japanese Rule	71
Chapter 9: Jews in the Japanese-Occupied Territories during the War Years	84
Chapter 10: A Japanese Righteous Gentile: The Sugihara Case	117
Chapter 11: The Japanese Policy toward the Jews in Japan's Home Islands	129
Chapter 12: "The Jewish Question" in Japanese-German relations, 1936-1945	138
Chapter 13: The Japanese, the Holocaust of European Jewry, and Israel	149
Selected Bibliography	178
References	198
Index	214

Preface

Among the tens of thousands of publications about the Holocaust, including memoirs, diaries, official documents, research papers, and historical volumes, comparatively few are devoted to the history of the Jews in East Asia during that era, and even fewer deal specifically with Japan's attitude, policies, and behavior toward Jews in the years 1933-1945. Most of the works dealing with the fate of the Jewish communities in East Asia are devoted to the history of the two largest Jewish communities in the region, those of Harbin and Shanghai, which had been growing since the late 1930s. Other communities, including the tiny one in the Japanese home islands, are nearly completely neglected.

This dearth of material derives perhaps from the fact that the number of Jews who found themselves living within the Japanese Empire in East and Southeast Asia in the years preceding and during World War II was very small. Another reason may be that most of these Jews, who numbered some 40,000 in all, survived the war and were treated by the Japanese in a somewhat more humane manner than European Jews were by Nazi Germany during the Holocaust. The Jews of East and South East Asia, like other foreign settlers who were not nationals of Germany and Italy, were put in detention and even concentration camps, prisons, and prisoner-of-war camps, but apart from several thousand Jews in Shanghai, none of them were put in ghettoes. The Japanese never built or operated extermination camps and crematoria, nor did they murder Jews because of their race or religion. The idea of genocide against this group of foreigners never crossed their minds.

Another reason for the near-total lack of research has to do with the fact that until recently, Israeli scholars and laymen had very little interest in the fate of Jews in Asia during the war. For most Israelis, the Holocaust took place in Europe. Most did not even hear of what happened to Jewish communities in Asia. There were no tales of feats of heroism and resistance, nothing like the Warsaw Ghetto Uprising or the Jewish involvement in anti-Nazi partisan warfare in Poland and other parts of Eastern Europe. In fact, the Jews of Asia do not appear to have displayed any resistance to the Japanese forces at all. Nor did they suffer from death marches. Virtually all of the Jews who survived the war in Asia emigrated at its conclusion to the United States, Canada, Britain, or Australia. Some went back to the countries from whence they came—Holland, France, or even Germany. Few of them immigrated to Israel, and thus few Israelis were available to perpetuate the memory of their brethren who fell under the Japanese occupation of the countries in which they resided.

In Japan too there was an attempt to dissociate from Nazi Germany, and certainly Japan wanted no part of blame for the Holocaust, in which they had not been involved. The Japanese government claimed—and rightly so, as will be discussed later in this volume—that Japan never adopted Nazi-style antisemitism and that it did not take part in the implementation of Hitler's Final Solution; rather, it tried to behave humanely toward the Jews under its rule.

The present study attempts to trace the experience of the Jews under Japanese rule in the 1930's and 1940's. It raises and aims to address some of the following questions: What was the general attitude of the Japanese people towards the Jews, and what did they know about them? Why did they ignore repeated demands by Nazi Germany, their ally, that they harm the Jews? What was their policy toward the Jews living in the territories they captured during the Pacific War (Dec. 7 1941-Aug. 15 1945)?

At the outset of this work, it can be stated that although many Jews did experience Japanese brutality in the occupied areas, they were not persecuted because of their religion, and the fact that they were Jews did not single them out from other Western aliens under the Japanese occupation.

After the Second World War, as will be discussed, the Japanese people and even its government displayed no knowledge of the Nazi-perpetrated Holocaust that exterminated six million Jews. The Japanese did not display any special interest in the Holocaust, mainly because they were busy with adjusting to the results of their own "Shoah"—their crushing defeat in the war and the horrific results of the two atomic bombs dropped on Hiroshima and Nagasaki in August 1945. As Germany's allies during the war, they preferred not to delve into the terrible crimes committed by the Nazis.

The actions of a single Japanese official, Sugihara Chiune, who issued over two and a half thousand transit visas to Polish and Lithuanian Jews allowing them and their families to travel to Japan in the summer of 1940, thus saving them from extermination, won him the title of Righteous Gentile, a title bestowed by the Yad Vashem Holocaust Memorial Authority in Jerusalem. He is the only Japanese person to date who has received this unique honor and recognition.

Despite the virtual silence on this subject in literature, as strange as it may seem, there was antisemitism in Japan, a country with barely a thousand

Jews, at the beginning of the twentieth century, and it raised its ugly head once again toward the closing decades of that century. It may also have influenced the evolution of Israel-Japan relations, which were established in 1952.

The Hebrew version of this book was an outgrowth of a radio series broadcast in the framework of the University of the Air of the Israel Defense Forces' Radio station in 2008. I wish to express my gratitude to the editor of the series, Dr. Hagai Boaz, and to the heads of the Louis Frieberg Center for East Asia Studies at the Hebrew University, Professors Gideon Shelach and Yuri Pines, for their support and for the scholarship awarded me to complete work on this book. The editor of the Hebrew version was the always-meticulous Yishai Cordova. Thank you also to Igor Nemirovsky and Academic Studies Press, who are publishing the English edition of this book, and to the English editor, Sharona Vedol, who has been a great help in preparing the present volume for publication. It is also my pleasure to express my gratitude to Professor Chiharu Inaba of Nagoya University for his very useful comments and additions. Rabbi Marvin Tokayer, a pioneer in the study of Japan and the Jews, also provided some much-needed advice, as did Professor Kiyoshi Ueda of Hosei University. The Joint Distribution Committee Archives in Jerusalem was a source of many illuminating documents about the work of that organization in China, Japan, and the Philippines during the war years. I owe special thanks to my colleagues and friends Professors Ben-Ami Shillony and Rotem Kowner for reading the entire text, making very useful comments, and saving me from errors. Those errors that may have remained are naturally my responsibility.

Introduction

During the most horrific time in the recent history of the Jewish people, the destruction of European Jewry in what became known as the Holocaust, several nations stood out as bright rays in the darkest nightmare. The world witnessed the murder of some six million Jews by the German Nazi state and its collaborators in various European countries, and some brave nations tried to intervene. One was German-occupied Denmark, whose people prevented some seven thousand Jews from being sent to death camps in October 1943 by helping them escape by sea to neighboring Sweden, a neutral country that granted them shelter. Another country was Bulgaria: although its government collaborated with Nazi Germany, its leaders and people opposed the dispatching of some fifty thousand Bulgarian Jews to the death camps. A third country, Spain, was also a collaborator of Nazi Germany, but for various reasons its fascist government allowed some forty thousand Jews, mainly from the German-occupied parts of France and Vichy-ruled France, to pass through on their way to safer places. True, it was recently discovered that Franco's Spain provided the German government with the names of the six thousand members of the Jewish community living in that country during the war, but at the time the Spanish government took no action against those Jews living in its territory.

Japan—a country that was one of the three members of the Axis Alliance, with Nazi Germany and Fascist Italy—neither went out of its way either to rescue Jews from the European inferno nor sought out and destroyed those Jews who came under its rule from 1931 to 1945. It could have been assumed that Japan would agree to carry out the Final Solution ordered by Hitler against the Jewish people, but for a variety of reasons that will be discussed later, Japan basically ignored repeated German demands that it exterminate the Jews living in the Japanese home islands, the territories Japan had occupied since 1931, and those areas under its control during the Second World War. As was mentioned in the introduction, there was even one Japanese official—Sugihara Chiune—who granted over 2600 Japanese transit visas to Polish and Lithuanian Jews who were ostensibly on their way to the Caribbean Island of Curacao, then a Dutch colony. By doing so he enabled some six thousand Jews to escape incarceration in Soviet prisons or almost certain death at the hands of the Nazis. Some of those Jews remained in Japan even after the December 7, 1941, attack on Pearl Harbor, and many were sent by the Japanese authorities to Shanghai, where almost all survived the war in the Shanghai Jewish ghetto. Sugihara's role in saving Jews is still contested and will be examined in Chapter 10 in greater detail.

Until the early 1960's, not much was known about Japan's attitude to the Jews. Research at that time barely touched on issues dealing with the Jewish community in Japan: its human composition; the number of Jews who lived in Japan before the war; their impact (if any) on the Japanese social, political, cultural, and economic environments; what Japanese society knew about Jews; Japan's policy toward Jewish refugees escaping from Europe; the nature of the antisemitic literature that flourished in Japan beginning in the 1920's; or the reason it flourished in a country whose Jewish community numbered less than a thousand people (out of a population of some 74 million). What were the origins of antisemitism in Japan, and why didn't the Japanese government and military adopt any measures to harm the Jews? Why, furthermore, did it enable thousands of Jews to survive while millions of their brethren in Europe were being systematically exterminated in death camps? What was the nature and what were the dimensions of this anti-Jewish sentiment in a country that hardly had any Jews, and the majority of whose people had never seen or met a Jew in their lives?

Until the early 1960's, there was little attempt to perform an in-depth study of the nature of Japanese antisemitism and its dimensions in comparison to the enormous respect and appreciation many Japanese people had for Jews and Judaism, evidenced by the fairly large number of publications that sought to understand the roots of Jewish power and why the Jews had earned a name as movers and shakers in international politics and finance. Thus, the theme of fear, envy, and hatred of Jews coupled with curiosity and an admiration for and awe of Jewish power is one that will run throughout this study.

In 2012, Israel and Japan marked the sixtieth anniversary of the establishment of diplomatic relations, relations that today form a major asset in Israel's presence and standing in East Asia. The time is ripe to pose, once again, such questions as what Japan's policy toward the Jews was; whether the Jews living in Japan since the Meiji Restoration had any influence on Japanese political, economic, social, and cultural life; and above all, why Japan, rejecting repeated appeals by its Nazi allies, allowed some 40,000 Jews in the territories under its control since 1931 to remain alive.

In recent years, there has been a growing interest in Japan, Germany, and Israel regarding the topic of Japan's attitude toward the Jews during the Holocaust era. Inevitably, this has led to interest in the Japanese attitude toward the Jews since the opening of Japan in 1853. Two leading Israeli scholars have devoted considerable time and effort to the study of Japanese antisemitism. Professor Ben-Ami Shillony of the Asian studies department of the Hebrew University published a book on the subject.[1] He and Professor Rotem Kowner of the department of Asian studies at the University of Haifa have also produced many essays on this theme.[2] Yad Vashem has yet to undertake an in-depth study of Japan and the Jews during the Holocaust.

Interestingly, a number of studies written by German scholars have appeared in recent years, based on extensive use of German and Japanese diplomatic and consular documents as well as the protocols of the International Military Tribunals both in Germany and in Japan.[3] There is also extensive literature dealing with the history of the Jews of Shanghai beginning in the middle of the nineteenth century and mainly during the Second World War.[4] There are also a growing number of studies by Japanese scholars on this subject.[5]

The research undertaken so far points in various directions. Some scholars believe that Japanese antisemitism was in fact disguised anti-foreignism in general, and that after the Second World War it was a way to express anti-Americanism at a time when it was not politically expedient to be explicitly anti-American in Japan. Another theory is that Japan received its antisemitism from Nazi Germany, which some Japanese leaders sought to emulate. However, as we shall discuss, the origins of Japanese antisemitism predate Nazi Germany and appear to derive from White Russian exiles after the 1917 Russian Revolution, which some exiles claimed was inspired and led by Jews. Still another theory is that the attitude of the Japanese toward the Jews was no different than their general attitude toward foreigners (*gaijin*) at a time when the Japanese were trying to demonstrate their own uniqueness to the world. There are researchers who are convinced that antisemitic outbursts in Japan prior to World War II and even in the 1980's were due to the great admiration and respect of most Japanese people for the achievements of the Jews—in other words, they were manifestations of envy. Professor Ben-Ami Shillony feels that the fact that the Japanese and the Jews were the epitomes of "successful outsiders"—two non-Western, non-Christian people who successfully competed with the West in various fields of endeavor—was responsible for creating that sense of envy.[6]

At the outset of this study, it must be made clear that although antisemitic feelings did exist in this country with virtually no Jews, antisemitism was marginal among the average Japanese populace, mainly because the Jews were marginal in Japanese society. To the extent that it existed, it was mostly present among the educated strata in society, who sought to exploit antisemitic sentiments to promote radical right-wing, nationalist, and anti-Western ideologies to justify preparations for war against the United States and Britain, and even to justify some of the crimes committed against Chinese citizens during the second Sino-Japanese war (1937-1945). Antisemitic texts, starting with the forgery known as *The Protocols of the Elders of Zion* and extending to various books and essays written in the 1980s, have played a minor but at times influential role during the twentieth century.

Chapter 1

Early Jewish Settlers in Japan

Prior to the arrival in Japan of Jewish merchants from Europe and America in the second half of the 1850's, there is no evidence of Jewish presence in that country. Some writers conjecture that during the era known as Japan's Christian Century (1549-1638), Jewish seamen and merchants may have arrived in Japan either as crew members or as traders, mainly on board Dutch, Spanish, and Portuguese ships that called in Japan and anchored mainly off Nagasaki. A number of sources indicate that two Portuguese Conversos (Jews who had converted, whether forcibly or not, to Christianity) visited Japan in the sixteenth century. One of these two apparent Conversos was Mendes Pinto, a trader who came to Japan in 1537 and then proceeded to write a book about that country which became a major sourcebook for knowledge about Japan. The second, Dr. Luis Almeida, arrived in Japan in 1552 and was reported to have built the first European-style hospital there. He too produced a memoir. However, there is no mention of Jews in Japanese history books or memoirs of that era, nor are there Japanese Jewish graves or synagogues dating back to that period. Even in the Dutch history books that were translated to Japanese during the early part of the Tokugawa era (1600-1867), also known as the Edo period, there is no special mention or information about Jews.

Following the advent of the Tokugawa regime that took over Japan in 1600, the new ruling dynasty decided to close Japan to foreigners and to expel all of them—especially Christians—from their borders. The intention of this ruling was primarily to ensure the wellbeing and survival of the new regime and to prevent foreign intervention in domestic Japanese politics, which had been a serious problem in the years before Japan was reunited by the Tokugawa family. Trade with the West was permitted only via ships belonging to the Dutch East Indies Company, which were allowed to dock at an artificial island called Deshima in Nagasaki's harbor. Beginning in the the early eighteenth century, the Tokugawa regime permitted the translation from Dutch into Japanese of books dealing with science, medicine, geography, astronomy, military matters and warfare, navigation, coastal fortifications, and gunnery. However, it specifically forbade the translation of the New Testament and other works dealing with the Christian religion. The consequence of this rule was that even those few Japanese people who were exposed to the Dutch Learning School (*Rangakusha*) knew nothing about the Jewish origins of Christianity, Jewish history, or the connection between the Jewish people and the Land of Israel. Needless to say, there was no mention of Jews and Judaism in the Buddhist and Shinto texts more easily accessible.

Japan was formally opened to foreigners following the visit of an American flotilla commanded by Commodore Mathew C. Perry (1794-1858) in 1853. A treaty signed between Japan and the United States in 1854 specified that five Japanese port cities would be opened for trade and the settlement of foreigners, who would enjoy consular protection as well as the protection of the physical presence of their own troops. Among the ports to be opened in 1859 were those of Yokohama and Nagasaki. These soon attracted a number of Jews, the majority of whom initially came from South East Asia, China, the countries of Western Europe, and later from Eastern Europe and the United States.

The Nagasaki Community[1]

Jewish interest in the port of Nagasaki and its commercial potential originated among Middle Eastern Jews. It followed the growth and flourishing of the Jewish community in Shanghai after the first Opium War (1839-1842) and the opening of five treaty ports on the China coast. In 1842, shortly after the signing of the Treaty of Nanjing, which opened Shanghai to foreign trade, a number of Baghdadi Jewish merchants arrived in that port city. Among them were the Sassoon, Yehuda, Ezra, Kadoorie, and Hardoon families. The Kadoorie family is well known in modern Israel, having bequeathed money in the 1920's for the establishment of the Kadoorie agriculture school on the foothills of Mt. Tabor. Among its early graduates were three well-known Israeli figures: Israel Defense Forces chief of staff and later prime minister Yitzhak Rabin (1922-1995), general and later minister for foreign affairs Yigal Allon (1918-1980), and the writer-poet Chaim Guri (1923-).

The Kadoories and other merchants in Shanghai, Jewish and non-Jewish alike, heard of new business opportunities in Japan and decided to open branch offices for their companies in Nagasaki.[2] In February 1859, the David Sassoon and Sons Co. sent both cargo and an agent to Nagasaki to see if it could establish offices and warehouses in that port city. Its agent, M. Yehezkel, asked the local Japanese authorities for permission to obtain a site on Pier 4. Apparently that request was granted, but for reasons not specified the family decided not to station a permanent representative in Nagasaki and instead preferred to use the services of other companies. Perhaps the family sensed that Yokohama, nearer to Tokyo (then still called Edo), would become the central port for Japan and was thus the better place on which to focus their operations.[3]

Jewish presence and activity in Nagasaki started after the implementation of unequal treaties imposed by foreign powers on Japan. The first Japanese-American treaty was signed in 1854, and was followed by another in 1858. These led to a considerable growth in the number of foreigners in the Japanese port cities of Nagasaki and Yokohama. By 1860, an American Jewish trader by the name of Elias Tollman was active in Nagasaki. By the end of the decade, there already existed a Jewish section in the Nagasaki cemetery. The first Jew to be buried there was an American Jewish sailor by the name of Solomon Keeler. In the 1870's, a number of Jewish merchants who came from Eastern Europe by way of Shanghai and Harbin settled in Nagasaki. They focused on men's clothing and opened shops for the sale of hardware and construction material. Some opened inns which included taverns. At this stage, Jewish communal or social organizations and institutions were not yet established. The few Jews in Nagasaki were not wealthy enough to support communal institutions and activity, unlike some of their counterparts in Shanghai.

Soon there developed a communal leadership, made up of a certain number of people with means who were prepared to establish institutions and represent the community to the authorities. In the 1880's, two families that would play an important role in the Nagasaki community arrived in that port city: the Lassner family, headed by Sigmund David, who held Austro-Hungarian citizenship, and the Ginzburg family, whose ancestor Morris, a Russian Jew, escaped Tsarist Russia to avoid being conscripted into the army. In 1883 the latter family established the Ginzburg & Co. firm and began to trade with the Russian government.

Ginzburg & Co. helped the Russian government obtain Japanese coal for the Russian East Asian fleet, part of which anchored off Nagasaki during the winter because the waters of its home base in Vladivostok froze regularly. Soon the Ginzburg family obtained a concession to supply goods and services to the entire Russian fleet in East Asia, both the navy and merchant vessels. For his endeavors on behalf of Russia, Morris won three important things: amnesty for avoiding military service; a medal from the Tsar; and the right to trade inside Siberia. In 1892, Ginzburg purchased a plot in the Nagasaki international cemetery for the use of the Jewish community, and in September 1896 the community inaugurated its first synagogue, which was named *Beit Israel* (The House of Israel). The community continued to flourish, and soon a Jewish club and a welfare organization were established. By 1903, about a hundred Jews resided in Nagasaki, and their future looked bright.

However, a year later the Russo-Japanese war broke out, and since most of the Nagasaki Jews were Russian citizens and their main business was with the Russian fleet or non-governmental Russian companies, their fortune changed abruptly. As the war progressed, the Ginzburg family closed its business and left town. Nagasaki's Jewish communal leadership shifted to the Lassner family, Austro-Hungarian nationals, and it prospered. This era of prosperity was also short-lived. When the First World War broke out in August 1914 and Japan joined the Allies, Sigmund David Lassner—who held an Austrian passport—became an enemy national and was denied the right to conduct business, and his property was confiscated by the Japanese government.

Several Russian Jewish refugees arrived in Nagasaki after the Russian Revolution of 1905, and their numbers increased after the 1917 Bolshevik Revolution. Most of these new arrivals made their way to Yokohama and Kobe, which had now become Japan's two major ports. The Nagasaki community slowly dwindled, and by 1922 the remaining Jews there authorized the Shanghai Zionist Association to sell their communal property. Beit Israel synagogue was sold for $2,600 dollars (some half-million dollars today), and the check was sent to Nissim Benjamin Ezra, the president of the Shanghai Zionist Association. The synagogue's Torah scroll was given as a gift to the Kobe Jewish community. As of 1923, organized Jewish life in Nagasaki ceased to exist. When Japan and the Soviet Union established diplomatic and trade relations in 1925, the few remaining Nagasaki Jews were no longer involved in this trade. The decline and slow disappearance of the Nagasaki Jewish community paralleled the growth and strengthening of the Yokohama and Kobe communities.

The Yokohama Community[4]

The first Jews who settled in Yokohama were the Marks brothers, who arrived from Britain in 1861. One of them, Alexander Marks, even wrote articles about Japan for the London Jewish Chronicle. He became involved in importing wood from Australia, and apparently represented that country as an honorary consul. They were followed that year by the Baltimore-born Raphael Schoyer (1800-1865), who was a merchant and also established the first English language daily in Japan—*Japan Express*. The newspaper focused on shipping news and economic topics, and did not deal with Japanese politics and social issues. Schoyer also owned a printing press that printed Christian tracts in Yokohama. *Japan Express* barely mentioned one the greatest events in modern Japanese history, the 1868 Meiji Restoration, and continued to stick to the safer grounds of business and shipping news. Another American Jew introduced horse racing to Yokohama. At the beginning of the twentieth century, a family named Luria arrived from Russia, and its members became influential members of the community. More Jews arrived from America, Britain, and Russia.

The Meiji Restoration transformed Japan, through a series of reforms, from essentially an agrarian semi- feudal society to a major industrial and military regional and later a world power. By 1885, Yokohama had become the most important and largest port city of modern Japan, as it was situated next to Edo, now the newly renamed capital, Tokyo. Yokohama was thus attractive to foreigners in general as well as to Jews. Among the 16,000 foreigners who settled in Japan during the Restoration era were a number of Jews and the Jewish community of Yokohama grew and flourished. The community could now turn its attention to the establishment of communal institutions such as a synagogue, cemetery, and burial society. There is a Jewish grave in Yokohama dating to 1865, and the synagogue was inaugurated in 1892. By the 1870's, the community numbered some 70 families, who were seen by their Japanese neighbors as part of the Christian community, albeit one with its own unique religious rites that differed from those practiced by the Christians. The most important of these differences noticed by Japanese society was their observance of the Sabbath on Saturday instead of Sunday, their placement of mezuzot on their doorways, and the fact that they had their male children circumsized.

Another well-known Jew who lived in Yokohama was Benjamin Fleisher, who settled there in 1908. A scion of a wealthy Jewish family from Philadelphia, he bought and edited the *Japan Advertizer-Japan Times*, which he developed into the leading English newspaper in Japan. He also wrote for the *New York Times* and acted as a reporter for *United Press*.

Two German Jews played an important role in the development of the Japanese constitution and laws. The first was Albert Mosse (1846-1925), who arrived in Japan in 1886 and stayed for four years, advising the Japanese government on the development of a written constitution and on administrative law. He is well-remembered in Japan as a key member of the team that eventually wrote the Meiji Constitution, promulgated in 1889. During the Nazi era, the Japanese embassy in Berlin, aware that there was some discrimination against Jews in Germany, requested that the German government not discriminate against members of the Mosse family. Due to this intervention, the Mosse family was protected. The second prominent name is that of Ludwig Riess (1861-1928), who was invited to teach history at Tokyo University and stayed there from 1887 to 1902. The *Japan Biographical Encyclopedia* credits Riess with being the father of modern Japanese historiography. Mosse and Riess did not stress their Judaism and were not involved in the affairs of the Jewish community in Yokohama.

American-Jewish Capitalists and Russian-Jewish Soldiers

The 1905 Russo-Japanese War and the 1905 Revolution in Russia brought to Japan several hundred Russian Jews who escaped Tsarist Russia by way of Siberia and Manchuria, making their way east on the Trans-Siberian Railway that was completed after the Russo-Japanese War and facilitated their travel. The Russo-Japanese war also brought to Japan an awareness that Jews were different than Christians, even though many of them resided in Christian nations.

This process of slowly learning more about Jews occurred partly because the Russo-Japanese war also brought to Japan some 1,300 Russian Jews as prisoners of war, all of whom had been captured in Manchuria. This group was different from the Jews who already lived in Japan. They were soldiers, which was not an occupation the Japanese associated with Jews. The most outstanding among them was Lieutenant Yosef Trumpeldor (1880-1920), who had lost an arm in Port Arthur and set up a Zionist cell where Hebrew and the Bible were taught. The Jewish prisoners were placed in a prisoner-of-war camp at Hamadera near Osaka. The Jewish prisoners were divided into two groups: those who preferred to assimilate and join in with the non-Jewish Russian prisoners, and those, numbering several hundred, who were Zionist and were involved in Zionist activities under Trumpeldor's charismatic leadership. The religious needs of the Jewish prisoners were attended to by the Nagasaki, Kobe, and Yokohama Jewish communities, as well as by American Jewish organizations. It appears that the Japanese guards were quite impressed with the behavior of the Jewish prisoners, who preferred Hebrew and Bible studies to vodka and cards.[5]

The Russo-Japanese War caused Japan's leaders to take note for the first time of the economic capability and financial power of wealthy Jews in America and Britain and their influence on their respective governments. Shortly after the outbreak of the war, Japan's leaders realized that they would soon find themselves in a major financial crisis and would require massive international credit and loans to purchase weapons and ammunition, fuel, and food to continue waging the war. The deputy governor of the Bank of Japan, Takahashi Korekiyo (1854-1936) was sent to London in order to secure such loans. At a dinner party in London, he met the American Jewish millionaire Jacob Schiff (1847-1920), who was involved in business in Russia and had become interested in supporting liberal causes in that empire, hoping that the liberalization of the Tsarist regime would help Russian Jews. Schiff was a supporter of the more liberal policies of Finance Minister Sergey Witte (1849-1915), who espoused reforms and opposed the policies of Interior Minister Viacheslav Pleve (1846-1904).[6] Schiff was deeply affected by the anti-Jewish pogroms in Russia in 1903-1904, and was determined to help Japan defeat Russia in any way he could. Schiff's biographer, Cyrus Adler, explains that Schiff wanted to take vengeance for the pogroms and thought that if Japan won the war it would lead to greater social and political reforms, or even a revolution, in Russia, putting an end to the persecution of Jews. He undertook personally to help Japan win the war by securing her three loans from Jewish and non-Jewish bankers in London and New York. He responded to Takahashi's request for credit by setting up a consortium that mobilized a loan of £52 million sterling through having Schiff's own company, Kuhn, Loeb and Co., and others guarantee half that sum. Another £30 million sterling loan was granted by a group of Jewish bankers in London and New York, among them the Kassel and Warburg families. These loans helped Japan survive financially, even when Japan failed to win war restitution from the Russians in the Portsmouth Peace Treaty of September 1905.

Schiff was influential enough in Washington to intervene with President Theodore Roosevelt (1858-1919) and ask him to mediate between Russia and Japan, which led to peace negotiations in Portsmouth. He also helped members of the Japanese embassy in Washington reach the American media. Schiff's name became well-known among Japan's leaders. He visited that country after the war as a guest of the Meiji Emperor, who awarded him the Medal of the Rising Sun—the first time it was awarded to a non-Japanese person. The emperor even hosted Schiff in the imperial palace in Tokyo.

Years later, when Takahashi, who became the governor of the Bank of Japan and later finance minister and then prime minister of the country, sent his daughter to study in America, she lived with the Schiff family in New York City. This episode marks the beginning of the understanding (or myth) among Japan's political and economic elites that world Jewry is a tight-knit, powerful, and influential group with connections around the world—mainly in key western powers—and that when one needs to secure large sums of money, one should turn to them.[7]

The Russo-Japanese War and Japan's military victory over Russia had a major impact on Jews in Tsarist Russia and elsewhere, not to mention their impact on growing Asian and even Arab nationalism. Naftali Herz Imber, the author of "Hatikvah," the poem that became Israel's national anthem, even dedicated a book of his poetry to the Emperor of Japan. The Japanese victory, especially the naval victory in the battle of Tsushima shortly after the 1903-1904 pogroms, was seen as an omen. In his memoirs, Chaim Weizmann (1874-1952), the future first president of Israel, wrote that in 1905, while he was teaching chemistry at the University of Manchester, a Japanese student thought that he would be upset over the defeat of the Russian fleet by the Japanese navy in the battle of Tsushima Straits. The student kindly attempted to cheer him up, not realizing that Weizmann was in fact quite pleased by Russia's defeat.[8] The 1905 Revolution in Russia drove hundreds of thousands of Jews from the country. The majority of them immigrated to the United States, a few thousand went to Palestine, which was then part of the Ottoman Empire, and a few thousand more traveled to Siberia. Eventually, many of this last group settled in Harbin, some others in Shanghai, and a few in Japan.

Chapter 2

Jewish Settlers in Japan at the Beginning of the Twentieth Century

After the 1905 Russian revolution, the next major migration of Jews from Russia began in late 1917, when thousands of Jews fled after the October 1917 Bolshevik Revolution and the ensuing civil war. A large portion of these new refugees sought safety in Japan. Some five thousand of them made their way there, mainly through Yokohama, that being Japan's major port of entry. The majority of these then attempted to immigrate to the United States, and some even secured entry visas. Those lucky enough to do so departed alone, leaving their families in Japan until they would be ready to travel to America and join them. Many families in this situation found themselves destitute and sought help from the Yokohama Jewish community. In 1919, matters grew worse when American immigration laws were revised and became far more restrictive. Hundreds of families were stranded in Yokohama with no one but the local Jewish community members to provide for their basic needs. Some financial aid came from the American Jewish organization HIAS (Hebrew Immigrant Aid Association), whose major benefactor was Jacob Schiff, whose actions previously have been discussed in Chapter 1. HIAS sent a special emissary by the name of Samuel Mason to Asia to open offices in Manchuria, Kobe, and even Vladivostok to help Jewish refugees make their way to America. He was provided with an introductory letter from Jacob Schiff, which helped open Japanese government office doors for him. That in turn enabled many of the refugees to relocate to Kobe. From there, hundreds eventually left for America, some went to Shanghai, and hundreds settled in Harbin and other cities in Manchuria. A handful decided to travel to Palestine. Among the last group was Moshe Medzini, the father of the present writer.[1]

Some 1,700 Jewish refugees were stranded in Japan at the beginning of this period, but they were eventually able to either settle there or to use it as a transit point on their way to other destinations.

The Kobe Community[2]

The third-largest Jewish community in Japan was in Kobe. It grew mainly as a result of the decline of Nagasaki and the arrival in 1923, following the great Kanto earthquake which destroyed much of Tokyo and Yokohama, of many Jews who had previously lived in those two cities. In the 1920's and 1930's, Kobe became the largest and most important Jewish community in Japan. The original Jewish settlers in that port city, which had been opened to trade and settlement of foreigners in 1868, were Iraqi and Iranian, in addition to a few Russians. On the eve of the Second World War, there were some hundred Jewish families in Kobe, about half of them Ashkenazim (of European origins) and the other half Sephardim (of Middle East origins). They were prosperous enough to establish and maintain communal institutions, among them two separate synagogues and a ritual slaughterer who provided kosher meat. This community would play an important role in helping European Jews find temporary shelter in Kobe in the late 1930's until 1941. Being a port city, situated some thirty kilometers northwest of Osaka, Japan's second-largest city, Kobe also served as an exit port for those who sailed to America.

Prior to discussing the core issues relating to the prevailing Japanese attitude toward the Jews, it is useful to expand the discussion to when, and under what circumstances, ordinary Japanese people and their rulers might encounter Jews. We have already noted that Jews played no role in Japan before, during, or immediately after the Meiji Restoration. There is no evidence that Japan's future leaders who were sent to the United States and Europe with the Iwakura Mission (1871-1872) to study government, education, industry, economics, and law met American or European Jews in their travels. One Jew did have an impact on the development of the Meiji constitution: the German-Jewish law professor Albert Mosse, who was invited by Prince Ito Hirobumi (1841-1909) to come to Japan to help write it. Mosse, however, was viewed by the Japanese as a German and not as a Jew, and apparently made no mention of his Jewish origins.

Curiously enough, many Japanese people made their first indirect acquaintance with Jews through Shakespeare's *The Merchant of Venice*, which was first translated and staged in Osaka in 1885 and then became part of the English-language curriculum in Japanese schools. Therefore, many Japanese readers thought that the typical Jew was Shylock-like: clever, sly, untrustworthy, and given to devious intrigues and manipulations. This stereotype of the Jew as a super-manipulator will reappear again and in greater strength in the 1920's, 1930's, and even in the 1980's, when antisemitic literature enjoyed a revival in Japan.

Some of the modern scholars who have researched the phenomenon of antisemitism in Japan, chiefly David Goodman and Miazawa Masanori, attribute the great popularity of *The Merchant of Venice* not to any preexisting antisemitic concepts but to domestic Japanese developments. They argue that the rapid process of modernization in Japan in the second half of the nineteenth century increased local interest in money, finance, banking, trade, and the legal matters connected with them and those involved in them. This was in stark contradiction to the prevailing ideology of the Tokugawa era, which placed merchants in the fourth social stratum, after samurai, peasants, and artisans, and just above the pariahs.

Japan's rapid modernization and fast economic growth led to a change in the position and standing of merchants, who now played a key role in the economic and industrial development of Japan. Even though the figure of Shylock was seen in a negative light by most Japanese people, to some he portrayed the new entrepreneur, who deserved to be emulated and respected.[3]

Another way in which the Japanese public became acquainted with Jews and Judaism was through the Christian faith. In 1873, all restrictions on Christianity in Japan were lifted, but toward the end of the nineteenth century, Christians numbered less than one percent of the total population. Those few Japanese converts to Christianity were introduced to the religion partly through the study of the New Testament, which was translated into Japanese by missionaries in the mid-1880's. Those interested in Christianity were through the New Testament exposed for the first time to the Jewish origins of Christianity, and even some of its anti-Jewish contents. Although the small number of Christians in Japan meant that they did not have much influence, they nonetheless did enjoy special treatment, partly because Christianity was seen as a Western religion. Since the West was successful and was now being emulated by a growing number of Japanese, the new Japanese elite became more aware of this, its main religion.

Evidently, the few Jews who resided in the three communities of Nagasaki, Yokohama, and Kobe were not noted for their social contact with the local Japanese population, and therefore they left no impact on the Japanese environment. These Jewish communities had no influence on Japanese politics, society, media, universities, or even the economy, exactly the opposite from their Western European and US counterparts' huge visibility in all these sectors. They did not serve in the armed forces of Japan, while there were numerous Jews who served in various armies in Western and Eastern Europe and even in the United States.

The major reason for this strong separation, I believe, was the language barrier. Jews did not generally acquire command of Japanese, and thus could not become part of the local elite. They were basically seen as part of the foreign community, but even in that group they kept to themselves. This is one reason why Japan did not begin to ponder over the "Jewish Question" that plagued many Christian countries in Europe and even the newly-emerging nationalist movements in the Arab and Muslim countries.

The tiny minority of Japanese people who were interested in Christianity included some who started to wonder about the origins of the Christian faith after reading its bible. This led them to study the historic background of that religion and its development, and connect it to Judaism and the Holy Land. This is also a reason why the Japanese attitude toward Jews was not loaded with negative historic connotations, such as the canard that the Jews killed Jesus. The image of Jews among those very few Japanese people who thought or cared about them was one of an economically successful people, highly influential in Western societies.[4]

Chapter 3

Japanese Images of the Jews: Myths, Canards and Fears

We have noted the almost total absence of any Jewish influence on Japanese politics, culture, media, and academia, even in the three communities where the Jewish population concentrated—Nagasaki, Yokohama, and Kobe. However, it can be safely assumed that the strange religious practices of the Jews aroused some interest among Japanese people, who may have wondered about the differences between Christian churches and Jewish synagogues, special "kosher" food for Jews, special burial sites, and their practice of attaching mezuzot to the doors of their homes and even kissing them. Some may have noted that during prayers Jews wore prayer shawls and skull-caps and prayed towards the West in the direction of Jerusalem. To the extent that some Japanese people wondered about these practices and rituals, however, their general sense was that Judaism was just another Christian sect, albeit one with its own rituals, and therefore no special attention was devoted to them.

The Japanese as Descendants of the Ten Lost Tribes

Over the course of the second half of the nineteenth century, several members of the new Japanese intellectual elite became interested in the Jews and their history. This was due mainly to the increasing number of Jewish settlers and to the appearance of works by European writers who studied the origins of the Japanese people and occasionally likened those origins to Jewish history. One of these publications appeared in Nagasaki in 1879, and was called *Japan and the Lost Tribes of Israel*.[1] The book's author, Norman McCleod, was a British businessman of Scottish descent who had lived in Japan since 1867. He claimed that on the basis of his research there were many similarities between Japanese and Jewish culture. Shinto temples, he argued, were similar to ancient Jewish temples, and some Shinto rituals reminded him of Jews parading with Torah scrolls in their synagogues. On the basis of his evidence, he came to the conclusion that the Japanese people were descended from the ten lost tribes of Israel, who reached Japan after they crossed the Asian continent and captured China and Korea, where they established a Jewish kingdom. This, of course, had no bearing on reality, as has been shown repeatedly since then.

Strange as it may seem, interest in the bizarre theory that the Japanese were the descendants of the ten lost tribes was due to the growing influence of the Christian Western powers in Japan and their ability to dictate to that weak nation a set of unequal treaties which forced Japan to open its gates to trade and settlements of foreigners. Many Japanese people began to wonder about the roots of Western power and wondered whether there was a connection between Christianity and the building of an overseas empire. Two noted Christian Japanese scholars, Oyabe Zenichiro (1868-1941) and Sakai Katsutoki (1874-1940), studied theology in the United States, where they were ordained. They too claimed that there was a connection between Japan and the ancient Jews. After abandoning Christianity at the ends of their respective lives, the two argued that Holy Japan must be the spiritual leader of the universe and that the Japanese imperial family was the embodiment of the Messiah. They also wrote that the Japanese are the legitimate heirs of the ancient Jews and derive their heritage from those ancient Jews, rather than from the Jews of modern times.[2] These two scholars eventually supported radical Japanese nationalism in the 1930's and the early 1940's. In this bizarre manner, the connection between modern Japan and ancient Judaism became a political tool that served Japanese nationalism and militarism in the 1930's. It was also designed to showcase Japan as the repository of an ancient history at least as old as Jewish history, and thus was a tool to be used as an argument against some Western scholars who claimed that Japan was—unlike China—a relatively new country.

In 1980, an Israeli researcher and writer, Joseph Eidelberg, published a book called *The Japanese and the Ten Lost Tribes of Israel*, in which he examined most of the Japanese publications on this subject and proposed the existence of a Japan-Jewish connection dating to the seventh century. In it, he claims that the word Yamato, the center of ancient Japan, is similar to Yehoamato—the people of God. He argues that the ancient Japanese began their journey in history in a year called Kinoye Tora, which he connected with the Hebrew words Kenei Torah (Torah reeds). The title "Agata Noshi," awarded by a Japanese emperor to his nobles, was identified by Eidelberg as close to "Aguda Nassi," or "Nessi Aguda" (meaning "chairman of the association"). All this sounds far-fetched and not plausible, although it is certainly interesting.³

Russian Antisemitism and the Japanese

In the absence of a sizeable and influential Jewish community in Japan, it seems likely that if there was a growing Japanese interest in Jews and a growing preoccupation with the image of the Jews, these were primarily the result of Russo-Japanese contacts and the evolution of a complex relationship that developed between the two peoples in the first two decades of the twentieth century.

The first Japanese scholar who sought to understand the meaning of the so-called "Jewish Question" in Europe was Kamuyama Sentaro (1877-1954). In May and June of 1905, he published a series of articles in the highly respected and influential magazine *Chuo Koron* called "Antisemitism and Zionism." In it, he argued that the Jews were a persecuted minority in Russia, that the Tsarist regime of that empire was inciting the masses to undertake pogroms against them, and that among the Jews there had developed a national movement called Zionism. He was probably drawn to this field because of the growing interest in Jews, and particularly in Jewish financial power, during the Russo-Japanese War.⁴

The first phase in the introduction of antisemitism to Japan took place in the years immediately following the October 1917 Bolshevik Revolution in Russia, the toppling of the Tsarist regime, and the occupation of parts of Siberia by Japanese forces starting in 1918. The Bolshevik revolution came as a huge shock to Japan. During the First World War, Russia and Japan were fighting on the same side against the Central powers and signed a number of agreements, dealing mainly with Japan's war-time aspirations in China, which were embodied in the 1915 Twenty-One Demands. The 1917 Russian Revolution created a huge void in the Far East that aroused hopes among some senior Japanese military officers that their country could profit by it. However, it also heightened fears of what could happen in the region now that Russia had become the Soviet Union and the Tsar and his entire family had been executed.

Into this complex situation the Jews were drawn, indirectly and for various and at times opposing reasons. They were seen as the most visible national element among the makers of the Bolshevik revolution, and thus as directly involved and perhaps even responsible for the murder of the

Tsar. The brutal elimination of the autocratic Tsar and the entire imperial family in early 1918 stunned many in Japan and was seen as regicide. This execution, it was feared, could serve as a model for the elimination of the Japanese imperial family, which was at the heart of the Japanese *Kokutai* (national essence).[5]

Additional military and political developments in the Russian Far East were even more important and urgent than these concerns. To the collapse of the Tsarist regime and the withdrawal of the Soviet Union from the war there was added the fear that the newly-created Soviet Union would seek to avenge Russia's defeat by Japan in their recent war, barely thirteen years in the past. There was a great deal of discussion in Japan, as well as in the United States and the countries of Western Europe, of the "Red Peril," a phrase reminiscent of what was once called the "Yellow Peril."

Beginning in January 1918, when Lenin signed the treaty of Brest-Litovsk, resulting in, among other things, the withdrawal of Russia from the war against the Central powers, the Allied powers were determined to keep Russia in the war at least in Asia. One reason for this goal was so that the 60,000 men of the so-called "Czech Legion," consisting of Czech prisoners of war held by Russia, could escape from Russia via East Asia back to Europe to help the Allies fight Germany. This was the main reason given to justify the decision to land British and American troops in Vladivostok (in addition to other sites in European Russia). These troops arrived in early August 1918, and Japan was invited to participate in the expeditionary force. In the Japanese leadership there were arguments not over the principle of participating in this venture, but over the goals, the scope, and the dimensions of the intervention, how many troops should be committed to Siberia, how far they should advance, and how long they should remain there.

Some in Japan supported the intervention in order to gain control of the Trans-Siberian Railway. Among these was the Russian director-general of the Chinese Eastern Railway, Piotr Horvat. Through its participation, he argued, Japan's position in Manchuria would be strengthened. General Tanaka Giichi (1864-1929), who would become Japan's prime minister in 1927, along with some of his colleagues, including generals and admirals as well as other senior Japanese army and navy officers, began to dream about the creation of a Japanese Asian empire extending all the way to Lake Baikal. Japan finally decided to send troops, double the the number that the Allies had initially requested. Officially, this move was made in concert with the United States, Britain, France, and Canada, and was designed to protect the interests of the Western powers after the overthrow of the Tsarist regime and the murder of Nicholas II. At the height of its presence, the Japanese expeditionary force numbered some 72,000 soldiers. But even this large force was unable to stem the advance of the Red Army toward Vladivostok, the main base of the Japanese army. In this port city, and in some surrounding Siberian towns, there remained "White" Russian forces—forces loyal to the old regime—under the overall command of Admiral Alexander Vasilyevich Kolchak (1874-1920) and his chief local commander, General Grigori Semyonov (1890-1946), who planned to establish an anti-Bolshevik government in Siberia. After the end of the war in Europe, the Western Allies withdrew their forces from Siberia, asking Japan to do the same, but Japan's government prevaricated and the force remained in place until 1922. By then it was becoming obvious that Japan's adventure in Siberia was unfruitful, as it had cost a fortune and had not achieved any significant political, territorial, or economic gains.[6]

The Protocols of the Elders of Zion[7]

Over the course of the almost four years of Japanese military presence in Siberia, Japanese officers were exposed to the White Russians' searing hatred for the Bolsheviks and also their animosity toward the Jews, whom they accused of being the main culprits responsible for the Bolshevik Revolution and the total collapse of the ancient order in Russia, as well as the execution of the imperial family. It was the White Russian officers who supplied Japanese expeditionary force officers with antisemitic tracts, most notably the *Protocols of the Elders of Zion*.

The origins of this document are murky, despite the fact that in recent years its history has been thoroughly researched. The text itself is an uncredited and altered copy of a book that was initially published in France during the reign of Napoleon III and contained material that ascribed dangerous intentions to Napoleon. The book was translated to Russian by the Russian secret police, the Okhrana, and after pertinent adaptations it was released to explain to the Russian people that the Jews were responsible for all the ailments that beset Russian society, including its defeat in the Russo-Japanese war. The aim was to prove that many of Russia's problems were the consequences of an international Jewish plot to destroy the Russian state. The core of the story is a series of twenty-four lectures delivered in the old Jewish cemetery in Prague by a figure referred to as the Chief Rabbi, whose audience consists of the representatives of the twelve tribes of Israel—the

Elders of Zion. This group is ostensibly a secret Jewish government that plans to destroy and then take over no less than the entire Christian world.

This document first appeared in Russia in 1905 as an annex to the Russian mystic Sergei Nilus' (1862-1929) book *The Great in the Small: The Coming of Anti-Christ and the Rule of Satan on Earth*. A further edition of Nilus's book appeared in 1917, and was called, "It's Close to Our Doors." The connection between the Jews and their influence on the Bolshevik Revolution was clear. That Revolution was seen as the direct result of a plot concocted by world Jewry, meant to first destroy the Russian empire and then take over the entire Christian world and kill its leaders, starting with the Tsar. The tract in fact absolved the heads of the Tsarist government from all blame, because they never had a chance to resist this horrific Jewish plot. The presence of so many Jews among the leaders of the Bolsheviks and in the new Soviet leadership only supported the claim that the Revolution was a key part of a Jewish scheme.

The Protocols of the Elders of Zion was distributed in large numbers among White Russian soldiers and officers, and received a great deal of interest and credence. After Russian military personnel in Siberia shared the tract with their Japanese counterparts between 1918 and 1922, copies of it found their way to Japan, where excerpts were published in 1920 in a series of articles called "The Jewish Peril" in the publication *Shinrei*.

Some scholars wonder to this day about the secret of the success of an untruthful antisemitic document in Japan, a country which had barely a thousand Jewish residents and no antisemitic tradition, where Jews had never been suspected of threatening the state, its culture, or its religion. The circulation of the *Protocols* in Japan, in fact, increased Japanese interest in Jews and Judaism. Some Japanese scholars wondered how the Bolsheviks, theoretically controlled by Jews, were able to take over the vast Russian empire so rapidly. Furthermore, it was thought, if indeed the Jews controlled the international economy and held enormous influence over the governments of the major powers, perhaps it was time that more Japanese should learn more about them. The reaction reads like a combination of the Red Scare and the Jewish Peril.[8]

Another reason for the growing interest in the *Protocols* was the development of severe domestic Japanese problems at the end of the First World War. After years of economic prosperity caused by the war, during which Japan had supplied the Allies and other countries with goods and services, Japan's economy stagnated, leading to rioting in Tokyo and other Japanese cities. These outbursts, known as the "Rice Riots" of 1919, were seen as an expression of the growing dissatisfaction of the Japanese people with the spiraling rise of the price of basic commodities. Some Japanese leaders, mainly the more conservative among them, felt that the unrest was influenced by the new doctrines of socialism, communism, and even anarchism emanating from Russia. The doctrines were initiated by Jews, they argued, who played key roles in the development and expansion of communist doctrines, starting with Karl Marx (1818-1883) and ending with the new rulers of Communist Russia—Leon Trotsky (1879-1940), Lev Kamenev (1883-1936), Grigory Zinoviev (1883-1936), and Karl Radek (1885-1939), to name a few. They knew that in various other European countries Jews stood out as leaders of communist uprisings, such as Rosa Luxemburg (1871-1919) and Karl Liebknecht (1871-1919) in Germany and Bela Kuhn (1886-1938) in Hungary. Thus, Jews were seen as leading an international revolutionary movement that was spreading its tentacles in many countries. Fear spread among some Japanese leaders that there would be growing demands in Japan for greater democracy and civil rights, something that could endanger their rule, the spirit of the *Kokutai* — the national essence and structure — undermine Japan's social makeup, and lead to anarchy. Naturally, Jews were accused of spreading such ideas as democracy, equality, and progress. A group of Japanese leaders, among them Prince Konoe Fumimaro (1891-1945), future prime minister and scion of an ancient aristocratic family, were in Paris in 1919 for the Peace Conference. In a series of articles written from Paris, Konoe complained that Japan was being humiliated by the Western powers, who were determined to preserve their colonial and imperial standing in their Asian and African holdings while demanding of Japan that it give up its claims to parts of China, mainly in the Shandong Province, and renounce the 21 demands it had presented to China in 1915.[9] Konoe and others in the Japanese ruling elite and the military high command saw the West as a clear threat to Japan's aspirations on the Asian continent. These elites, who still bore the legacy of the oligarchy of the late Meiji period, feared that the social unrest in Japan was partly due to new Western ideas imported from the West and from Russia: socialism, liberalism, democracy, communism, anarchism, and the desire for a pluralistic and secular society. Some of them identified Jews with the Western regimes because of their perceived influence on their social and economic policies. Thus, Jews were identified with those in the West who were determined to undermine the Japanese social and political structure and also prevent them from taking what they considered their rightful place in Asia.

After Konoe committed suicide in December 1945 and his journals were published, it emerged that his antisemitism was mainly due to fear of Bolshevism and the fact that he considered Marxism a "Jewish disease." In this respect he was similar to a large number of influential Germans who claimed that their country was defeated in the First World War by a "stab in the back" from its Jewish population. As evidence of Jewish might and influence, these Germans cited the April 1922 Rapallo Friendship Treaty, signed between the Soviet Union and Germany, which created the military cooperation that helped build the Red Army. They noted that this treaty was signed by German Foreign Minister Walther Rathenau (1867-1922), a German Jew, and on the Soviet side by Foreign Minister Grigori Chicherin (1872-1936), a non-Jew. Here was additional proof that a Jewish foreign minister ran the affairs of a major power. Senior Japanese staff officers feared the growing strength of the Red Army created and initially led by Leon Trotsky (born Lev Bronshtein). It was easy to conclude that influential Jews in the West and certainly in the Soviet Union had joined together to keep Japan as a second- or even third-rate power.

Herein, however, lies the paradox. On the one hand there existed among the Japanese ruling elites a keen interest, verging on admiration, for Jews, who they saw as possessing vast amounts of influence over various governments. They thought of them as the clever, intelligent, crafty Jews with special talents mainly in finance and international politics. This was another Western "contribution" to Japan: in the West as well, Jews were seen at best as possessing vast powers far exceeding their numerical strength. Some key Japanese leaders also considered them highly influential and well-placed in strategic positions. Many Japanese civilian and military leaders knew well the action undertaken by Jacob Schiff and his associates to rescue Japan from financial ruin during the Russo-Japanese War. Some also expressed fear that American and European Jewish bankers might help shore up the Soviet Union in revenge for the pogroms carried out during the era of the Tsarist regime. There was anxiety that major Jewish financial concerns run by Jacob Schiff, Felix Warburg (1871-1937), and the Lehman, Goldman, and Sachs families would underwrite or even guarantee loans taken out by the new communist government of Russia. Such fears were encouraged by White Russian soldiers and officers in Siberia, who made sure these ideas would be passed on to Japanese forces in Siberia during the era of Japanese presence in that part of Russia.

Not everyone in Japan was convinced that the *Protocols* was a genuine document. As early as 1921, after it was translated into English and found its way to Japan in that language, there were some who argued that the historic foundation of the text is basically false. One of these skeptics was Yoshino Sakuzo (1878-1933), a respected law professor at Tokyo University, who wrote two articles on the subject in the magazine *Chuo Koron* in May-June 1921. In them, he argued that there was no basis for the assumption of an international Jewish plot, and that the distribution of the Protocols in the West was an opaque attempt to blacken the name of the Soviet Union by attacking the Jews who held central positions in the newly created Soviet government.[10]

As was mentioned above, the *Protocols* was first translated into Japanese in 1920, and excerpts appeared in a series of articles in *Shinrei* called "The Jewish Peril," written by Higuchi Tsuyanosuke (1870-1931). Higuchi attended a Russian Orthodox Seminary in Tokyo, and was later ordained as an Orthodox priest by the Theological Seminary in St. Petersburg, Russia. It is likely that during his studies in Russia he became imbued with antisemitic ideas. Since he was fluent in Russian, he was attached to the headquarters of the Japanese forces in Siberia as a Russian affairs specialist and served there for three years as an interpreter. The entire *Protocols of the Elders of Zion* was later translated to Japanese by Major (later Colonel) Yasue Norihiro (1881-1950), who was at the time serving in the headquarters of the fifth Japanese Army in Siberia, attached to the headquarters of the White Russian General Grigory Semyonov.[11] He translated 120 pages of text and wrote an eighty-page introduction, under the pseudonym Ho Koshi. He called the combined text *The Seamy Side of the World Revolution*. He ignored the fact that in 1921 it was already generally understood that the *Protocols* were a forgery and lacked any historic or factual basis or validity. He was convinced that it was genuine. Yasue had been sent by the Japanese army to study Russian in the Foreign Languages School in Tokyo when the army had decided to train a number of Japanese officers in foreign languages. Incidentally, another student of Russian there at the time was a Japanese civilian named Sugihara Chiune (1900-1986), who later heroically provided thousands of Polish and Lithuanian Jews with documentation they needed to escape the Nazis. Perhaps it was during his Russian language studies that Yasue began to show an interest in the Jews.

Two other Japanese officers also played an important role in disseminating antisemitic tracts. One was the naval officer Captain Inuzuka Koreshige (1890-1965),[12] and the other an infantry officer, General Shioden Nobutaka (1897-1962).[13] The latter became the most outspoken and well-known antisemite in Japan during the twentieth century. They, along with

Yasue, were staff officers under the command of Major General Higuchi Kiichiro (1888-1970), and as part of their work as liaison officers to the Semyonov headquarters they read antisemitic publications in Russian. They may also have been influenced by antisemitic ideologies they learned from Semyonov and his soldiers. They began to use terms such as "Jewish Peril" and discuss the need to undertake severe measures before the Jews took over the entire world through means of revolutions, murder, and mainly by subverting, undermining, degenerating, and atrophying the cultures of the West and Japan.

Later in the 1920's, antisemitic publications entered Japan from other sources. One, translated into Japanese in 1927, was Henry Ford's *The International Jew*, which contained segments of the *Protocols*. Ford (1863-1947) had been publishing antisemitic articles since the early 1920s, mainly in local publications in Michigan that included citations from the *Protocols*. His fear of Jews derived from, among other things, the role they had played in setting up trade unions in America and in demanding unionization of the automotive industry in order to protect workers' rights. He saw unionization as a Jewish plot—hence his antisemitism. The publication of Ford's book in 1927 may have been seen by some Japanese people as giving them a green light for antisemitism. If the American tycoon Ford was allowed to publish such tracts in democratic and liberal America, they may have thought, then why couldn't Japan, at the time also struggling against the rise of trade unions and fearing strikes in essential services, adopt his stance against the Jews? The problem, of course, was that, unlike in Europe or the United States, there were no Jews involved in the creation of the Japanese trade union movement. Only after Japan's defeat in the Second World War did Jews become involved, in the capacity of some of General MacArthur's (1880-1964) senior political advisers during the occupation of Japan. Among this group were at least two Jewish advisers who suggested that the American occupation authorities immediately release imprisoned trade union leaders and permit the creation of trade unions in Japan. MacArthur agreed.

A further source for the spread of the antisemitic theories of the Russian school were the thousands of non-Jewish White Russian refugees who escaped from Communist Russia after the revolution and found shelter in some of the major cities of Manchuria, chiefly in Harbin, and in Tianjin and Shanghai in China. Few arrived in Japan proper. The refugees had a burning hatred for anything that smacked of communism due to the loss of their way of life, property, homes, and—above all, since they were

Russian patriots—their homeland and their adored Tsar. For their survival these refugees, embittered and resentful, found themselves dependent on the good will of others. In the major cities of Manchuria they saw flourishing Jewish communities, including some very wealthy Jews, and contrasted them to their own destitute community. This only added to their anger and antisemitic feelings.

The combination of the White Russian forces of Kolchak and Semyonov, and the few Japanese staff officers who became interested in the "Jewish problem," proved to be pernicious, although anti-Jewish sentiment in Japan never reached the destructive dimensions of the antisemitism of Nazi Germany.

New Political, Social, and Economic Reality—and the Long Arm of the Jews

Another cause for the rise of interest in Jews and the growing antisemitism in Japan were the unexpected domestic developments in that country after the First World War. These years witnessed an ongoing struggle between those who demanded growing liberalization, democracy, and greater freedom in Japan and those who opposed these demands, between those who wanted to see Japan pursue a foreign policy based on international cooperation with the Western powers under the leadership of the League of Nations and those who argued that the West was determined to prevent Japan from attaining its rightful place under the sun and to prevent it from gaining any footholds anywhere on the Asian continent. Some Japanese politicians and senior army officers watched with growing concern the close ties that began to develop between the Chinese nationalist party, Chiang Kai-Shek's (1887-1975) Kuomintang, and the Soviet Union through the Comintern (Communist International), which sent to China a number of political advisers, military experts, and revolutionary ideologists. Among these emissaries were a number of Jews, including Adolph Yoffe (1883-1927), Lev (Leo) Karachan (1869-1937), and Michail Borodin-Gruzenberg (1884-1952). The combination of Chinese nationalism and Soviet Bolshevism was enough to alarm those in Japan who aspired for an active imperial role for Japan on the Asian continent in general, and on the Chinese mainland in particular.

An additional struggle was taking place in Japan between those who wanted to open the country to modern Western culture and those conservatives who feared for the impact of these ideas on Japanese youth. Among those who were determined to reconstruct what they considered to be sacred Japanese values and traditions was Kitta Ikki (1883-1937), who in 1919 wrote a book titled *General Structure for the Reconstruction of Japan*. This book had a vast influence on young Japanese officers, who were trained to worship the emperor and the homeland and to defend them against all enemies from within and without.[14]

No wonder, then, that at a time of growing restlessness, severe economic problems, a devastating earthquake that almost destroyed Tokyo and Yokohama in 1923, and the failure of the government to take immediate relief actions after it, many Japanese people sought culprits for their country's predicament. Japan was struggling with labor disputes and strikes, a steep rise in the price of food and other essential commodities, a growing social gap, and a constant struggle between conservatives and radicals, and all this contributed to the rise of the type of ultra-nationalist elements who normally flourish at such times. Part of the blame was aimed at foreigners in general, those from the West and in particular the Jews, although most Japanese people had still never laid eyes on a Jew. The antisemitic publications of the 1920's had been read mainly by a few individuals in the higher echelons of the Japanese army: they never filtered down to the general public and the Japanese masses. Most of the Japanese population was still agrarian, and the peasants certainly had never seen a Jew. Unlike in Europe, where certain social phenomena encouraged hatred of Jews, in Japan there was no phenomenon of the Jewish landlord, loan shark, trade union activist and organizer, editor or journalist, banker, industrialist, or political activist, and certainly there were no Jewish academics. There was nothing in Shintoism or Buddhism that was remotely anti-Jewish.

It was previously noted that one of the few Jews to have taught in a Japanese university up to that point was the German Jew Professor Ludwig Riess, who lectured at Tokyo University from 1887 to 1902. Riess was a student of the leading historian Leopold von Ranke (1795-1886), and went to Japan because he was unable to secure a teaching position in Germany. He was also the guiding spirit of the journal of the Association for the Study of History in Japan. While it is true that he was well known, he was considered by Japanese society to be a German, and his Jewishness was overlooked.[15]

Unlike in other countries, there were no Jewish writers, musicians, playwrights, film makers, doctors, lawyers, or accountants in Japan of this period. Jews did not pursue these occupations mainly because most of them did not know the language well enough to communicate with prospective clients and made no effort to learn Japanese. Few thought of Japan as their permanent homeland, many seeing it instead as a way-station to Western Europe, or preferably America. Jews never served in the Imperial Japanese army or navy. They were mainly agents of foreign companies. They barely had communal institutions, and did not have their own Jewish school system—their children attended international schools, some of them run by Christian missionaries. There was almost no intermarriage with the native Japanese populations. They spoke the languages of their countries of origin. Few joined the Zionist movement, and none are known to have been suspected by the Japanese police of un-Japanese activities or disloyalty to the country.

The 1920's were a period of growth and relative security for many Jewish communities in Europe. Thus, few Jews wanted to relocate to foreign countries. Those who wanted to immigrate to Palestine had no difficulty doing so, as the gates of that country were open at the time. The only country that did not allow Jews to emigrate was the Soviet Union. This meant that in the 1920's, Japan was not experiencing a major and urgent Jewish refugee problem.

In 1924, the United States closed its doors to migration from Eastern Europe, affecting predominantly Jews. The few thousand Jews who decided to resettle in East Asia generally preferred at first Harbin, and later Shanghai, where there were already prosperous Jewish communities with health, welfare, educational, and religious institutions and facilities, where Jews spoke German, Russian, and English, and above all, where the Jewish community members were ready to help in the absorption of new arrivals. In Japan, apart from Kobe, there were no such hospitable Jewish communities, and the Japanese government did not make it easy for foreigners to enter its territory. Part of the new difficulty was due to Japan's reaction to the draconian American immigration law of 1924, which allowed an annual quota of only several hundred immigrants from Japan. This was seen in Japan as a major national insult based on race, and Japan responded by effectively closing its gates to foreigners, a policy that in fact remains informally in force until today. Those who were hurt by the new American immigration laws were mostly European Jews who sought shelter in the United States after the rise of Hitler in 1933.

Why was there such a positive echo in some Japanese quarters to antisemitic theories? Part of the answer lies in the failure of the Japanese intervention in Siberia and the Western demand that Japan renounce its claims to Shandong. Another part is the general ignorance most Japanese people had at the time of the history of foreign nations. Although the school curriculum in Japan did include the study of Western countries, some of what they learned was tainted with anti-Western contents that stressed the uniqueness of Japan and the superiority of the Japanese race under the emperor—who was seen as superior to other dynasts, and who would implement Japan's destiny to purge Asia of Western presence and influence. As Japan failed to cope properly with the world economic crisis that began on Wall Street in October 1929, there was a growing need to seek someone who could be blamed for its plight.

As there developed among conservative intellectuals and the middle class a growing fear of the Western materialistic lifestyle and of Western influence and capitalism, some tended to connect these forces with Jews and consider both the antithesis to the spirit of Japan. Antisemitism in Japan in the 1920's can also be interpreted as a part of the era's general anti-cosmopolitanism and support for traditional Japanese culture, values, and way of life. Perhaps Jews were also seen as feeling negative toward war, a problem in a country that glorified war as a highly positive and purifying phenomenon, as an integral and even central part of the Japanese tradition.

However, Jews were never seen as a fifth column determined to destroy Japan's civilization, and in fact it would have been hard to claim that Jews ever endangered Japan. Since Japan was among the victorious nations in World War I, it was impossible for Japan to blame the Jews for all the world's ailments in the way that Germany blamed them for its defeat in that war. Due to the barriers mentioned above, it was obviously impossible for Jews to play any role in the creative spirit of Japan as they did in Europe. The worst that the Jews' detractors could say about them was that they were purveyors of individualism, a concept that was abhorrent to Japanese nationalists. Some writers blamed the Jews for publicizing Western-style democracy, but it was impossible to accuse them of being a force bent on the disintegration of the Japanese state. Whereas in Europe and even in the United States, Jews were seen as exploiters, usurers, loan sharks, or real estate owners, the Jews in Japan did not engage in the types of pursuits that might lead to such accusations. Some even saw the Jews as bearers of Anglo-American self-centered individualism and materialism, two tendencies in total opposition to the Japanese notion of the supremacy of the collective, the triumph of spirit over matter. Nonetheless, it has to be admitted that in the writings of many anti-Western Japanese thinkers, there is hardly any reference to Jews or Judaism.

Jews were never seen in Japan as part of the body politic. They were at best part of the foreign community, and therefore they did not arouse the passionate, often hysterical, response they encountered in Nazi Germany. Since they were never seen as an integral part of Japan, and subsequently were not viewed as enemies of that country, Japan's society saw no need to destroy them. The so-called "Jewish Question" was virtually non-existent there: no one wanted or needed to save Japan from the Jews. Unlike the situation in Germany, where Jews were very active in the socialist and communist parties, in the media, in academia, among the judiciary, and at the helm of some of the major corporations in Germany, not to mention the banks, in Japan the Jews were not a major part of public life.

One Japanese thinker who was interested in Judaism was Hiraizumi Kiyoshi (1895-1984), a professor of history at Tokyo University who in 1924 expressed doubts over the manner in which Japanese history was being taught in Japan. He focused on the study of culture and its influence on the spirit of the times, and rejected the trend of objectivity. He lived briefly in Germany in 1930, and learned much about Judaism from his Jewish friends in Berlin. He was quite impressed with the manner in which the Jews preserved their ancient religion, customs, culture, rites, and language, and sought to understand the role of rites and prayers as preserving the Jewish people even after their expulsion from their ancient homeland by the Romans two thousand years earlier. He thought that the source of Judaism's strength was the Jews' preservation of their spirit and their history, and became convinced that the preservation of tradition is critical for a nation, even one deep in the process of modernization and renewal (*ishin*). He became a strong advocate of Japanese expansionism in Asia, and in 1937 was one of the founders of a university established in Manchuria by the Kwantung Army. Later, he blamed the defeat of Japan in World War II on the failure of the spirit (*seishin*). He was one of very few thinkers in Japan who made an effort to understand Jewish history and religion.

The so-called "Jewish Question" in Japan suddenly came into being with the rise of Hitler to power in 1933. From then on, thousands of German Jews sought asylum in any country that was prepared to grant it to them. The Japanese government had not yet adopted any official stand toward Jews, either those already residing in Japan or those wishing to enter it. We have seen that antisemitism was virtually non-existent in Japan in the 1920's, apart from the circulation of tracts translated mainly from Russian. The Jews were never a topic of national concern or debate.

There were, in fact, a number of intellectuals in Japan who thought that antisemitism lacked any valid foundation. In an academic symposium held in Tokyo in 1928 that dealt with the "Jewish Question," a number of well-known scholars, among them Uchimura Kanzo (1861-1930) and Hasegawa Nyozekan (1875-1969), came out openly against antisemitism. The conclusions of their position were published in the magazine *Heibon* in an article which stated that the *Protocols of the Elders of Zion* was a forgery, that the Zionists had no intention of conquering the world, and that the idea of an international Jewish plot was a fantasy.[16]

Nonetheless, at the same time antisemitic ideas began to seep into social and political discourse in Japan. Antisemitic writers were able to propound these ideas, which often fell into open ears. The deep social and economic frustrations of the late 1920's and early 1930's were placed at the feet of what became known as international Jewry. The severe social crisis that accompanied Japan's rapid process of modernization and industrialization, the growing economic difficulties that followed the world economic crisis, and Japan's growing entanglement in China led Japan on a path of nationalist radicalism, leading to the nurturing of native and unique Japanese values and—above all—belief in the emperor and fear of the West and its values.

The economic crisis would lead Japan to occupy Manchuria in what turned out to be the first shot that eventually led to the Pacific War. Japan also sought allies in Europe. This search soon led her to the arms of Nazi Germany and Fascist Italy, which some Japanese civil and military leaders saw as two other "have not" powers, emasculated by the Treaty of Versailles. Germany, some of these leaders argued, could become a partner to Japan's political and even global ambitions and plans as well as her ideological values. It is obvious that closer ties with Germany would have an impact on Japanese antisemitism, and it is to these changes that we now turn.

Chapter 4

Nazi Antisemitism and its Influence in Japan in the 1920's and 1930's

In spite of the social tensions evident in Japan after World War I, Japan enjoyed a certain economic prosperity in the 1920's. This was due partly to the conciliatory policies of its foreign minister Shidehara Kijuro (1872-1951), who advocated international cooperation and closer ties with the Western democracies under the umbrella of the League of Nations, in which Japan was a major player, being one of the Big Five and a member of its Council. This conciliatory policy was also helped by the absence of a visible threat to Taiwan and Korea, Japan's colonial holdings in Asia. As long as it was uncertain whether China's nationalist leaders under Chiang Kai-Shek would be able to unite that country, it was difficult for right-wing nationalist-militarist groups to fault the government of Japan. The mid-1920's witnessed the height of the so-called Taisho democracy, named after Emperor Taisho (personal name: Yoshihito; 1879-1926), who reigned from 1912 to 1926 but was confined to the palace due to illness beginning in 1921. We have seen that Japan had terminated its Siberian intervention in 1922, and it went on to renounce its claims to the Shandong peninsula in China, established diplomatic relations with the Soviet Union in 1925, signed a number of international treaties to reduce armaments, accept the political status quo in East Asia, and even signed the 1928 Kellog-Briand Treaty that formally outlawed war.

It was probably Japan's low-profile foreign policy that enraged those of its citizens who called for an activist and tougher policy against those whom they viewed as Japan's enemies. Top among these enemies were the Chinese nationalists, the Soviet Communists, and the Western democratic powers. Those who supported right-wing radicalism argued that Japan faced a mortal "red" danger from the Bolsheviks and a similar "white" danger from Western democracies. The leaders of both threats were perceived by some Japanese people to be Jews. Jews were seen as endorsing universal as opposed to national values, supporting trade unions and strikes in vital services, and espousing women's equality, freedom of the press, and modernization in all spheres of life. It is only in view of this that it is possible to explain the interest that a number of Japanese thinkers began to show in antisemitism in this country with barely any Jews.

Right-wing thinkers claimed that Japan faced a major threat from the rise of forces over which it had no control: Chinese nationalism, which aspired to unite all the forces in China and terminate Japanese ambitions in that country, international communism, which supported Chinese nationalism, and the Western powers that denied Japan a foothold in their colonies in Asia—Britain in India, Burma (today's Myanmar), Malaya (now known as Malaysia), and Hong Kong; France in Indochina; Holland in Indonesia; and the United States in the Philippines. It became evident to those thinkers that while the West spoke highly of democracy, equality, and progress, it applied these lofty ideals only to Europe and North America—not to their overseas colonies. The Western democracies were thus accused of hypocrisy and "double-speak." Japan now found itself classed with Germany and Italy as a "have not" country, facing the superiority of the Western militaries, led by those of Britain and France. The Soviet Union was still boycotted in the international community and had not yet been admitted to the League of Nations. The United States chose to remain isolationist.

However, as long as Japan's economy functioned properly, right-wing thinkers found it hard to influence the moderate policies of its civilian leaders. When the Japanese economy began to show signs of growing pains, which started with the 1927 banking crisis and increased sharply with the collapse of the international economic system after the October 1929 Wall Street meltdown, much depended on the response of the Japanese government to the internal and external crises. However, the failure of successive Japanese governments to deal effectively with the deepening economic crisis, the collapse of the market for silk, which was Japan's major export, and the dramatic growth in unemployment and growing poverty in the agrarian sector led to increasing demands from the middle class for the establishment of a strong government that would know how to deal with the existential issues that now faced Japan. The direction was evident: the Japanese armed forces were seen as patriotic, possessing a virtuous spirit and samurai values, and being a pure non-corrupt body, and it was widely felt that they would be the institution that would save Japan from its loss of direction, economic collapse, national degeneration, and social disintegration.

In the mid-1920's, a number of Japanese scholars began to show interest in the theories of a right-wing nationalist party in Germany, little-known at the time, called the National Socialist Workers Party. It was headed by an Austrian-born former corporal named Adolph Hitler (1882-1945), who was unknown outside Germany but who was making a name for himself in radical right-wing German politics.[1] Few in Japan, though, read his book *Mein Kampf* ("My Struggle"). The first part of the book was written while Hitler was serving a prison term in Bavaria's Landsberg jail following the failure of his attempted putsch (uprising) in 1923. The second part was written in 1925-1927, after his release.

If those Japanese people who did pay attention to the book had delved into it deeper, they would have found some unpleasant and basically negative descriptions of their own country and race and of Asian people in general. Parts of *Mein Kampf* were translated into Japanese as early as 1925 and apparently provoked little interest.

One of the many problems with the tract had to do with Hitler's racist doctrine and his attitude to the "Yellow" race. Racism stood at the heart of his beliefs, which were based on the inequality not only of individuals but also of entire races. The Aryan race, headed by the Germans, was of course considered the master race. They were the elite of humanity, the "creators of culture." The Jews were described as the exact opposite, "destroyers of culture." All other nations, including Japan, were at best "transferers of culture." Those who read the Japanese translation may have noted the distinction Hitler made between Aryans and other races, ascribing to the "Yellow" races an inferior position. After Hitler's rise to power in 1933, and when *Mein Kampf* was again distributed in Japan in 1937, Hitler's views on the Asian peoples were largely not made available to Japanese readers. His position, though, had not changed: the Japanese were placed between the master race and the hated Jews.

Doubts lingered in Japan over the validity and true value of Hitler's racial doctrines. It was also somewhat difficult for Japanese readers of *Mein Kampf* to relate to Hitler's views of the Jews as the sources of all evil and enemies of not only Germany but also the entire world, partly because they had little experience with Jews, and those very few who had more experience with them generally had a positive view of them.

But as Japan slowly became isolated from the Western world, some sought the culprits responsible for this situation. Thus it was easy to sell Hitler's ideas about the Jews to a growing number of Japanese officers, intellectuals, and even academics. The new Japanese antisemites now accepted the idea that Jews were headstrong and known for their practice of mutual assistance. It was bandied about that while they refused to assimilate into other peoples, the Jews penetrated every sphere they could, dominated the Western banking system in order to dominate capitalist countries, directed the international economy, media, cinema, theater, literature, and arts, and exploited the entire world through the capitalist and nation-undermining Marxist theories. The Jews were seen as disseminators of liberal, secular, universal, democratic, and Marxist ideas. One writer, Sakai Shogun (1870-1939) argued that Christianity, which emerged out of Judaism, destroyed the Roman Empire, and that religion was a Jewish reactionary notion. Jews, he argued, were attempting to subjugate the world by denying nationalism and extolling cosmopolitanism and universalism. Similar charges were leveled at Jews by the Soviet communists at the same time.[2]

Another Japanese scholar argued that the Jews had already succeeded in dominating Britain and the United States and had caused those two nations to degenerate. Now they were trying to undermine Germany from within. The Jews were the ones who had stabbed Germany in the back at the end of the First World War by spreading the poison of revolution in the German army and navy, they were the ones who had pushed the United States into the war, and furthermore they had spread communism.[3] Such ideas fell on open and willing minds in Japan of the mid-1930's, especially after many Japanese people began to feel that the West was trying to rein in Japan's expansionist ambitions on the Asian mainland. The best proof of this effort on the part of the West was the policy of Western nations towards Japan's seizure of Manchuria beginning in 1931.

The Occupation of Manchuria and the "Jewish Question"

On September 18, 1931, a number of Japanese officers belonging to the Kwantung Army planted an explosive device on the main line of the Southern Manchurian Railway near Mukden. The explosion caused minor damage but served as the signal for the takeover of all Manchuria by the Japanese army, a feat completed in early 1932. The reactions of foreign powers were tepid at best. They were satisfied with dispatching a commission of inquiry (the Lytton Commission) to the region to investigate the causes of the crisis. That commission's recommendations were focused on the restoration of the status-quo-ante. Japan responded in March 1933 by seceding from the League of Nations. This was the first nail in the coffin of that international body at the ripe old age of barely fourteen, and it heralded the collapse of the world order created in Versailles in 1919. Germany would secede from the League a year later, and Italy would do the same in 1936 after the League failed to sanction its occupation of Ethiopia.

As the Western powers persisted in their objection to the occupation of Manchuria and the creation in 1932 of the puppet-state called Manchukuo, some Japanese leaders continued to claim that the West was influenced by Jews, and that the goal of the Jews was to dominate the entire world in general and block Japan's aims in East Asia in particular. Much of Japanese anti-foreignism was directed at the United States, which—although it was not a member of the League of Nations—some Japanese leaders accused of pursuing an anti-Japanese policy motivated by Jews who controlled the American economy, media, culture (especially the film industry), and political establishment. These leaders were mainly incensed at the US Secretary of State, Henry Stimson (1867-1950), who had proclaimed the doctrine of "non-recognition" of Manchukuo, which was interpreted by many Japanese people as part of an effort to isolate Japan and prevent its southward march into China.

From there, the road to adopting some of the Nazis' antisemitic ideas was relatively short. Needless to say, the charges made against American Jews had no basis in fact. Most American Jews were busy trying to survive the Great Depression, and most of Roosevelt's Jewish aides were involved in creating the New Deal—which had nothing to do with foreign policy. Many senior state department officials in the Roosevelt era harbored antisemitic sentiments themselves, as demonstrated later by their anti-Zionist policies regarding the establishment of a Jewish state in Palestine. They also blocked any changes in America's immigration policies, thus shutting the doors on Jews fleeing Nazi Germany.

Japanese Officers and Antisemitic Ideas

A major German Nazi ideologist whose doctrine reached Japan and influenced some writers there was Alfred Rosenberg (1893-1946). He was born in Riga, Latvia, and fled to Germany from that country after the Bolshevik Revolution. In Munich he joined fringe right-wing groups that saw the Jews as the chief culprits responsible for the disaster that had befallen Germany and forced her to surrender to end the First World War. His 1920 tract *The Traces of Jews over the Generations* made his argument that the Jews were the root of all evil in Europe, that they were a foreign element in Germany, and that it was imperative to deny them participation in Germany's cultural life. At that time, he also called for the emigration of German Jews to Palestine. In 1930 he published *The Myth of the 20th Century*, in which he called for the elimination of all Jewish presence and influence in Germany. He became the chief ideologist of the Nazi party and the editor of its daily newspaper *Volkischer Beobachter*.[4] Those Japanese people who were familiar with his ideas were also impressed by his geo-political notions, his expression of the need for *Lebensraum* (space for living) and his statement of the duty to fight international communism, whose flag-bearers were Jews.

One of the reasons for the spread of antisemitic ideas from Germany into Japan had to do with the fact that the new Japanese Imperial army was built on the model of the Prussian army, and that many of its instructors in the nineteenth century were German officers. After the First World War, in which Germany and Japan were formally enemies and Japan took over control of German territories in China and in the Pacific Ocean, relations between the two countries resumed, and training in Germany became a desirable goal for Japanese officers who knew that promotion depended partly on training in Germany. The flag-bearer of antisemitism in Japan in the 1920's was General Shioden Nobutaka, who had also been influenced by the ideas of French antisemitic writers when he had served as Japan's military attaché in Paris during the war. It can be argued that he became the father of modern Japanese antisemitism. He espoused radical Japanese nationalism, idolized the Emperor, and fought for what was called in Japanese *Kokutai*, broadly translated as the "national essence." He thought that the Emperor of Japan should rule not only his own country but the rest of the world, as he was heir to the only unbroken dynastic chain that had been in existence some 2600 years. Even after he retired from the Japanese army in 1928, Shioden maintained his contacts with Nazi officials and continued to write about what he perceived as Jewish issues. He visited Germany again in 1938 and while there attended a Nazi conference in Erfurt. There he met with Julius Streicher, the editor of the main Nazi antisemitic newspaper *Der Sturmer* in Nuremberg, during a party day rally held in that city—the city that gave its name to the racial laws of Nazi Germany.

Nazi Racism and Japanese Racism

An additional reason for the growing interest in the Nazi's racial doctrines in Japan was their so-called scientific base. Both Hitler and Rosenberg based their ideology on scientific theories that had been developed in France and Britain, not to mention Germany, at the end of the nineteenth century. Since there was a great deal of admiration in Japan for Germany's scientific achievements in various fields, it seems that certain Japanese scholars were also impressed by the Nazi antisemitic doctrines, which appeared to them to be scientifically valid. As early as the second part of the Meiji era, some Japanese writers began to develop racial doctrines that were aimed at explaining to the Japanese people the divine origins of the Yamato race and its uniqueness, and mainly its holy mission to purge Asia of foreigners and establish a new order on that continent in which Japan would be the leading nation. The basis of this belief was the argument that since the Yamato race is the race of the gods, and Japan is the land of the gods and the rising sun, the Yamato people of Japan have the privilege, the right, and the duty of leading the Asian nations.

A number of Japanese people who were acquainted with the so-called "Jewish Question," including General Higuchi Kiichiro, in whose headquarters both Colonel Yasue and Captain Inuzuka served, knew Germany from previous service there or from occasional visits. General Higuchi had served in Germany as the military attaché in the Japanese Embassy in Berlin in the 1930's. Colonel Yasue visited Germany during the very same 1927-28 trip in which he visited Palestine. Captain Inuzuka was in Germany in the late 1920's. Since these officials were already considered experts on Jews and the "Jewish Question" even before they arrived, they wanted to broaden their knowledge on Jewish matters while in Germany and read everything available. Naturally, in the antisemitic atmosphere of Germany in the 1920's and especially in the 1930's, they were bound to be influenced by what they heard, read, and witnessed. Initially it was somewhat difficult for the Japanese visitors to accept the Nazi racial doctrine. As noted earlier, this doctrine created problems for Germany in its relations with Japan, since ideologically the Japanese race was seen as inferior to the Aryan one. Asians were relegated to the role of "transferers" of culture, and thereby were placed a notch below the German master race but still well above the despised Jews, who were at the bottom. This second-rate position was unacceptable to Japanese academics, intellectuals, diplomats, and even traders who resided in Germany. Since each country was interested in developing commercial relations with the other, there was a need to somewhat blunt this part of the Nazi racial ideology. Shortly after the ascent of Hitler to power in March 1933, the German foreign ministry invested much effort in relieving the sensitivities of Japanese diplomats and assuring them that Germany had no intention of acting against Japan in any way. On the contrary, Germany was seeking Japanese friendship and support against the Western powers and the Soviet Union. Germany was still smarting from its defeat in 1918, and Japan felt that the other Western countries were determined to keep it a second- or third-rate power,[5] and so they were in some ways natural allies.

However, while the Nazi racial doctrine spoke of the need to eliminate Jewish influence, and later of the Jews themselves, some Japanese diplomats and army officers questioned whether Japan should be far more cautious about the way it viewed the Jews, since they apparently played a key role in the world's economy and exercised a great deal of influence over Western leaders, especially in the United States. As a result, they suggested, perhaps it would be a good idea to maintain good relations with at least some influential Jews in the United States. One of the nightmares of all Japanese governments was that the United States would impose economic sanctions against Japan because of her expansionist policy on the Asian continent. Eventually the nightmare would come true, and the economic sanctions imposed on Japan by the United States in 1941 were among the main causes for Japan's fateful decision to attack the United States. However, in the 1930's some Japanese leaders, certainly the more moderate ones, thought that if the Jews played such a key role in the international economic system, it would be counterproductive to hurt them or take steps against them. Once again, the absence in Japan of deep knowledge and understanding of Jewish matters is glaring. Since there were only a few hundred Jews living in Japan at the time, they were still seen as merely a part of the foreign community and not viewed specifically as Jews. The majority of the Jews who resided in Japan held German, Austrian, British, American, French, or even Russian passports. Why, then, these leaders asked, should they quarrel with the Jews instead of using their international connections to help Japan's cause? This approach would be evident in the late 1930's in what two American writers would later call the Fugu Plan.[6]

In the early 1930's, Nazi antisemitism and—to a greater extent—Hitler's racial doctrines were greeted with growing skepticism by the Japanese public and the international media. Some writers, both academics and journalists, failed to understand the depth of Nazi hatred for the Jews and raised doubts about the intent of their anti-Jewish doctrine. Perhaps, some wrote, Hitler was trying to unify the German nation, to purge it of pernicious thoughts, to provide it with a sense of direction and guidance, and above all to instill a new spirit in the German people. Antisemitism, they argued, was merely being used as a lever to enhance Hitler's control of Germany.

The reports that appeared in Japanese and international media on the rise of the Nazis to power and the beginning of the persecution of Jews elicited a number of responses from liberal Japanese academics. It appears in retrospect that they, too, failed to understand Hitler's intentions, the nationalist-racist ideology of the Nazi party in Germany, and above all Hitler's aspirations regarding the future of Europe and Germany's leading role on that continent. Some Japanese correspondents even thought that like Japan, Hitler needed the Jews due to their pivotal role in the international economy. Indeed, like some Japanese leaders, Hitler and his associates in their first few years after acceding to power were careful not to antagonize what they considered international Jewish economic and financial interests (mainly in the United States) so as to avoid harming their own economy, which was still reeling from the 1929 crash. Some scholars in Japan even thought naively that Nazism in Germany was a passing phenomenon, and that very soon the German voting public would realize what it did to itself by choosing Hitler and his antisemitic ideology.[7]

Another reason for the growing uncertainty over what was occurring with the Nazi persecution of German Jews was the growing number of questions asked in Japan regarding what would happen if anti-Jewish persecution caused hundreds of thousands of German Jews to leave Germany. Since it was obvious that they were not wanted in Western Europe and they were virtually barred from the United States, Britain, and countries of the British Commonwealth of Nations such as Canada, Australia, New Zealand, and South Africa, some of them would surely try to make their way to East Asia and might even seek shelter in Japan. Japan's reputation as being neutral on Jewish matters was already known in Europe and supported by its policies. If a wave of Jews sought to settle in Japan, that country could find itself burdened with an acute "Jewish Problem," something that Japan had never before faced, apart from dealing with some 15,000 Jews living in Manchuria.

Nazi ideas began to infiltrate into Japan mainly at the end of the 1930's. *Mein Kampf* was retranslated and once again distributed there in 1937. Alfred Rosenberg's *The Myth of the Twentieth Century* was also retranslated and widely distributed in 1938. All this aroused greater awareness and even some fear of the Jews, irrespective of the fact that there were hardly any Jews in Japan.

Reports of the first days of the Nazi regime in Germany appeared in the Japanese media, encouraging a group that was seeking a new course for Japan. This group consisted mainly of army officers who were developing an idea that became known later as the "Showa Restoration." Their intention was to return political power to the emperor, taking it away from the corrupt politicians and business tycoons who they perceived as having it. In addition, of course, they wanted to see the reins of government being granted to the armed forces, the only pure and patriotic element in Japan that knew exactly what the Imperial wishes were. A growing number of Japanese officers, mainly in the junior and middle ranks, watched with great interest as the Nazi party slowly took over all German government institutions, eliminated criticism and opposition, purged the universities, the bureaucracy, and the judiciary from their Jewish professors, civil servants and jurists, instituted new content in the state educational system, and strengthened the German national spirit, and they wondered if Japan should not emulate this model. These ideas aligned well with other forces—the fear and hostility felt for Western liberal democracies and resentment at what was seen as the West's determination to block Japan's ambitions in Asia. However, there were a number of military leaders who feared that Japan was not yet ready to embark on a road that would lead it to inevitable military confrontation with the West. It was obvious to many army and navy officers and senior civil servants that Japan was not in the same position as Germany. At its head stood an emperor with links to the nation's mythological founding gods; there was no charismatic leader like the German Führer or even the Italian Duce Benito Mussolini (1882-1945). There was no single mass party that ruled in Japan: its government was in the hands of a coalition consisting of political parties, the armed forces, the bureaucracy, and heads of large corporations (known as *zaibatsu*). Unlike Germany, Japan had not been defeated in the recent war, had never been occupied by foreign powers, and had never been forced to submit to humiliating terms such as those imposed on Germany by the victorious allies (including Japan herself) at the end of the First World War.

What was the place of Jews in the thinking of the average Japanese citizen? Unlike Germany, where the Jews became the main focus and target of the Nazi regime from its inception, there continued to be no "Jewish Question" in Japan. Most Japanese people had still never seen a Jew in their lives, and thus knew nothing about and subsequently had no interest in this issue. Very few studied, knew about, or understood the "Jewish Question." Among the minority who did was the small group of officers who became specialists or experts on Jewish affairs. The initial goal of their research on this topic was to help the Japanese military authorities deal with Jews in Manchuria. As time went on, however, they came to play an important role in formulating Japan's policies toward Jews until 1945.

Chapter 5

Japanese Experts on Jews, Judaism, and Zionism

We have noted that in Major General Higuchi Kiicihiro's headquarters in Siberia there were a number of officers who specialized in Jewish affairs. The need for specialists in Jewish affairs arose when soldiers and officers belonging to the Japanese expeditionary force in Siberia had to deal with tens of thousands of Jews who lived in Siberia and Manchuria. The need to gather intelligence about this community was great, if only to prevent clashes between White Russians and Jews in Manchuria. Jews could also be a source of intelligence about the Soviet Union. After the departure of Japanese forces from Siberia in 1922, the Japanese military presence on the Asian mainland was concentrated in the Japanese-leased territory of Liaotung in southern Manchuria. Japanese army units had been stationed there as part of the 1905 peace treaty between Japan and Tsarist Russia that had ended the Russo-Japanese War. The units posted there were called the Kwantung Army, and their mission was to safeguard and advance Japanese interests in Manchuria, expand them if the opportunity arose, and obtain intelligence on all elements that could stand in the way of Japan's goals.

Initial intelligence about Jews came from White Russian refugees, some of them civilians but most of them former Tsarist soldiers and officers who had escaped from the Soviet Union after the Bolshevik Revolution. These individuals had a pernicious influence on the Japanese officers with whom they came into contact, and were the only channel though which Japanese officers could glean intelligence about Jews. Their negative opinions were due to their hatred of the Bolshevik regime, which they claimed was led by Jews. There were in fact many Jews in the upper echelons of the Soviet leadership, such as the head of the NKVD internal security agency Genrich Yagoda (1891-1938), Stalin's deputy Lazar Kaganovich (1893-1991), Stalin's personal secretary and later the editor of *Pravda* Lev Machlis (1889-1953), Leningrad party boss Grigory Zinoviev (1883-1936), Politbureau member Lev Kamenev, and Stalin's arch-rival, Red Army founder Leon Trotsky.

Among the leading Jewish intellectuals, artists, writers, and poets who were part of the establishment there stood out the film director Sergei Eizenstein (1898-1948), journalist Ilia Ehrenburg (1891-1967), and poets Isaac Babel (1894-1940) and Ossip Mandelshtam (1891-1938). In Stalin's inner circle were Jews such as Paulina, the Jewish wife of prime minister and later foreign minister Vyacheslav Molotov. Such a high concentration of Jews in the highest echelons of the Soviet regime only strengthened fears among Japanese officers regarding the influence of Jews on policy- and decision-makers of the Soviet Union. This was also a proof of the Jewish ability to penetrate into the highest levels of a rising power—in this case the communist Soviet Union, a potential enemy of Japan.

Two Japanese officers became known as the country's leading experts on Jews. Both served in Higuchi's headquarters, which was responsible for special duties and was mainly used for gathering intelligence. One was Colonel Yasue Norihiro and the other Naval Captain Inuzuka Koreshige.[1] The role of these experts was to advise the Japanese command on what they should do with the thousands of Jewish refugees who escaped from the Soviet Union after the Bolshevik Revolution and settled primarily in Manchuria's main city, Harbin, whose Jewish community in the early 1920's already numbered some 15,000 souls. It must be noted that the military careers of these two experts were not stellar, and that they did not stand out in any way apart from their linguistic abilities.[2]

Yasue was born in 1888 to a samurai family. At age 19 he entered Japan's Imperial Military Academy, and despite poor health managed to graduate in 1909. His military career was unexceptional, but in 1917 he was sent to study Russian at the Tokyo Foreign Languages School. His knowledge of Russian led to his assignment to Siberia in 1918, where he served as a liaison officer to Semyonov. This gave him the chance to meet a number of White Russian, anti-Bolshevik, and antisemitic officers, and thus began his career as a Jewish affairs specialist.

Inuzuka was born in 1890. He joined the navy after graduating from high school, enrolling in the Imperial Naval Academy, from which he graduated in 1912. During the First World War he served on board a number of vessels in the Mediterranean Sea, and at the end of the war he was stationed aboard a warship anchored off the port of Vladivostok. There he read *The Protocols of the Elders of Zion* for the first time, and was impressed with the "authenticity" of this forged document.

While Inuzuka never served in Siberia, Yasue did and used his Russian language skills to converse with Harbin's two largest foreign communities: the

White Russians and the Jews. In the 1920's he and Inuzuka, after many conversations with White Russians and much consideration of Russian material on Jews, came to the conclusion that the Jews had become a major force in the world in the early parts of that decade, and that Japan must adopt a restrained policy towards them and attempt to win their goodwill in order to promote the continental interests of the Empire and win sympathy and understanding in America.

Their acceptance of the concept that the Jews possessed vast political and economic power was due partly to the antisemitic ideas adopted by Yasue and Inuzuka from the White Russian émigrés. Yasue undertook to translate the *Protocols of the Elders of Zion* to Japanese in 1924, and in the introduction to this infamous tract he in fact demonstrated that he subscribed to some of the antisemitic ideas contained in it. However, he also learned to appreciate and value the imagined and real power of the Jews and counselled his superiors to beware of their influence. He began to warn his superiors of the slow penetration of Jews into Japan in the guise of refugees, and suggested the possibility of their slow penetration into the nascent trade union movement and the Japanese Communist Party, which was established in 1926. In this manner, he warned, the Jews would add to the social upheaval and instability that already prevailed in some areas of Japan's major cities. Of course, none of this ever happened.

In the mid 1930's, Inuzuka was stationed in Shanghai and came into contact with the large Jewish community of that city. This familiarity strengthened his belief in the vast powers of world Jewry, and he supported the scheme of mobilizing German Jews to settle in Manchuria. In 1939, on the eve of World War II, Captain Inuzuka published an article in which he claimed that Japan faced a grave danger from the Jews. This danger began, according to him, in the days of Marco Polo—described by Inuzuka as Jewish—and later by another Jew: Christopher Columbus. Like Yasue, he argued that if Japan pursued an adroit policy, it could derive much benefit from the Jews. He too was influenced by Nazi racial doctrines. From March 1939 to April 1942, he served as the head of the Japanese Navy Advisory Bureau on Jewish Affairs and was deeply involved in formulating Japan's policies on the Jews of Shanghai.

There is no evidence that these two Jewish affairs experts ever made an attempt to study Jewish history in depth, to read books and articles on Judaism, learn rudimentary Hebrew or even Yiddish, or to understand the major foundations of the Jewish religion, such as the Jewish Bible and the commentaries of the Talmud. Since they received much of their knowledge of

Jewish affairs from White Russians—and mainly White Russian officers—many of whom were openly antisemitic, it could not be expected that they would be educated on the positive aspects of Judaism. Nonetheless, for the requirements of their superior officers, their knowledge seems to have been sufficient. They were expected to deal with the leadership of the Jewish communities in Manchuria and later in Shanghai in order to ensure their support for Japan's policies in Asia. They were also expected to obtain intelligence on the Soviet Union, to be gathered from Jews in Harbin who still had many relatives in Russia.

However, there were other people in Japan who became interested in Jews and Judaism. Some Japanese intellectuals even displayed a friendly and positive interest in Zionism. Among them were Uchimura Kanzo (1861-1930), Nitobe Inazo (1862-1933), Tokutomi Kenjiro (1868-1927), and Professor Yanaihara Tadao (1893-1961). The latter lectured on colonial policy at Tokyo University, and wrote in one of his articles that, "The Zionist Movement is no more than an experiment to guarantee the Jews the right to emigrate and to settle, in order to create a center for Jewish national culture." He added that the Zionist claim that the Jewish people deserve a national state of its own reflects a true national problem, and that the cooperative system of the Jewish settlements in Palestine was worthy of adoption by Japan.[3]

The Specialists and Zionism

In the framework of acquiring knowledge on Jews and Zionism, the experts sought information that would help them establish Japan's policy toward the Zionist movement and wished to study what exactly the Zionists were aiming to achieve in Palestine. It turned out that some Japanese officers had already been introduced to the ideology of the Zionist movement over the course of the Russo-Japanese War by Japan's most famous Jewish prisoner of war, Yoseph Trumpeldor, who organized a Zionist cell and study groups in the Hamadera prisoner-of-war camp near Osaka. It is not known if the officers who guarded the Hamadera camp shared what they learned with higher military authorities or the Japanese government. The interest of the Japanese government and people in an independent state for the Jews in particular, and in problems of the Middle East in general, was virtually non-existent. Japan had few consular or diplomatic representatives in the Middle East, and had little information on the rise of the Arab national movement—which surprisingly had drawn much encouragement from

Japan's victory over Russia in 1905. Until World War I, the Japanese government had no cause to take a stand regarding the Zionist movement and its aspirations, partly out of sheer non-interest and partly because no authorized Zionist body ever suggested that it do so. The leaders of the Zionist movement had many more immediately relevant things to think about during the first decade of the existence of the World Zionist Organization.

There is no evidence of any contact between Japanese officials and the Zionist Association that was established in Nagasaki in 1905, which offered assistance with food and Hebrew texts to Trumpledor and his fellow Russian Jewish prisoners of war. The need to obtain Japan's support of Zionist aspirations in Palestine arose toward the end of the First World War, when Japan joined Britain, France, Italy, Tsarist Russia (until January 1918), and beginning in April 1917 the United States as a member of the coalition against the German, Austro-Hungarian, and Ottoman Empires. Since a major foundation of Japan's foreign policy was its treaty of friendship with Britain, it appeared to the Zionist leadership to be a power that could play a potentially important role in shaping the post-war arrangements.[4]

The Zionists, who were obviously focused on the future of Palestine, realized that the power that was about to conquer Palestine from the Turks was Britain. In the early stages of the War, they had already concluded that they would have to link the fate of Zionism and its goal of establishing a Jewish state in Palestine with the British Empire, and their major achievement was the Balfour Declaration of November 2, 1917. Following this proclamation of support for Zionist aims by the British government, the Zionist leadership sought to obtain declarations of support for the Balfour Declaration from other major powers. The Shanghai Zionist Association was charged with the task of seeking the support of the three independent nations of Asia—Thailand, Japan, and China. The Japanese government expressed its support in various ways on a number of occasions. In fact, on September 24, 1918, the president of the Shanghai Zionist Association, Elie Kadourie, wrote to the Japanese embassy in Paris to seek the support of Japan for the Balfour Declaration. That embassy replied on December 27 that Japan's foreign minister Uchida Yasuya (1865-1936) stated that "the Government of Japan was happy to hear of the deep desire of the Zionists to establish a Jewish national homeland in Palestine and that it sympathizes with the implementation of their aspirations." Another expression of support was in the form of a reply to a letter written on January 3, 1919, to Japan's Ambassador to London Chinda Sutemi (1857-1929) by the

Chairman of the Zionist Federation of Great Britain, Dr. Chaim Weizmann, seeking Japan's support for the Balfour Declaration. Chinda replied three days later saying that his government noted with pleasure Zionist aspirations to establish a national Jewish homeland in Palestine and viewed with favor the implementation of this aspiration on the proposed basis. Chinda also noted that the Japanese government had already sent a letter in this spirit to the Zionist Association of Shanghai in December 1918.

On the eve of the meeting of the four superpowers in San Remo in April 1920 to decide upon the granting of the Mandate over Palestine to Britain, Japan supported the granting, and Uchida Yasuya had already instructed Japan's consul general in Shanghai to write a letter on his behalf to the local Zionist Association congratulating the Zionists for this achievement. He added that he had followed closely the progress of the Zionist movement, which had won this noteworthy achievement. When the plenary session of the League of Nations voted on July 22, 1922, on granting the Palestine mandate to Britain, Japan translated its verbal support into political action and voted in favor. For his role Uchida was honored by the Zionist Movement, which inscribed his name in the Golden Book of the Jewish National Fund in Jerusalem. On the tenth anniversary of the Balfour Declaration, in November 1927, the Shanghai Zionists once again sought a declaration of support from the Japanese government. This time, Prime Minister Tanaka Giichi sent his greetings and noted the impressive achievements of the creation of national Jewish institutions in Palestine.

Why did Japan support the Zionists' aspirations in the 1920's? What lay behind the early Japanese support for Zionism? There were a number of very sober and well-calculated policy considerations involved. Four main reasons stand out: First, Japan was an ally of Britain during the First World War, and supported Britain's territorial demands and interests in the Middle East hoping to receive in return British support for its territorial ambitions in East Asia and the Pacific. Therefore, maintaining good relations with Britain was a cornerstone of Japanese foreign policy since the signing of the first Anglo-Japanese Alliance in 1902. Second, the highly exaggerated assessment and image of the well-connected wealthy Jews and the help they provided Japan during the Russo-Japanese War had to be considered, and perhaps was even rewarded in this manner. Third, the ability of the Zionist Organization to obtain the Balfour Declaration and subsequent declarations of support by the French and American governments impressed the Japanese government deeply. Japan saw the Zionist Organization as a powerful instrument of world Jewry which had vast influence over various governments. Fourth, it is important to note that the price paid by Japan for its support of Zionism was meager. Its support did not cost it the friendship of the Arabs (which it would have in the 1950's or later). Japan began to show growing interest in the Arab states only beginning in the mid-1920's. The absence of interest, knowledge, and understanding in Japan of Arab national aspirations helped the Zionists gain Japan's support. Furthermore, this support did not require of Japan any political, financial, or military effort. At most it was expressed in letters of support written to Zionist associations and in favorable votes in the League of Nations. Perhaps another reason had to do with the Shanghai Zionist Association, headed by Elie Kadourie (1865-1922), a member of the well-known and wealthy Jewish family which had large-scale business interests in Japan.[5]

The Japanese media showed almost no interest in Zionism or Palestine, and the few reports made on the topic demonstrated a lack of understanding. An outstanding example of this can be seen in coverage of the visit of Israel Cohen, who visited Japan, China, and Australia between May 1920 and May 1921 as an emissary of the Zionist Executive in London. He spent ten days in Japan in December 1920, held two public meetings with the Jewish communities in Yokohama and Kobe, and met with the British ambassador in Tokyo, but made no contact with the Japanese government. After the meeting in Yokohama, the daily newspaper *Asahi Shimbun* wrote that the Jews had held a meeting in the office of the Jewish community of Yokohama to discuss the creation of a "Jewish Kingdom" (sic). The same paper also called Cohen a member of the Jewish royal family.[6]

Contact between the Jewish community of Palestine and the Zionist Executive in Jerusalem in the 1920's was maintained through the consul general of Japan in Port Said, who visited Palestine in 1926 to gather intelligence. Various reports emanating from Palestine prompted the Japanese government to learn more about that country and the Jewish enterprise there. Some officers may have heard about the Zionist effort from the Jews in Harbin who maintained close contact with the Zionist leadership in Palestine. It is not coincidental that the job of learning more about Palestine fell on Colonel Yasue.

After returning to Japan from Siberia and Manchuria, Yasue had published a number of articles on Jewish subjects under a different name, because as an active-duty officer in the Japanese army it would have been inappropriate to publish under his own name. One of the articles was called "The Movement for the Establishment of a Jewish State." Yasue was later promoted by War Minister Shirakawa Yoshinori (1869-1932), who posted him to the imperial military headquarters in Tokyo. In the spring of 1927, Yasue was dispatched to Europe and Palestine to gather intelligence on what was already known as the "Jewish Question." He arrived in Palestine on December 8, 1927, accompanied by the pastor Sakai Katsuhisa (or Shogun). Their arrival was noted in the *Palestine Weekly*. They spent twenty-four days in Palestine, five of them touring the country, guided by a local journalist, Moshe Medzini (1897-1983, the father of this writer), who had been asked by the Zionist Executive to be their guide. Born in Irkutsk, Medzini had studied in Harbin and lived for a year in Japan in 1919, and was able to speak Russian with Yasue and English with Sakai.

They toured Jerusalem, Tel Aviv, and Haifa, saw a number of moshavim and kibbutzim, and visited some of the new industrial plants of the Jewish community. They also visited the newly opened Hebrew University campus on Mt. Scopus in Jerusalem. Their visit seems to have been important to the Zionist Executive, and they met with the Head of the Executive Colonel Frederick Kisch (1888-1943) and with the British High Commissioner Lord Plumer (1857-1932). During their visit they also had talks with Chaim Kalvarisky-Margaliot (1868-1947), the head of the Arab Department of the Zionist Executive.

Upon their return, Yasue published several articles on his impressions of Palestine (and Europe), in which he expressed his admiration for what he saw and the Jewish ability to make the desert bloom. The American Jewish scholar David Kranzler, who read Yasue's diary, noted that Yasue wrote that in his reports to the Japanese government he had expressed his view that the Zionist enterprise in Palestine was part of an international Jewish plot, and explained that his hosts in Palestine sought to conceal this fact from him.

Pastor Sakai gave a number of lectures about Palestine upon his return to Japan, and even wrote to Kisch suggesting that the World Zionist Organization present Emperor Hirohito (1901-1989) with a gift on the occasion of his coronation in 1928. Kisch referred to Sakai as the "crazy Gentile" ("Meshugener Goy"), but thought that an album of photographs depicting the Jewish community in Palestine would be a fitting gift. It is not clear if the gift was ever sent to the Emperor. Hirohito's coronation was noted by the *Israel Messenger*, the publication of the Zionist Association of Shanghai, edited by Nissim Benjamin Ezra. The article written for the occasion expressed hope that a Japanese consul would be appointed to New Judea, and that Japan would actively assist the implementation of the Zionist dream in New Judea.

However, the interest of the Japanese government in Zionism and in Palestine cooled somewhat after this point. Other, more pressing, concerns arose that occupied its attention. One notable exception had occurred already in the early 1920's after an outbreak of violence in Palestine, when the under-secretary general of the League of Nations, a Japanese diplomat named Sugimura Yotaro (1884-1939), granted an interview to the *Israel Messenger* in Shanghai. He deplored the lack of law and order in Palestine and identified himself as a strong believer in the renaissance of the national Jewish spirit. He claimed that Japan had made a commitment to help implement the dream of a national Jewish homeland in Palestine and was fully aware of the key roles played by Jews in human history and what all of humanity owed them. He even mentioned Albert Einstein (1879-1955), who had visited Japan in 1922. But on the whole, the Japanese government refrained from making pro-Zionist statements and was content to let the British administer their mandate over Palestine and thus determine the fate of the Zionist effort in that country.[7]

In the 1920's and 1930's the Middle East was a very low priority on Japan's foreign policy agenda. It is true that Japan imported large quantities of raw cotton from Egypt, and exported to Egypt as well: between 1921 and 1924 the Japanese exports to Egypt grew from 2.5 million to 13.5 million USD. In 1931, at the height of the global economic crisis, Japanese firms exported to Middle Eastern countries goods worth 20 million USD, and four years later the sum rose to 43 million. Japanese goods, mainly textiles, began to enter markets in Middle East nations such as Turkey, Iran, Trans-Jordan, and even Palestine. This trade convinced Britain to pressure the Egyptian government to abrogate the most-favored-nation clause in its relations with Japan. Japanese goods did not have a good reputation and were known for being shoddy.[8] Despite the increase, even at its height, exports to Middle Eastern countries constituted only 3.3% of Japan's overall exports.

Did the experts on Jews play any role in determining Japan's policy on Palestine? Most likely they did not. They were far more concerned with establishing and maintaining ties with the Jewish refugees who were beginning to arrive in Manchuria in growing numbers and with the leaders of the Harbin Jewish community. There is no record of Japanese statements referring to the 1936-1939 Arab rebellion in Palestine, to the Peel's Commission recommendation of partitioning Palestine in 1937, or to the 1939 White Paper policy that severely limited Jewish immigration to Palestine and forbade the sale of land to Jews in a large part of that country. Since Japan withdrew from the League of Nations in 1933 over the Manchurian crisis, it was no longer represented in the League's Mandates Commission, a body to which the British were to provide an annual report on developments in the Palestine Mandate. Beginning in the mid-1930's, Germany replaced Britain as the focus of Japan's quest for alliances. In November 1936, Japan joined Germany in the Anti-Comintern Pact against Soviet Communism.

After the outbreak of the second Sino-Japanese War in July 1937, Japan experienced increasing problems with Britain in China, including British arms shipments to Chiang Kai-Shek's nationalist forces via the Burma Road. Palestine and its Jewish community were now relegated to the lowest priority in Japan's diplomacy. Japan was not yet dependent on Arab oil, as it would become starting in the mid-1950's, and so there was even less reason to be concerned with the Middle East. Japan's major interest, as far as Jewish matters was concerned, was focused on the Jewish community of Manchuria, which since 1931 had become the direct responsibility of the Japanese government. Harbin was the key city of this large community.

Chapter 6

Japan and the Jews of Manchuria Beginning in 1931[1]

As we discussed briefly above, the first contact between Japan and a relatively large Jewish population took place during the Japanese Siberian Intervention, from 1918 to 1922. That operation was designed to help White Russian forces defeat the Bolsheviks and destroy the newly established Communist regime in that country. At the time, some 25,000 Jews living in a number of cities in East Siberia found themselves between the hammer and the anvil following the Bolshevik Revolution. On the one hand they were hounded by the newly established Far East Republic which was soon replaced by the Communist regime, which charged them with anti-Bolshevik tendencies, and on the other they were charged by the White Russians, the enemies of the Reds, of being loyal communists who supported the new regime in the Soviet Union and were busy spreading communist ideology in East Asia. After the Japanese troops returned home from Siberia in 1922 and the communist regime stabilized itself in Siberia, the fate of the Jews in that part of Russia was akin to that elsewhere in the Soviet Union: they were tolerated by the new regime, but their religion, language, and school system were proscribed. Zionism was outlawed, and emigration from the Soviet Union became highly restricted.

Of the 25,000 Jews in Siberia, several thousand fled south across the Manchurian border. This area, formally under Chinese sovereignty, had been increasingly under Russian influence since the beginning of the twentieth century. Even before the Russo-Japanese War the Jews there had enjoyed a special status under the Tsarist regime, which had encouraged them to settle in cities like Harbin, Mukden, and Dairen to cement the Russian presence in Manchuria.

By 1900 approximately 45 Jews lived in Harbin. The community grew to 300 only two years later, and in 1915 the number of Jews residing in Harbin was estimated at 12,000 souls. They made their living in trade, services, and exports and imports, with a few working in industry or the hotel business. The community was well-organized and maintained synagogues, schools, and health, welfare, and charitable institutions. Community members spoke mainly Russian. Among them were the Olmert family, including the grandfather and father of Ehud Olmert (1945-), who would eventually become prime minister of Israel.

After the October 1917 Bolshevik Revolution, the legal status of the Jews of Harbin became problematic. Some were now Soviet nationals, but the majority of them were in effect stateless and thus under the protection of the local Chinese warlord Chang Tso Lin (1876-1928). In the absence of a strong central government, they had few defenses from their virulent enemies the White Russians, who like the Jews were exiles from the Soviet Union. The White Russians embarked on a systematic campaign to turn the Japanese government and officers belonging to the Kwantung Army headquarters in Manchuria against the Jews. The Kwantung Army was responsible for the security of the Japanese enclave in the Liaotung Peninsula, whose major cities were Port Arthur and Dairen. On the eve of the Japanese occupation in 1931, a White Russian fascist party was established in Harbin. The Japanese army wanted above all to ensure stability and social order in Manchuria. Intercommunal tensions were highly undesirable for them.

After the Occupation of Manchuria by Japan

After Japan's occupation of Manchuria in late 1931 and early 1932 and the establishment of the puppet state of Manchukuo, the Jews of Manchuria found themselves under direct Japanese rule. Since many lacked any nationality, and those of Russian origins were formally Stateless Russian Emigrants, they were at the mercy of the Japanese army, the true masters of Manchukuo. They sought the protection of the Japanese army mainly from the White Russian émigrés, who never tired of accusing them of various crimes, including maintaining contact with the enemies of Japan and disloyalty to the new puppet regime of Manchukuo. When the Soviet Union sold its holdings in the Southern Manchurian Railway to Japan in 1935, the Russian government no longer felt any obligation to protect the Jews of Soviet nationality, resulting in the departure of almost half of the Jewish community from Harbin, Mukden, and other towns. The number of Jews in Manchuria dwindled to less than 6,000. Many of the emigrants went south to Shanghai, a few traveled to the United States, and some even immigrated to Palestine. At this stage, however, the economic position of some of the wealthy Jews remained intact. Among the wealthy families were the Zykman, Skidelsky, and Kavalkin families. The Jewish leadership understood very early that in order to survive it would have to collaborate with the puppet regime of Manchukuo, and that this meant it would truly be collaborating with the headquarters of the Kwantung Army. The commander of that force became Japan's ambassador to Manchukuo, and was thus the de-facto ruler of that country, which by 1937 was recognized only by Japan, Germany, Italy and El Salvador.

Among the officers who served in the Japanese supreme command, and mainly among that group that became known as the "Manchuria Faction," a number of ideas were discussed regarding how to exploit the Manchurian Jews to help Japan gain recognition of the Manchukuo puppet state by additional countries and above all how to obtain foreign economic aid for the development of Manchuria's industry. Among those who supported this line of thought were Colonels Itagaki Seishiro (1885-1948) and Ishihara Kanji (1889-1949).

Quite early in the occupation, it dawned on the Japanese leadership that the hopes they had pinned on the quality of Manchurian coal and steel were highly exaggerated.[2] In order to develop these two key resources, vast sums of money would be required, and some officers thought that it would be possible to mobilize international Jewry to raise the necessary funds. The minimal amount required was estimated at between two to three billion dollars, an astronomical sum and even more so for those times. Those Japanese officers and civilian bureaucrats who supported the idea hoped that wealthy Jews, mainly in the United States, would invest in Manchuria. Hence, it was imperative not to harm the Jews in Manchuria in any way.

Once again, Japan's ignorance and total lack of understanding of world Jewry was evident. Even the few officers who were considered Jewish experts failed to realize that while Jews were wealthy in certain countries, their political clout even in the United States was almost non-existent. They were even unable to change America's drastic immigration laws to allow tens of thousands of German and Austrian Jewish refugees to find haven in the United States. In the midst of the Great Depression, there was no chance that any wealthy Jew would invest in the development of Manchuria's industries, let alone promote an aggressive Japanese policy in East Asia.

The idea of using the power of rich Jews was not new; it had initially been discussed by a number of Japanese foreign ministry officials in 1921. Now it surfaced again. At this time the officers discussing the situation basically thought that it would be beneficial for Japan to establish good working relations with the Jewish community in Manchuria, and allay their fears that the Japanese might support White Russian hooliganism and even antisemitic outbursts in that country. They feared that anti-Jewish incidents, if mentioned in the American media, would create an unpleasant image for Japan at the very time that it wanted to demonstrate the benevolent nature of its rule in Manchuria. The local Jewish leadership under Dr. Abraham Kaufman (1885-1971) recognized the need to collaborate with the Japanese authorities in order to ensure the survival of the slowly diminishing Jewish communities of Harbin, Mukden, and Dairen.

For their part, the Japanese authorities adopted a "divide and rule" policy regarding the Jews and the White Russians. They did not ban the Russian fascist party, but they did restrict its activities. On a number of occasions they used White Russians as special police officers to spy on the Chinese, Koreans, and Jews. The Japanese authorities also permitted the publication of a fascist Russian publication *Nash Pot* ("Our Way"), which called for killing the Jews.

During the 1930's and early 1940's, the main enemies of the Manchurian Jewish communities continued to be the White Russians. This dire situation meant that the Jews had to rely on the Japanese authorities to protect them from the Russian ultra-nationalists. This suited the Japanese rulers of Manchuria well, and to counterbalance the Russians, they now encouraged Zionist bodies such as the Beitar Youth Movement.

The Fugu Plan

At the same time as Japan was considering the benefits of seeking Jewish capital, the President of the Southern Manchurian Railway Matsuoka Yosuke (1886-1946) and the Chairman of the Manchurian Heavy Industries Association Oikawa Yoshisuke (1880-1967) toyed with the idea of settling some fifty thousand European Jews in Manchukuo. They would, it was believed, bring with them not only capital but also technological know-how and managerial skills. The idea was developed in an article written by Oikawa in 1934 called "A Plan to Settle Fifty Thousand German Jews in Manchukuo." The underlying assumption was that the Jews Germany wanted to get rid of would be seeking a refuge wherever they could settle and invest their capital. Here, Oikawa stated, was an opportunity for Japan to steer a highly desirable population to Manchukuo. It is highly doubtful that he had ever heard of the so-called "Transfer Plan" arranged by the

World Zionist Organization and the German government in 1933, whereby the newly installed Nazi regime of Germany would allow Jews to immigrate to Palestine and transfer their capital to that country.

Key Japanese officials such as finance ministry official Kishi Nobosuke (1896-1987), a future minister in Tojo's wartime cabinet and later prime minister of Japan in the late 1950's, supported this idea, as did other finance ministry officials.

The idea—which never amounted to an operational plan in its full meaning—was described in retrospect by writers Marvin Tokayer and Mary Swartz in their 1979 book *The Fugu Plan*. Fugu is a word for blowfish, which has some poisonous flesh and some edible parts, and which is a much sought-after delicacy. The idea was suggested by Inuzuka's January 18, 1939, report to the Navy General Staff, which stated that "The Jews are just like a fugu (blowfish). It is very delicious but unless you know well how to cook it, it may prove fatal." The reference indicated that Jews spread poison in the societies in which they lived, but that they could also be highly beneficial if properly monitored and controlled. In the end, this idea remained on paper and was never accompanied by a serious, detailed, and well thought-out operational plan. Those who espoused it never determined who would be responsible for obtaining the necessary permits from the government in Tokyo, who would prepare the required infrastructure in Manchuria, who would approach and recruit those German Jews deemed eligible and mobilize their capital, and who would contact the Nazi regime to start things moving. There was never any serious effort by a responsible Japanese government body to interest German Jews and attempt to persuade them to migrate to Manchuria. The proponents of this idea never even contacted international Jewish organizations such as the World Jewish Congress, the American Jewish Congress, or the World Zionist Organization.

The causes for the failure of the idea to get off the ground were varied, and were partly the result of the planners' inability to implement such an ambitious and grandiose plan. There was also a total lack of basic knowledge on the topic, and no one had even begun to prepare the ground-work for such an undertaking. But the main reason seems to be the reticence of the Japanese government in Tokyo as well as the puppet regime of Manchukuo and their reluctance to become involved in such a scheme. In Tokyo there was less and less enthusiasm for collaborating with Jewish factors because of the government's growing ties with Nazi Germany, especially after the signing of the Anti-Comintern Pact in 1936. As German-Japanese ties grew stronger and warmer, and Germany became a strategic asset to Japan, any measure that could be interpreted as helping Jews or encouraging German Jews to remove their capital from Germany was seen as counter-productive.

Meanwhile, the Japanese military authorities in Manchukuo may have thought that the settlement of German Jews there would be a positive step in the development of that region, but they may also have feared that it would endanger their ties with the White Russian population in that country, a population far larger and more influential than the local Jewish community. They followed a policy designed to avoid alienating the two communities and acted to alleviate the fears of the Jews by making sure that there would be no outbreak of violent antisemitism. At the same time, they also made strong efforts not to alienate the local White Russian community. The final outcome of this policy was contrary to what they wanted to achieve: not only did it fail to attract German Jews, but it caused a growing flight of wealthy Jews from Manchuria, many of whom resettled in Shanghai, where entry visas were not required. By the middle of the 1930's the Harbin Jewish community had shrunk from 15,000 to less than 3,000 individuals. Even the intervention of the Japanese consul general in Harbin, General Morishima Morito (1896-1975), who met with the leaders of the community periodically in order to pacify them, did not yield any results.

The idea that the settlement of such a large number of Jewish refugees in Manchuria would improve Japan's image in the American media was preposterous from the beginning, and naturally backfired. Those who toyed with it failed to understand that American Jews had no intention of investing in Manchuria in the depths of the Great Depression. Furthermore, an investment in Manchuria would only anger the American government, which opposed the occupation of that country by Japan and in 1932 had adopted a policy of non-recognition (also known as the Stimson Doctrine).

There were also several Japanese officers who argued that Japan must distance itself from anything connected to Jews and Judaism in view of what they believed to be the Jews' constant scheming to control the world through their nefarious activities. This group based its arguments on *The Protocols of the Elders of Zion*, which as noted had been translated into Japanese in the mid-1920's. How could Japan seek Jewish help to advance its economy at the same time that the rootless Jews were considered the world's greatest danger by the Germans—Japan's own allies? Those who opposed turning to the Jews claimed that many Jews were disguised Soviet agents who could undermine Japanese society from within. The counter-view was that at least an effort should be made to harness the Manchurian Jewish community to promote Japan's interests. The task was assigned to officers in the

Intelligence Section of the Kwantung Army, and specifically in the Special Services unit, whose main role was to spy on Russians suspected of supporting the Soviet Union, mobilize White Russians, and create anti-Soviet front organizations. In 1934 this unit established the Office for Russian Émigrés and made sure that some of its members obtained senior posts in the Russian Fascist Party, which was otherwise made up of anti-Bolshevik, antisemitic White Russian émigrés. One of the first measures they took was designed to stop attacks on Jews by White Russians, attacks that had reached their peak in the years 1931-1932 with the kidnapping and subsequent murder of the son of a wealthy Jew by the name of Kaspe, who owned the largest hotel in Harbin, the Moderne.[3]

Attacks on Jews in Manchuria led to criticism by various Jewish communities overseas, mainly that of Shanghai. One of the Shanghai community's leaders, Nessim Benjamin Ezra, the editor of the *Jewish Messenger*, was received by Japan's Deputy Foreign Minister Shigemitsu Mamoru (1887-1957) in the fall of 1934 to protest these attacks. Shigemitsu promised that Japan would maintain law and order in Harbin. The Japanese government feared adverse news items on this topic in the American media, and attributed these stories to Jewish sources—hence the need to appease the Jews.

The Far Eastern Jewish National Congress[4]

Another reason Japan felt the need to mobilize the Manchurian Jews was the fear that they, too, would join the boycott against Nazi Germany's goods that had been proclaimed by international Jewish organizations, mainly in the United States, following the onset of anti-Jewish persecution in Germany. The boycott of German goods proved, to those Japanese who believed in it, that the Jews had vast power and influence and could severely harm Germany's economy if they so desired. The boycott issue became more acute after Japan joined Germany in the Anti-Comintern Pact of November 1936. Now there grew the realization that it would be useful to organize a regional Jewish body that would help advance Japan's goals in Manchuria, China, and even in South East Asia. The position of those who called for the utilization of imaginary Jewish power won over those who advised Japan to keep away from any thing that smacked of Jews.

The task of organizing the Jewish communities in Manchuria and later in all of East Asia fell to Japan's number-one Jewish expert, Colonel Yasue

Norihiro. Since his visit to Palestine in 1927 he had fulfilled a number of mid-level roles in the Japanese army, but apparently he was not that busy, as he also found time to write books and articles on Jews and deliver lectures to civilian and military groups. In his publications he wrote that the Jews endangered the world, spread dangerous thoughts, and were planning a global revolution to destroy the existing world order and establish a universal socialist regime that would help their cause.

The need to mobilize the Jews of Manchuria became more significant after the outbreak of the Second Sino-Japanese War in July 1937, a war that caused much anger in the United States and Britain, especially at the end of 1937 following the atrocities committed by Japanese troops in Nanjing. Yasue was assigned to the Kwantung Army Headquarters as an expert on Jewish affairs and once again served under Major General Higuchi Kiichiro, who was chief of the Intelligence Bureau of Harbin for the Kwantung Army. One of the first things he did was shut down the Russian language newspaper *Nash Pot*, the mouthpiece of the Russian antisemites in Manchuria. Higuchi had previously served as military attaché in the Japanese embassy in Warsaw, had a number of Jewish friends, and was aware of the plight of the Polish Jews. When he arrived in Harbin he developed friendly ties with Dr. Abraham Kaufman, the veteran leader of the Jewish community there.

The Jewish experts also helped prepare a position paper for the chief of staff of the Kwantung Army, General Tojo Hideki (1884-1948), who would later serve as Japan's wartime prime minister from 1941-1944. The document contained detailed instructions to the Japanese authorities in Manchukuo intended to ease the entry of a certain number of Jewish refugees into that territory. It was determined that the entry of Jews who had a certain amount of funds would be permitted. The implementation of these instructions was left to the discretion of local border officials, mainly in the border town of Manchuli, on the Manchurian-Siberian border where the Trans-Siberian train stopped. This train carried many of the Jews who chose the Siberian route to escape from Central Europe. Since they did not have a visa to Japan or entry permits to the Soviet Union, it was evident that if they were not allowed into Manchuria they would be sent back to Germany or Austria. Tales of their plight reached Harbin, and Dr. Kaufman was able to persuade Higuchi to allow a large number of these refugees to enter Manchuria. They were met at the Harbin station by members of the Zionist youth movements and were housed temporarily in a Jewish-owned hotel called Astoria. They were then taken to Dairen, from whence they sailed to Shanghai.

Japan's attitude toward the Jewish refugees now became an important issue, since it also involved German-Japanese relations. The problem, as noted above, was how to avoid doing anything positive for the Jews that would harm Japan's ties with Nazi Germany while also avoiding alienating American Jews, whose economic power was seen by Japan as dominant. In view of such conflicting considerations, the Japanese high command had to navigate the political waters carefully, and once again they turned to their chief expert.

Yasue's recommemdation was to establish a regional council of the Jewish communities in East Asia, which would serve as the umbrella organization for the Jews of Manchuria, Northern China, and even Japan. For that purpose he recruited the heads of the Harbin Jewish community, led by Dr. Abraham Kaufman and Lev Zykman. Colonel Yasue was aware that Dr. Kaufman had contacts with the World Jewish Congress and various American Jewish organizations, as well as with the Zionist Executive in Jerusalem. Another possible reason for the creation of this organization was that the Jewish experts believed that the Manchurian Jewish leadership would be able to establish ties with American Jewry, which was seen as highly influential at the time. The American media was full of stories about the atrocity known as "rape of Nanjing," and the Japanese government felt the necessity of limiting the damage done by the publicity of the crimes committed by Japanese troops in the Chinese capital.

The culmination of this activity was the convening of the First Congress of the Jews in East Asia in Harbin on December 26, 1937, with over five hundred people in attendance. Among those present were a number of senior Japanese officers, headed by General Higuchi, and there were even some White Russian observers. Order was maintained by uniformed members of the local Beitar Youth Movement. The gala opening session of the congress was covered by Japanese reporters. The speeches given by the Japanese officers stressed the need for the Jews to identify with Japan's struggle for peace and harmony. In East Asia, its fight against Bolshevism, and its demand for a rightful place in the sun. The Jewish speakers expressed their strong identification with Japan's "rightful struggle" and supported its desire to achieve for itself a place in the sun (defined in this case as becoming the leading regional superpower).

Major General Higuchi stressed in his speech that the government of Japan and the Japanese people held no prejudices against Jews and did not subscribe to racist ideology. He stated that they welcomed close, friendly ties with the Jews and were prepared to cooperate with them in the economic and commercial spheres in Japan as well as in other countries.

In his response, Dr. Kaufman emphasised the fact that Jews residing in Japanese-controlled areas enjoyed full equality and were not discriminated against because of their race. They were willing to cooperate with Japan and Manchukuo in an effort to create a new order in East Asia under Japan. At the conclusion of the three-day conference, a governing body was established, led by Dr. Kaufman but under the close supervision of Colonel Yasue, who became the link between the Japanese authorities and the congress. As noted above, one of the immediate results was the granting of transit entry permits into Manchukuo for thousands of Jewish refugees who were stranded in Manchuli on the Soviet border on their way to Shanghai, the United States, and any other destination that would accept them. Years later, Kaufman (who immigrated to Israel in 1961) explained that the Jews of Harbin had no choice but to collaborate with the Japanese authorities in order to survive. This argument was repeated by his son Theodore (1923-2012) in his own memoirs.[5]

The Congress met again in December 1938 and December 1939. The fourth gathering was due to take place in Dairen in December 1940, but the German government asked Japan to cancel it. Japan, having signed the Axis Pact with Germany and Italy ten weeks earlier, decided to comply. This marked the end of this body, which was in reality an instrument of the Japanese army meant to control the Jews or at least gain some propaganda benefits. Yasue was removed from his post as Jewish expert in Dairen. Captain Inuzuka would emerge later in Shanghai, once again as a Jewish expert. One of the results of the Far Eastern Congress, however, was salutary. The Japanese army in Manchuria and Northern China understood that the highest echelons of their commanders were involved in this enterprise, and thus the Jews were left on their own in that part of China, their institutions untouched until Japan surrendered in 1945.

In their capacity as heads of the Congress, Kaufman and Zykman visited Japan a number of times during 1938-1940 and met with Japanese cabinet members. Yasue and Kaufman even came up with the idea of sending Zykman to America to meet the heads of the American Jewish Congress as the representative of the East Asian Jews. Their plan was to mobilize the American Jewish leader Rabbi Stephen Wise (1874-1949) in an effort to improve Japan-American relations. The Japanese officers apparently thought that Zykman could have a mollifying effect on American Jewish leaders, and that they in turn could prevent the worsening of commercial ties between Japan and the United States and even avert the possibility of economic sanctions against Japan that would seriously harm Japan's military preparations for a future war against the United States. Zykman's role would be to tell American Jewish leaders that Japan treated the approximately 15,000 Jews under its control in East Asia fairly. Wise's angry response was written on November 22, 1938, some two weeks after "Kristallnacht" in Germany, and rejected outright the notion that American Jews would support Japan, a fascist state like Germany and Italy. He informed Zykman that he was not even prepared to discuss the matter, regardless of the reasons that Zykman was seeking his help. This setback did not deter Yasue, who continued to maintain close ties with Dr. Kaufman.[6]

Another Japanese idea was considered in 1939 by Yasue, Inuzuka, and the Japanese foreign ministry official Ishiguro Shiro. It regarded the possibility of creating an autonomous Jewish area near Shanghai, similar to the Soviet Jewish autonomous region of Birobijan. It is unclear how seriously the Japanese government treated this idea, which was never implemented, but it is indicative of the thinking of the two experts on Jewish matters in the Japanese army.[7]

After Japan joined Germany and Italy in the Axis Pact in late September, 1940, Lev Zykman was invited on December 31 to dinner at the home of Japan's Foreign Minister Matsuoka, the man who more than any other Japanese leader had pushed for Japan to join the Axis pact. Matsuoka, who knew the Manchurian Jewish leaders from his tenure as chairman of the Southern Manchurian Railway, attempted to allay Zykman's fears that Japan might also adopt some of Germany's antisemitic policies, saying that Germany's racial policies did not obligate Japan, and that the Jews in Japan and the territories under its control would not be harmed by Nazi-style anti-Jewish measures. He made it clear that he was speaking on behalf of the Emperor of Japan, and added that neither Hitler nor Ribbentrop had ever asked Japan to adopt Nazi Germany's racist policies toward the Jews. Zykman, who held a Polish passport, reported on what was said at this meeting to the Polish ambassador in Tokyo, Thadeusz Romer, who in turn reported it to the American ambassador Joseph Grew.

Two years earlier, in December 1938, the government of Japan reached the conclusion that it had to adopt a more precise policy regarding the thousands of Jewish refugees who were now crowding its consulates and embassies in Europe, desperately seeking to escape from the Nazi terror. Japan's diplomatic and consular representatives in several European capitals requested clear-cut guidelines regarding issuing visas to the growing number of Jewish refugees. A committee of five ministers convened for that purpose issued a statement that said in clear terms that expelling the Jews from Japanese-held territories would violate the principle of racial equality and that Japan would refrain from doing so. It also added that in view of the need to mobilize foreign capital for the purpose of Japan's war economy, the Jews in China, Japan, and Manchukuo would be treated fairly and the migration of valuable people, such as engineers and capitalists, would be encouraged. The decisions of this committee will be described in greater details in the following chapter. On February 27, 1939, Foreign Minister Arita Hachiro (1884-1965) stated in Japan's Upper House that "Jews residing in Japan will be treated like other foreign residents.... Jews reaching Japanese shores must obey Japan's immigration laws but they will not be denied entry only because of their race."[8] However, the instructions sent out to Japanese consular officials told them to severely limit the issuing of entry permits to Japan and Manchukuo.

Manchurian Jews during the Pacific War

By early 1941 there remained in Harbin, Mukden, and Dairen some two thousand Jews, who had managed to survive the entire Pacific War without persecution and were even able to maintain their communal institutions intact because they collaborated with the Japanese army and because they were treated by the Japanese as Russian citizens. During the war, the Japanese authorities appointed an adviser to every Jewish organization. His task was to approve various requests, mainly in the sphere of cultural and religious activities. These were usually permitted. The Harbin community, although cut off from the rest of the world and receiving no outside financial help from the American Joint Distribution Committee or other Jewish organizations, maintained itself. In 1943, the Japanese authorities rejected a request by the Zionist Revisionists in Harbin to hold a commemoration ceremony for the World Zionist Revisionist Movement founder and revered leader Zeév Jabotinsky, who had died in America in September 1940. The authorities' explanation was that he had died in America, with which Japan was at war. Dr. Kaufman explained that Jabotinsky was an anti-British freedom fighter who had even been jailed by them in Palestine in 1920 and later exiled from that country. The ban was rescinded and the ceremony was held.

Two years earlier, as a token of their appreciation, on March 14, 1941, the Jewish community of Manchuria had even registered Major General Higuchi and Colonel Yasue in the Golden Book of the Jewish National Fund in Jerusalem in recognition of the help offered to Jewish refugees who sought shelter in Manchuria. Even the small German community in Harbin, which spawned a Nazi youth movement, maintained good relations with Jews who escaped from Germany and remained in Harbin for the duration of the war. The Harbin Jewish community managed to carry on its normal life through the war unscathed. Some of its members even continued to go to their summer homes on the seashore.[9] Fifty Jewish children from Shanghai were invited to a summer camp in Dairen in the summer of 1940. Harbin also escaped the carpet bombing of most major Japanese cities by American bombers.

A week before Japan surrendered, on August 8, 1945, the Soviet Union declared war on Japan and the Soviet army invaded Manchuria. The Russian authorities wasted no time in arresting Jews of Soviet nationality, but most of them were soon released. With the onset of civil war in China between the Nationalists and the Communists, most of the Jews fled to Shanghai, Israel, or the United States. Dr. Kaufman was captured by the Russian army in 1945 and served as a doctor in forced labor camps in Siberia until he was released in 1956. The Manchurian Jewish community ceased to exist for all intents and purposes after the establishment of the People's Republic of China on October 1, 1949.

The Jewish Community of Tianjin[10]

Another small Jewish community existed in Tianjin (also known as Tientsin) and miraculously survived the war almost intact. Its origins go back to the mid-nineteenth century, when Russian Jews began to arrive there. In 1890 a Russian Concession was created in Tianjin, and in 1901 the "Tientsin Hebrew Association" was established. A plot for a Jewish burial ground was purchased in 1904. The number of Jews swelled after the 1917 Russian Revolution and Manchuria's occupation by Japan, and by the mid-1930's the Jewish populaton grew to some 3,500, boasting well-known primary and secondary schools that had been established in 1925. Almost the entire community consisted of Russian Jews, and Japan's determination not to strain its ties with Russia helps explain why they survived the war. Before the war, the community members traded mainly in furs and lived in an area known as the British Quarter. On the eve of the Pacific War the community, although it dwindled in numbers from 3,500 to 1,500, maintained a country club and a synagogue. Jewish holidays were observed, and a Zionist chapter was created. The Tianjin community also served the needs of the few Jews who lived in Beijing and Qingdao.

Quingdao

The first Jewish settlers in Qingdao were German Jews who arrived after the German government took over the Shandong province as part of its sphere of influence at the end of the nineteenth century. More came after the October 1917 Russian Revolution, the majority of them stateless Russian Jews. Japanese records show the existence of a Jewish school that catered to some 220 children. Tiny Jewish communities also existed in Manchuli, Dairen (Dalian or Dalny), Mukden, and Hailar. Their populations consisted predominantly of Russian Jews who arrived after the Bolshevik Revolution, as they did not have to travel far. They looked to the Harbin community as their source of education and kosher food.

Beijing

China's northern capital had never possessed a Jewish community or a synagogue. This can be explained by two reasons: the first was the absence of wealthy Jews who could support communal institutions and welfare societies as they did in other areas of China. The second was the fact that Beijing was never included in any concessions arrangement with the foreign powers and was not a treaty port, and thus few Jews had any incentive to settle there. Several German Jewish professors, however, did teach in Beijing University, among them Rudolf Lowenthal (1904-1996). In 1938 it was estimated that around 120 Jews lived in Beijing, among them 40 French citizens, 30 British, 20 Americans, and 10 Soviets. The rest were classified as stateless—in most cases, Russian Jews whose passports had been revoked. Many Jews in Beijing probably represented foreign companies.

As a rule, the Jews who lived in Manchuria and China proper did not become involved in local politics. They played no role in nationalist or communist party politics and showed no visible interest in what was happening in China in the interwar era. One of the main reasons for that behavior was, of course, lack of knowledge of the language; the second was the desire not to become involved in issues that mattered little to them. Key to this is the fact that most of the Jews in China never viewed China as their permanent home (with the exception of the Baghdadi Jews in Shanghai and Hong Kong). The Russian Jews did not see China as the end of their travels, and nor did Jewish refugees fleeing from Nazi Germany starting in 1933. Both groups hoped to seek refuge in western countries, and indeed did so immediately after the war ended in 1945.

The Jews who lived in Manchuria and China had no special antipathy to the Japanese occupiers. On the contrary, the Japanese military attempted to protect them from the White Russians and did not go out of its way to persecute them after occupying the major cities of China beginning in July 1937 and increasingly after Pearl Harbor. As we shall see, the Japanese allowed Jews to travel through Japanese-controlled areas, mainly to Shanghai, and did not create a separate Jewish ghetto in that city until the spring of 1943.

Chapter 7

Passports, Entry Visas, and Transit Visas: Japan's Policy toward Jewish Refugees (1935-1941)[1]

Japan's immigration laws in the 1930's stipulated that nationals of foreign countries would be admitted to Japanese territory if they possessed a valid passport and an entry or transit visa for Japan issued by a competent Japanese consular authority. Visitors also had to show that they possessed the financial means to cover their stay in Japan. The interior ministry was in charge of implementing this law, but visas were issued by Japanese consulates world-wide, thus making the foreign ministry the dominant factor.

Until Hitler's rise to power in Germany in January 1933, the Japanese authorities did not have to deal with the problem of a large number of Jews wishing to reside in or travel through Japanese territories. Their policy toward Jews was similar to that applied to all other foreigners. During the early years of the Nazi regime in Germany, there was no need to formulate a special policy toward Jewish refugees, since until 1935 the number of German Jews who wanted to leave Germany and settle in Japan or Manchukuo was tiny. But after 1935, and especially after the enactment of the Nuremberg Laws in September of that year, Japanese diplomats predicted that the number of Jews wishing to leave Germany would increase, and that dealing with them would require certain changes of policy. And indeed, after the anti-Jewish laws were enacted in Germany the trickle of Jews wishing to leave Germany grew into a stream and Japan now faced, for the first time in its history, the question of how to deal with Jewish refugees seeking shelter in Japanese territory. The stream soon became a torrent consisting of hundreds and then thousands of Jews who desperately wanted to either settle in Japan or its territories or to travel through Japan to other destinations.

A special policy toward German Jews was also urgently required in view of the fact that their status as holders of German passports had changed.

Until 1935, Jews possessing German passports had not required entry visas to Japan because of prevailing agreements between the two countries that had exempted their nationals from the need for them. After 1935, however, the German authorities began to revoke German citizenship from Jews wishing to leave Germany—they became effectively stateless. In order to overcome this hurdle, Japan's foreign minister of the time, Hirota Koki (1878-1948), issued a ruling that Jewish refugees whose German nationality was cancelled but who had been issued with "*laissez passer*," similar to other refugees, and with this document were able to leave Germany, would be allowed to enter Japan. Even though this was a purely administrative regulation, it did express Japan's policy of not discriminating between Jews and non-Jews, and in that way demonstrated that Japan had no obligation to follow Germany's antisemitic policy.

Events in Europe soon required a more detailed and clearer Japanese policy toward Jewish refugees. Following the annexation of Austria by Germany in March 1938 and even more so after the pogroms known as *Kristallnacht* on November 9 of that year, the number of Jews who sought Japanese entry visas soared to new heights. Since the gates of the United States and Canada, their preferred choices of haven, were closed, they sought visas to any country that would be willing to accept them. The new situation was noted by Yamaji Akira (1896-1970), Japan's consul general in Vienna, in a cable he dispatched to Tokyo in September 1938. He reported a significant growth in the number of those seeking entry visas to Japan and asked for clearer instructions on how to deal with the new situation.

The Jewish and Muslim Question Committee[2]

In order to formulate a new policy toward Jewish refugees, in the spring of 1938 the Japanese foreign ministry established the "Jewish and Muslim Affairs Committee," whose task was to produce the guidelines and principles required to deal with the refugee problem in view of new international developments. There is no apparent reason why the Japanese lumped together Jews and Muslims. There were no known Muslim refugees from Germany or any other country seeking shelter in Japan, or anywhere for that matter. The Japanese authorities may have been thinking of the three hundred million Muslims in Asia at the time, the majority in India, Indonesia, and Malaya, whom they wanted to mobilize against the western colonial powers Britain and Holland. Over the course of 1938, additional bodies were created to deal with Asian Muslims, among them the Greater Japanese Muslim League, and in October 1938 the Institute of Islamic Areas was established in Tokyo. This body produced a number of publications, among them *Islamic Area*. Some attention was also paid to the millions of Muslims residing in China. This fit nicely with the concept of Japan leading the Asian nations in expelling western colonialism and fighting Soviet Bolshevism. It was also in line with the policy of the New Order in East Asia announced by Prime Minister Konoye in November 1938. A mosque was opened in Tokyo in May 1938, but it is not clear how many Muslims living in that city at the time used it for prayers.

The committee consisted of representatives of the foreign ministry as well as representatives of the army and navy. They were instructed, along with their other tasks, to produce a position paper on the question of Jewish refugees who found shelter in China. They were greatly assisted in this by the two veteran Jewish experts, Colonel Yasue and Captain Inuzuka, and their views influenced the committees' discussions and recommendations.

At the conclusion of their deliberations, the committee members formulated general principles designed to establish a more detailed policy toward Jewish refugees, as requested by Consul General Yamaji in Vienna and some of his colleagues in other European capitals. In a foreign ministry circular dispatched to all Japanese diplomatic and consular posts, it was made clear that as a rule Japan did not want foreigners expelled by Germany and Italy to reach its territory. Hence, no visas should be issued to stateless refugees (including German Jews whose nationality was revoked). The committee also decided that those Jews still holding valid German and Austrian passports should be persuaded to seek shelter in other countries rather than Japan. It was also determined that Jewish refugees from other European countries would not be entitled to obtain a Japanese entry visa. This was aimed mainly against those Czech Jews trying to travel to Japan on the eve of that country's occupation by Germany in March 1939. But there was an exception: any refugee already holding an entry visa to a third country would be permitted to obtain a transit visa to Japan valid for fifteen days as long as he had the sum of 250 yen to cover his expenses in Japan during those two weeks.

The committee's recommendation clearly showed a change for the worse in Japan's policy toward Jewish refugees and a growing tendency to limit their movement toward Japan.

Two major developments account for this change. The first was the growing ties between Japan and Nazi Germany, expressed by Japan joining

Germany in the November 1936 Anti-Comintern Pact, which Italy later joined as well. The second was the dramatic rise in the number of Jewish refugees beginning in the mid-1930's. It can be assumed that the committee members sensed that Japan found itself caught berween contradictory pressures and sought a policy that would enable them to deal with these pressures effectively. On the one hand was the need not to harm the growing ties with Nazi Germany in any way, and on the other was the need to avoid alienating the Western democracies, mainly the United States, Britain, and France, whose relations with Japan were deteriorating, especially after the outbreak in July 1937 of the second Sino-Japanese War and then the Nanjin Massacre carried out by Japanese troops in December 1937. The Western democracies were now convinced that Japan was totally and consistently violating the "Open Door" policy that had been in existence in China since 1900, and that Japan's expansion into China seriously endangered their economic interests in that country.

Although the growing anti-Japanese policy of the United States and the threat that Japan could face American-imposed economic sanctions were not directly connected with American Jews, somehow the "Jewish Question" was in the back of the minds of some Japanese diplomats, and they assumed that if Japan pursued a flexible policy toward German Jewish refugees, that would have a positive effect on the policy of the United States. Once again they repeated their mistake regarding the influence of American Jews when they assumed, probably based on the advice of their experts, that the Jews had vast influence on the governments of the United States and the Soviet Union, when in reality the influence of American Jews on the Roosevelt administration was marginal, and the Jewish influence in the Soviet Union and other countries where Jews were seen as a minor factor was totally nonexistent. Not only were American Jews not influential, but the policy of the Department of State, headed by Secretary of State Cordell Hull (1871-1955), was that America should close its gates to Jews from all countries.

The Five Ministers Committee[3]

The Japanese decision-making process regarding the Jews was, therefore, influenced by various, often contradictory, factors. Some officials maintained vague stereotypical ideas regarding the political and financial clout of the Jews and the influence they wielded on the governments in those countries where many of them lived. There were also other, more sober and pragmatic considerations. Clearly Japan's relations with Nazi Germany carried weight, although it is hard to evaluate the dimensions and influence of this factor. There were in Japan some serious doubts about the racial policy of the Nazis, mainly because it relegated the Japanese and Chinese to an inferior position as a "Yellow" race. But a number of thinkers in Japan sought to ignore this slur and focus on other issues, among them the Jewish threat.

We have noted that in the 1930's there had already been a flowering of antisemitic literature and populist ideas that portrayed the Jews in a highly negative light. Various societies and associations active at the time played a role in spreading antisemitic ideas. The International Political-Economic Society, established in 1934, aimed at carrying out research on the "Jewish Question" and published a newsletter called *The International Secret Force*. In 1941 they began to issue a monthly publication named *Jewish Studies* that contributed its share to creating a hostile atmosphere against Jews. However, Jews were never seen as an element that endangered Japan's very existence, traditions, and values. The populist anti-foreign concepts focused mainly on the hundreds of millions of Chinese citizens believed to desire to harm Japan's interests on the Asian continent and to be aiming to undermine Japan's efforts to attain a leading role there. Even the attempt to link the Jews with America, a country that was gradually emerging as Japan's leading enemy, did not take hold in the minds of most Japanese people, who had never seen a Jew in their lives.

Similar to what often happens in countries whose regimes see the need to channel social unrest toward the "enemy of the nation," thus strengthening their holds on the people, in Japan, too, populist ideas were a mixture of lies and half-truths aimed at convincing the masses through the use of incitement, hatred, and irrational motives. The regime sought to assure the people that it was looking after their welfare and keepimg them safe from terrorist and subversive elements. Antisemitic mottoes, influenced partly by Nazi ideology, had a certain role in the populist-propaganda tapestry, but not a major role. The effectiveness of antisemitism in Japan in this connection was basically marginal and minor.[4]

At that time, there were a number of governmental organs that dealt with the Jewish issue, among them the foreign ministry, whose consular officers issued the required entry or transit visas; the home (interior) ministry, whose officials were in charge of admitting foreigners to Japan and issuing them with landing and residence permits; the finance ministry, some of whose heads still toyed with the idea that they would be able to mobilize Jewish capital to be invested in Manchuria; the Imperial Army and Navy, whose officers were the de facto rulers of the Japanese-occupied areas in China and later in South East Asia; and the Japanese authorities in Manchuria, which was the first stop in Asia for many Jewish refugees. Finally, the Japanese government decided that the principles of the policy toward the Jews would be formulated and adopted by a small body consisting of five ministers that met in Tokyo on December 6, 1938. The significance of the issue was seen by the fact that the most important ministers in the imperial government of Japan participated. These were Prime Minister Konoe Fumimaro; Army Minister General Itagaki Seishiro; Navy Minister Admiral Yonai Mitsumasa (1880-1948); Foreign Minister Arita Hachiro; and Finance Minister Ikeda Shigeaki (1867-1950). They were charged with adopting a clear-cut and precise policy and formulating instructions to be sent to the relevant Japanese officials in Europe dealing with requests for visas.

In the discussion, it was clear that a number of approaches to the problem existed, some of them contradictory. One concept was expressed by Foreign Minister Arita, who argued that Japan must do everything within its power not to harm the country's close relations with Nazi Germany in any way, and called for limiting considerably the number of Jews who would be admitted to Japan and the areas under its control. The opposite view was expressed by Finance Minister Ikeda and Army Minister Itagaki. They claimed that hurting the Jews could have a negative effect on Japan's relations with the United States, because American Jews controlled the economy and media. The Jewish experts, who also took part in the meeting, stressed the vast Jewish influence on President Franklin D. Roosevelt (1882-1945) and his administration, and the ensuing need not to harm the Jews, even if it annoyed the Germans. Once again the irrefutable idea that Jews controlled America was in evidence at the highest level of Japan's decision-making process.

Finally, as often occurs in Japan, a compromise proposal containing some ideas of both schools of thought was adopted by consensus. In principle, it was decided that although Japan's close ties with Germany and Italy did not allow her to demonstrate a sympathetic and positive attitude toward Jews, Japan would not treat the Jews the way those two countries did: it would not institute policies that discriminated against Jews. On the contrary, the treatment to be accorded to Jews already living in Japan, Manchukuo, and the occupied areas of China, would not differ from the treatment of other foreigners, and there would be no special effort to expel them. As for Jews wishing to enter Japan, Manchukuo, and Japan's occupied areas in China for the purposes of residence or transit to other countries, Japan's attitude toward them would be determined according to the prevailing Japanese immigration laws. Japan would make no special effort to attract Jews to the areas under its control apart from refugees termed "attractive"—businessmen and professionals whose contribution to Japan's economy could be useful. It is interesting to note that at no time was the possibility of settling Jews in Taiwan or Korea (Chosen) even mentioned, let alone discussed in detail. As a rule, foreigners were banned from these two Japanese colonies.

Upon the adoption of this proposal, the Japanese foreign ministry dispatched instructions to all its diplomatic and consular representatives regarding the spirit of the Five Minister Committee decisions. The foreign ministry instructed its consular officers to issue Jewish refugees entry visas to Japan only in special cases, which were not specified. Transit visas would be issued only to those holding a valid entry visa to a third country to which they were proceeding via Japan. Jews would not be granted residence visas to Japan, but the issuing of transit visas was permitted in the situation specified. This arrangement proved to be highly beneficial in saving the lives of thousands of Jews. After the outbreak of World War II in Europe in September 1939, and the signing of the Axis Alliance in September 1940, Japanese consular officials in Berlin, Prague, and Vienna continued to issue transit visas to Japan, thus saving numerous Jews from almost certain extermination by the Nazis. Over two thousand, two hundred such visas were issued in the summer of 1940 by the Japanese consul general in Kaunas, Lithuania, whose name was Sugihara Chiune. His story will be discussed in Chapter 10.

Chapter 8

The Jews of Shanghai under Japanese Rule[1]

The Jewish Community Prior to the Japanese Occupation

The largest Jewish community in East Asia in the mid-1930's resided in Shanghai, the hub of China's international trade, where the largest concentration of foreign residents in general lived and worked. This was partly due to the existence of the International Settlement quarter that was created in 1842, under the protection of eleven foreign powers and administered by a municipal council representing them. Formally, this settlement was under Chinese sovereignty, but in reality the settlement's foreign residents were not under the authority of the Chinese police or other local governmental institutions, and enjoyed the protection of the consuls of France, Britain, the United States, Japan, and Russia. There was also a French Concession where some Jews found refuge, and where effective Chinese sovereignty was also non-existent. Additionally, there was the Hongkew zone of Shanghai, which for decades had been part of the International Settlement, but which came under direct Japanese rule in August 1937. Finally there was the rest of Shanghai, a city of 4.5 million inhabitants administered by a pro-Japanese puppet Chinese government but in reality controlled by Japan. The special character of the foreign settlement and the possibilities of finding both refuge and business opportunities there attracted many foreigners, among them Jews.

The first wave of Jewish settlers who established the Shanghai Jewish community arrived in the middle of the nineteenth century. Some came from Iraq and Persia via India. Many had British passports, and soon a number of families stood out for their wealth and communal leadership. Among them were the Sassoon, Kadoorie, Hardon, Elias, Gubai, and other families. In 1902 the *Ohel Rachel* (Rachel's Tent) synagogue was inaugurated, named after the late wife of Sir Jacob Sassoon. The Hardoon family built the *Beit Aharon* (The House of Aaron) synagogue, named after Aaron Hardoon (1851-1931). The Zionist movement had an active branch there, and its publication, *The Israel Messenger*, is a highly credible source for the history of this community as it grew bigger and richer. On the eve of the First World War, it numbered over a thousand individuals.

The second wave arrived after the Bolshevik Revolution in 1917, in the form of several thousand refugees from Russia, among them hundreds of Jews. Shanghai was convenient for those who sought haven because there was no need for entry and residence permits, and there was also a supportive Jewish community already there and ready to help. In addition to the Jews there were also hundreds of White Russian émigrés who brought with them antisemitic doctrines and literature which placed the blame for the Russian Revolution squarely on the Jews. The Jews were also accused of the murder of the Tsar and his family, and all of the social and political ills and upheaval and turmoil that followed the 1917 Revolution were attributed to them as well. The Jews already residing in Shanghai, many of them originating in Central and Eastern Europe, were not enthusiastic about the growth of the Russian Jewish community, which on the eve of the Second World War numbered some five to eight thousand people, a huge increase from the several hundred who were present in the 1920's. Their spiritual head was Rabbi Meir Ashkenazi, a Lubavitcher Chassid who came from Vladivostok by way of Harbin. Many of this new wave of Russian Jews came from Harbin, Mukden, and Dairen after Manchuria was occupied by the Japanese in 1931. They preferred living in a city where Western culture and a greater sense of law and order prevailed to remaining in the Japanese-occupied areas. The Russian Jewish immigrants at once set out to establish their own communal institutions and built an old-age home that served meals for the needy, which by then meant some 400 people. They also established their own burial society, religious schools, and a charitable fund for the needy.

In 1931 an organization called the Shanghai Ashkenazi Relief Association (SACRA) was established. It claimed to represent the entire Jewish community in that city, but in reality it was distinctly separate from the old-time wealthier Sephardic community. In 1937, on the eve of the second Sino-Japanese War, SACRA won recognition from the Chinese nationalist government. Parallel to this body there also existed the *Judische Gemeinde*, the umbrella organization of Jews who came from German-speaking Europe. It was this organization that began to deal with the growing number of Jewish refugees from Nazi Germany after the rise of Hitler to power in 1933.

After Shanghai's Occupation by Japan

Shanghai's occupation by Japan in August 1937 left the legal status of the foreign settlements intact: the Foreign Settlement and the French Concession retained their autonomous status under the protection of the Western powers and the Soviet Union. Since Japan did not want to provoke the Western powers and the Soviet Union, there was no attempt by the Japanese to harm Central European, Russian, or Sephardi Jews in Shanghai, especially those who were either Soviet citizens or stateless persons under Soviet protection. Japan's basic policy toward the foreigners in Shanghai was to treat them fairly while maintaining close surveillance over their activities, mainly through the control of their communal organizations.

The growth of the German Jewish community in Shanghai can be traced to the events of 1934, a year after Hitler's ascent to power, when a small number of German Jewish physicians arrived in China and found work in Shanghai and other cities that were yearning for medical doctors. Some traveled to China via the Soviet Union on the Trans-Siberian Railway, continuing south from Manchuria. Others came directly by sea, sailing on board Japanese and Italian vessels, mostly those of the Italian Lloyd Triestino. The growing number of Jews arriving in Shanghai at this time can also be explained by the policy of the Gestapo, which encouraged Jewish emigration mainly from Austria, a policy led by the rising Nazi official Adolph Eichmann (1906-1962) and his aides.

Eichmann was at the time in charge of getting rid of the Jews of Austria. He and his associates met with foreign consuls in Vienna, including those of China and Japan, and encouraged them to issue visas to Austrian Jews. They also urged shipping companies to allocate additional places on their vessels to accommodate Jews, and to arrange for extra journeys. Another source of the Jews arriving in China were the visas issued by the Chinese Consul General in Vienna, He Feng Shan (1901-1997). The records of the Shanghai police show the arrival in 1938 of 1,374 Jewish refugees. A year later the number grew to 12,089, but in 1940 the figures declined to 1955 and in 1941 only 33 are listed. When Japan attacked America in December 1941, followed by Germany and Italy's declaration of war against America, this channel of travel shut down entirely.

During the four years 1938-1941, 15,450 Jewish refugees arrived in Shanghai. They joined the existing community, and in early 1942 there was a total of 27,000 Jews in Shanghai, comprising about a third of all foreigners living there at the time. The majority resided in the Hongkew neighborhood in central Shanghai.

Since 1938, the organization that looked after the refugees had been the Committee for the Assistance of Jewish refugees in Shangahi, or the CFA. They provided help in finding housing, employment, schooling, and kindergartens for the refugees and their children and acted as mediators in the many conflicts that arose between the newly arrived refugees and the older, more established members of the Jewish community. Among the major donors to this body were Sir Victor Sassoon and Eli Kadoorie. American Jewish organizations such as the Joint Distribution Committee and HIAS also sent funds that in 1940 were estimated at half a million dollars. Some of the refugees also received funds from their family members living in the United States.

On the eve of the Pacific War, a number of Japanese officers, including the Jewish experts, understood that the wealthy Jews of Shanghai could be of use to Japan in implementing its new policy, the Greater East Asia Co-Prosperity Sphere. This was a rehash of similar ideas that were previously discussed about making use of the Jews of Manchuria in the late 1930's. In Shanghai there lived a number of very wealthy Jewish families with vast international business connections. Perhaps they could be mobilized to help Japan's economy, or at least to advance Japanese economic interest in the areas it occupied in China beginning in July 1937.

In May 1939, three Japanese officers met with Sir Victor Sassoon, recognized by all parties as the uncrowned leader of the Jewish community, to discuss the plight of the 12,000 Jewish refugees in the Shanghai area. One of them was Colonel Yasue, the second Captain Inuzoka, and the third Japan's consul in Shanghai, Ishiguro Shiro. A meeting was required as the Japanese officials and the Jewish leaders of Shanghai were becoming increasingly concerned over the rising tide of German, Austrian, and Czech Jewish refugees. The issue became more acute with the growing flow of refugees, partly because various foreign consuls residing in Shanghai recommended to their governments, as was their right to do during this era of the International Settlement and the French Concession, that it would be wise to halt the flow of Jews to that city. These recommendations were not to the taste of the Japanese authorities, who did not want Japan to be tainted with the negative image of a country that is oblivious to the plight of refugees. As usual, they wondered how the refusal to accept refugees would be seen by American Jews, who were perceived to have vast influence over public opinion in America through their control of the media in that country. By 1939 and 1940 several ideas began to be discussed in Tokyo, among them the notion that Japan could concentrate the Jews into a special section in Shanghai and make it into a Jewish puppet state, similar to Manchukuo. It was also assumed that this would make it easier to control the Jews of Shanghai, with the help of the existing local Jewish organizations. Since the Japanese navy was responsible for Shanghai, it did not come as a surprise that Captain Inuzuka was asked to become involved. His first step was to establish, in January 1940, a special bureau for Jewish affairs.

After Pearl Harbor

On December 7, 1941, the Japanese attacked the US Navy's Pearl Harbor in Hawaii, and Japan entered into Germany and Italy's war against the Western democracies. The Japanese army now occupied the International Settlement and the French Concession, ending the international control that had existed there since 1842. A day after Pearl Harbor, Inuzuka seized the office of Victor Sassoon and turned it into his headquarters. But at this stage there were no indications that the Shanghai Jews were to be subjected to special treatment. Indeed, until 1943 there was little anti-Jewish discrimination. The main concern of the Shanghai Jewish community was how to handle the refugees in that city, to whom were now added several hundred who arrived from Kobe, having gotten their transit visas to Japan by the Japanese Consul in Kaunas, Sugihara Chiune. They had been unable to leave Japan for Curacao or other destinations before Pearl Harbor, and were transferred by Japan from Kobe to Shanghai after the war against the United States began. As we shall see later, the movement from Kobe to Shanghai started in early 1941, and was paid for by the Joint Distribution Committee in New York at the specific request of the Kobe Jewish community. Among the refugees was the entire Mir Yeshiva, consisting of several hundred students and teachers. The Judische Gemeinde assisted the local community by feeding the refugees, using funds that continued to come from the United States through the Joint Distribution Committee until 1943, apparently with Japan's knowledge and encouragement. The funds were sent through neutral Switzerland. The representative of the JDC in Shanghai, Laura Margolis, maintained cordial ties with Captain Inuzuka and operated freely until she was interned as an enemy alien in February 1943 and repatriated to the United States in September 1943.

Until the summer of 1942, there was no attempt to harm the Jews in Shanghai. Quite the contrary: the vast literature that exists on the Shanghai Jewish community during the war describes in great detail the ongoing and endless internal struggles and constant fighting among the various Jewish organizations over such issues as financial aid to refugees, school curriculae, the style of prayers in synagogues, and the distribution of funds that came from the United States. In order to qualify for aid, one had to register with the Judische Gemeinde, and two thirds of the community did so. In May of 1942, the Japanese occupation authorities demanded that all Jews register with the government and list their residences and occupations. A document from that time, a 1941 census, shows that among the Jewish refugees in Shanghai there were 220 physicians, 180 dentists, 120 nurses, 22 milliners, 130 engineers, 1100 merchants, 150 chefs, 140 people in the meat trade, and 100 chauffeurs. Japanese representatives began to participate in meetings of the local Jewish organizations to exercise control, demonstrate the government's presence, and ensure that there would be no manifestations smacking of anti-Japanese sedition, mainly in the Jewish publications that began to appear in Shanghai. They also aimed to ensure that there would be absolutely no contact between the Jews of Shanghai and enemy countries, mainly the United States and Britain. In order to facilitate control over the Shanghai Jewish communal organizations, the Japanese authorities decided in May 1943 to place the Judische Gemeinde and the Ashkenazi social welfare body (SACRA) under the leadership of Dr. Abraham Cohen, a Romanian Jew who studied medicine in Japan and spoke fluent Japanese. He was the rare exception – a Jewish leader fluent in Japanese.

German Extermination Plans

The relative calm which the Shanghai Jews were enjoying was about to end. From testimonies gathered after the war, it appears that the German government pressed Japan to take measures aimed at dealing with the Jews under its control. Fritz Wiedemann (1891-1970), who served as the German Consul General in Tianjin but was in fact the key German intelligence officer in China between 1941 and 1945, testified in 1951 that he had no doubt that German pressure brought about a change in Japan's previous policy toward the Shanghai Jewish community. His testimony was supported by a Japanese naval officer by the name of Takeshima, who had served as an intelligence officer in Shanghai. In July of 1942, the ardent Nazi Gestapo Colonel Josef Meisinger (1899-1947) arrived in Shanghai.[2]

In the 1930's, prior to his arrival in Shanghai, Meisinger had been head of the Nazi office dealing with matters relating to abortions and homosexuality. After the outbreak of the war he served in Poland, where he earned the sobriquet "the Warsaw Butcher" for his actions in organizing the Warsaw ghetto and mainly for his responsibility for the deaths of thousands of Jews in the Polish capital. In 1941 he was appointed to the German Embassy in Tokyo as police attaché. He was, in fact, the senior representative of Germany's Gestapo in Japan, seeking enemies of Nazi Germany within the German community of Tokyo. He also served as the liaison between the Gestapo and the Japanese intelligence services. In Tokyo he befriended the Soviet spy Richard Sorge (1899-1944) and became a major source of information for Sorge (who was captured by Japanese counter-intelligence agencies in October 1941 and executed three years later). In 1942 Meisinger was sent to Shanghai, where he took upon himself the task of dealing with the Jews of that city. He was assisted by an SS officer called Hans Neiman who at the end of the war was responsible for the Bergen-Belsen concentration camp. Another aide was an officer named Adolph Pottkamer, who was in Shanghai in the guise of commercial attaché at the German embassy in Tokyo.

In early 1942, the Japanese naval authorities responsible for the Shanghai area had already come to the conclusion that Japan's control over foreigners in general and Jews in particular would have to be tightened, and that perhaps it would be useful and easier to concentrate some 20,000 Jews in one neighborhood and eventually get rid of them (and the non-Jewish Russians) altogether. The German officers probably heard from the Japanese navy that they were wondering how to better control the foreigners in Shanghai.

From sources within the Japanese consulate in Shanghai, some Jewish leaders learned as early as August 1942 that Meisinger had proposed to a number of Japanese officers that they begin to act against the Jews in the spirit of the Final Solution. He suggested a number of concrete courses of action. One was to send those Jews who were once German nationals to Japan to work as forced laborers for the Japanese war effort. The second was to use Jews as guinea pigs for experiments on human beings. The third and most lethal was to put thousands of Jews aboard cargo ships and either starve them to death on board or sink them in the China Sea. Another remote idea was to transfer the Jews to Nazi occupied Europe where they would be exterminated. But as a first step, and prior to taking drastic measures agains the Jews, they should be concentrated into one area.

The experts thought it would be easy to round up all the Jews on the eve of the Jewish New Year, since many of them would be in synagogues.

Among those present at the discussions with the Germans on this topic was the Japanese Vice Consul Shibata Mitsugu, who decided to alert a number of Jewish communal leaders to the plot being hatched by the Nazis. One of those leaders, Dr. Abraham Cohen, had already heard of the plan from his own sources, including some Japanese officers whom he had befriended. He met with a Japanese officer, Kubota Tetsuma, who promised to see what could be done to thwart the plot. Shortly thereafter Meisinger's ideas were leaked to a local Chinese-language newspaper and published. This caused great deal of anger in the Japanese navy headquarters. The navy resented the publicity, as they were not sure whether the German method was the right way to go about resolving the "Jewish Question" in Shanghai.

It is not clear if the Japanese authorities were indeed interested in undertaking such radical measures against the Jews, which could have meant the arrest, detention, and even extermination of some 27,000 people, most of them of European origin. It can be assumed that they did not want to harm the wealthy Sephardi Jews who held British or American passports and who were already interned in detention camps until the end of the war. Russian Jews were automatically excluded, so as not to harm the delicate relations with the Soviet Union.

The Japanese authorities were furious over the leak. Vice-Consul Shibata was arrested, as were some leaders of the Jewish community. They were all released after a few days, but the Japanese authorities were probably terrified by how easily this German-inspired plan could be leaked and thus foiled. Shibata was detained for several months, sent back to Japan, and then dismissed from the Japanese Foreign Service. It was now evident that some Japanese naval officers as well as Japanese diplomats did not view with favor the idea of Japan doing the bidding of the Nazis regarding the Jews. This too had to be taken into consideration when the time came to make a decision.

The Creation of the Hongkew Ghetto

Over the course of late 1942 and early 1943, Meisinger continued to pressure the Japanese authorities in Shanghai to take action against the Jews, and they finally chose what they may have considered the lesser evil: they decided to set up a Jewish ghetto in Shanghai, which was politely called a "designated area." The reason for choosing this option probably had to do with their reluctance to follow the Nazis in their anti-Jewish policy of extermination, although the Japanese were not aware of the dimensions of the Holocaust and the extermination already taking place in Auschwitz, Treblinka, Majdanek, and other death camps. They may have feared that exterminating some 20,000 Jews of European origin would create furor in the West. They also did not see much sense in killing the wealthy Jewish families of Shanghai, who might in the future be useful for Japan's economic plans. Above all, they recoiled from killing scores of Jews who held British and American citizenships, fearing terrible retribution after the war in case Japan lost. The decision was made in early 1943 and was based on prior Japanese thinking, which had considered the possibility of a Jewish ghetto in Shanghai. By then, the tide of the Pacific war had begun to turn against Japan. However, there is no evidencd that the turning of the tide in any way influenced Japanese thinking regarding the "designated area."

On February 18, 1943, an ordinance was issued relating only to the approximately 14,000 stateless refugees who had come to Shanghai after September 1939. They were ordered to move to a "designated area for stateless refugees" adjacent to the international settlement Hongkew. The words ghetto and Jews were never mentioned, but the intention was quite clear. Those affected were stateless Jewish refugees from Germany, Austria, Czechoslovakia, Hungary, Poland, Latvia, Lithuania, and Estonia. Russian Jews were totally excluded from this ordinance. Several Jews who held Polish passports requested that they be treated as Russians, claiming that they had come from areas occupied by the Russians in 1939. The Japanese consul Kubota met with the heads of the Jewish community and asked for their cooperation in moving the designated groups of Jews to the ghetto. They had no choice but to comply. Within a few weeks some five thousand Jews were moved to Hongkew, including three hundred Mir yeshiva students who continued their studies in a building they renamed "Beit Aharon." It can be conjectured that Meisinger and his assistants were involved in this move, but the implementation was totally in the hands of the local Japanese authorities.

The Japanese officer responsible for the ghetto was Goya Kano, who had previously worked in the Japanese office responsible for stateless refugees. He was mainly in charge of issuing entry and exit permits to the ghetto and had four Jews on his staff. He was apparently a somewhat eccentric individual, who liked to call himself the King of the Jews. Many who survived their internment in the ghetto recalled him as a moody person and noted that they behaved towards him accordingly. Some thought he was a psychopath.

Unlike the Jewish ghettos in Eastern Europe, the Shanghai ghetto was not that difficult to exit or enter during the two years and four months of its existence. One witness, Yosef Tekoa (1925-1991), future Israeli diplomat, Israeli ambassador to the Soviet Union and the United Nations, and president of Ben-Gurion University of the Negev, remembered no difficulty entering and leaving the Hongkew ghetto.[3] Life for the five thousand Jews crowded into Hongkew was harsh—they lived in cramped quarters, few had income, and food was scarce—but they were not physically molested or harmed. They had to endure chilly winters and hot and humid summers. A number of Jewish newspapers, mainly in German, were published in the ghetto in those years. Not involved in the ghetto, the Russian Jews who had established a social club in 1931 maintained it even after Japan occupied Shanghai and turned it into an officers' club. The Russian Jews were undeterred and continued their club from the local Masonic chapter and in 1943 numbered some 450 people among its members.

Responsibility for maintaining law and order in the ghetto was given to the Jews themselves. Starting at the end of 1943 the Japanese once again allowed American Jewish organizations to send funds to China even though the United States was an enemy country. The Joint Distribution Committee resumed sending money through Switzerland. A hundred thousand Swiss Francs arrived from Switzerland in September 1943 through the channels of the International Red Cross, thereby alleviating the hunger of the Jews inside the ghetto. The transfer of funds was made possible by pressure exerted on the American State Department by the Union of Orthodox Rabbis in America. Most of the Jews in the ghetto were unemployed, and the prospects of finding employment, even outside the barbed wire wall that surrounded the ghetto, were virtually non-existent. Apparently some two thousand Jews died during the Japanese occupation of Shanghai, most of them from illnesses or old age. There is no evidence of executions or torture of Jews.

Those Jews in Shanghai who were not herded into the ghetto carried on their lives to the best of their ability under the Japanese occupation. Tekoa continued to attend the French university, his brother an American college whose gates were not closed by the Japanese. Virtually all the testimonies on this topic from people who were in Shanghai during those days—and there are scores—as well as the official documents and reports of Japanese consular officials and military officers and navy and army commanders confirm that the Japanese had no intention of exterminating the Jews under their control, but did not wish to make their lives easy either. Most likely the main reason for their caution was the growing realization of the Japanese leadership beginning in early 1943 that Japan was going to be defeated. They may have thought of their own personal future, and did not want to add to their war crimes against Chinese civilians additional ones against Jews. The Jewish complex in Japan was still alive: what would Japan do if the Jews, given their vast influence over Western governments, the media, and public opinion, accused it of implementing a Nazi-style Final Solution? In any case, many Japanese officials realized that they were already being demonized by the United States as bloodthirsty barbarians who committed atrocities not only against Chinese civilians but also against American civilians and prisoners of war in the Philippines in early 1942, specifically by forcing them to participate in the Bataan Death March. They did not wish to add charges of antisemitism against them at the end of the war.

Furthermore, after 1943, there is no evidence that Germany was in any way pressing Japan to persecute Jews in Japan, China, or other territories under Japanese occupation aside from Indonesia. That may be ascribed to the lack of cooperation between Japan and Germany in many spheres despite the fact that they were formally allies. Japan had already refused Germany's pleas to attack Singapore in 1940, and though Germany wanted Japan to invade the Soviet Union when that power was on the verge of collapse in October 1941, Japan maintained strict neutrality with the Soviet Union until a week before it surrendered. Japan did not see itself as committed ideologically or in any other way to the German policy of exterminating the Jews. It can also be assumed that Germany never revealed to Japan the details of the Final Solution or the manner in which it was carried out in Europe.

In other cities in China and Manchuria, Jews were not physically or otherwise molested, and the hundreds of Jews who remained in Harbin, Mukden, and Tianjin during the war did not report any assaults on them. On the contrary, Japan allowed the Jews in those cities (apart from Hong Kong) to lead their lives as before and did not destroy communal institutions, impose financial levies, or compel men to do forced labor. And so, while millions of European Jews were exterminated in death camps in Poland and other locations, the Jews under the Japanese occupation in China were spared from a similar fate and the majority survived the war. It is still a matter of debate whether there was an official Japanese government policy of protecting the Jews under their control, or whether the decisions were left to local commanders to make. It may seem symbolic, but the only 31 Jews killed and approximately 250 wounded in Shanghai were the result of an American air raid on Hongkew on July 17, 1945, a month before Japan surrendered. The wounded were treated in the Jewish hospital in the ghetto, which was was manned by Jewish doctors and nurses. The American bombers had sought to destroy a Japanese broadcasting station in the foreign quarter and missed their target.

Japan's Attitude toward the Jews in Other Parts of China[4]

Since late 1937 Japan had controlled about a third of China, mainly its northeastern parts and the key cities along the coast. It would be reasonable to assume that in order to solidify its control over these parts of China it would seek to launch a propaganda campaign against the West, and that the campaign would include some antisemitic sentiments, as similar campaigns did in Japan itself. Since the Kuomintang forces, in addition to sporadically fighting the Japanese forces, were also battling the Chinese Communists, whose center was in the Yenan enclave. However, unlike in Japan, where authorities used anti-communist sentiments (which were closely related to antisemitic sentiments) to describe part of the country's struggle against the West and the Soviet Union, in the occupied Chinese territories the Japanese refrained from using antisemitic propaganda. In any case the connecting line drawn between communism and Judaism would have meant nothing to the Chinese, who knew virtually nothing about Jews and Judaism. The Japanese propagandists could theoretically have used the fact that Karl Marx was a converted Jew, and that many of the Bolshevik leaders in Russia were Jews, a fact noted by Chiang Kai-Shek during his three-month-long sojourn in Moscow in 1923. The Japanese could have pointed out the fact that a number of the Comintern emissaries in China in the 1920's were Jews, but they chose not to do so.

It seems plausible that Japan's Jewish experts noted and advised their superiors that anti-Jewish propaganda and antisemitism would not strike a chord with the Chinese intellectuals and middle class. True, a number of Chinese Nationalist army officers and many students lived in Germany in the late 1920's and early 1930's, but they did not spread antisemitic ideas upon their return to China. Some may have refrained from doing so after noting that in *Mein Kampf* Hitler had written that "it was incorrect to believe that a Negro or a Chinese could ever take part in German life." When *Mein Kampf* was translated to Chinese in 1936, the offensive sentence was deleted. There was one faction in the Nationalist Party that did admire some aspects of Nazism, the Blue Shirts group, and they published allegations in their publications that "Germany's largest banks, newspapers, and other commercial enterprises are almost all controlled by the Jews."[5] However, even the New Life Movement, which did agree with some Nazi principles, basically ignored antisemitism.

It was also hard for the Japanese, even if they were willing to do so, to fault the Jews for many of China's ailments. There is nothing in Confucianism, Buddhism. or Taoism that could encourage hatred toward the Jews. Even Christian missionaries in China did not go out of their way to blame the Jews for killing Christ. In the few cases in which Jewish traders did compete with overseas Chinese traders in South East Asia, there is no evidence that the competition created antisemitic sentiments. The Jews were seen by and large as Europeans, and were not singled out or identified specifically as Jews. Like those in Japan, the Jews who lived in China never played any role in China's politics, media, academia, or arts. The Jews of China were mostly merchants, many of them involved with international firms. It would have been quite difficult to fault the Jews for the economic collapse of 1929 and the worldwide depression that followed. Therefore, those very few Jews who lived in China under the Japanese occupation—with the exception of those in Hong Kong and Shanghai—were spared the manifestations of antisemitism that could so easily have been encouraged by the Japanese occupation authorities. Even the Nazi party branches in China did not publicly engage in overt antisemitic acts.

Chapter 9

Jews in the Japanese-Occupied Territories during the War Years

General Observations

During the first six months of the Pacific War, Japan attained highly impressive achievements by any standards, and particularly by military standards. Japanese forces occupied Hong Kong and additional parts of China, all of Malaya, Singapore, the Philippines, Wake and Guam, all of the Dutch East Indies, most of Burma, and parts of New Guinea. They were even threatening Australia. They were on the threshold of India, the jewel of the British crown. Ceylon (now Sri Lanka) also came under threat, and if Japan had wanted to occupy Madagascar near the east coast of Africa, there was not much to stop her from doing so. The Japanese navy ruled the seas from Hawaii to Ceylon. It seemed at the time that there was no force that could stem the Japanese blitz.

Even before the surprise attack on Pearl Harbor in December 1941, broad policy guidelines were discussed in Tokyo on November 20, 1941, by an inter-ministerial committee regarding the future status of and administration policies in the territories to be occupied. It was decided that once the fighting was over, a military government would be established in the occupied areas to ensure the restoration of law and order and mainly to ensure a steady supply of rice, raw materials and oil to Japan. It was also decided that the Japanese military administration would honor local customs and act through local officials. In order to gain the trust of the local population, it was determined that in addition to showing respect for native traditions and languages, in certain areas the Japanese would make efforts to encourage local national liberation movements that would be willing to collaborate with them. In any case, it was decided that the Japanese military administration would act to uproot all traces of the former colonial administrations, so that even if Japan lost the war the West would not be able to return to play a significant role in Asia. Above all, it was unanimously agreed that policy in the occupied areas must focus specifically on helping Japan's war effort.

In general terms, it was decided that in the initial phase of occupation the territories would come under direct military administration. Later there would be further discussion of the territories' eventual roles in the Greater East Asia Co-Prosperity Sphere led by Japan. It should be recalled that these ideas were essentially an ideological and propaganda platform for Japan's basic intention of gaining political and economic mastery in East and South East Asia while erasing all vestiges of the Western colonial powers from these regions. Appropriate slogans would be coined to help convince each local population of Japan's determination to expel Western imperialism and colonialism, put an end to the rule of the white races, and support local national liberation movements working to achieve independence—whose target date was never announced.

This would enable Japan to use the natural resources that abounded in the region, mainly oil from the Dutch East Indies and rubber from Malayan plantations – so vital for Japan's war effort—in the most efficient manner. Obtaining the assistance of the local populations was necessary. They would have to be convinced that the white man's rule was over and that it would be in their best interest to collaborate with Japan in the coming days. Japan's initial goal was to ensure stability and calm in these territories. It was obvious that Japan would not only be in charge of the local administration, but would also dominate the economy and culture, and naturally local internal politics.

The principles formulated in November 1941 were general indications and guidelines for the actions to be undertaken by the occupation authorities in each area. The speed and relative ease with which Japan was able to capture these territories surprised even the Japanese leadership. Between December 1941 and May 1942 Japan captured territories that came with hundreds of thousands of Westerners, both soldiers and civilians: British, Americans, Dutchmen, and even Frenchmen, along with several thousand Jews. Local Japanese commanders were given a great deal of leeway in governing the new territories, and in fact made the key decisions on the details of how to deal with the local population and the thousands of foreign prisoners who were now their captives. The Japanese government had to address the more general question of how to treat prisoners, both civilians and military. The central idea was to exploit those who were willing to cooperate with Japan mainly in local administration and the production of oil, rubber, tungsten, and other raw materials. The initial decisions were obvious. Soldiers were to be imprisoned in prisoner-of-war camps, to be dealt with in accordance with the Geneva Conventions. This did not prevent Japan from using tens of thousands of prisoners as slave laborers. The best-known episode involving the use of slave labor was the laying of a railway from Burma to Thailand, which included building a bridge across the River Kwai.

Once Japan completed the occupation of those areas deemed vital for its war effort and broad policies, it was decided in Tokyo that Malaya and the Dutch East Indies would be governed directly by the Japanese army under the overall authority of the area commander, whose headquarters was in Singapore. Java and Madura would be administered by officers belonging to the 26th Army, whose headquarters was in Batavia (today known as Jakarta, Indonesia), and Sumatra would be administered by the 25th Army, whose headquarters was initially in Singapore, but in 1943 was transferred to Sumatra. Celebes and the Mollukas would be handled by the Japanese navy, whose command included New Guinea and the Bismark Islands. The Navy headquarters was on the Dutch East Indies port of Macassar.

As noted, while the main guidelines were determined by the government and military headquarters in Tokyo, the implementation of the policies was left to local commanders, including the commandants of the prisoner-of-war camps and civilian internment camps. Postwar evidence shows that a great dal of what happened in these camps and territories depended on the personality of individual commanders. Some behaved in a decent, humane fashion while others were brutal and did their utmost to humiliate the prisoners under their control, partly because the Japanese samurai ethos disdained those who surrendered rather than dying for their country.

The first priority regarding the newly occupied population was deciding how to treat the overseas Chinese (*Nanyang*) communities in Hong Kong, Indonesia, Malaya, Singapore, the Philippines, and Burma, which totalled some twenty-five million individuals. These *Nanyang* Chinese maintained strong links to the motherland, and among them were elements that supported the war effort of Chiang Kai-Shek against the Japanese invaders. Despite their political leanings, these communities were by and large prosperous and numerous, and so their economic activity was vital for the Japanese to ensure that the economies of the newly occupied territories continued to function. Thus the general interest of Japan was in maintaining social and economic order in these areas without causing shock waves. Special efforts were made to control the native communities by inciting them against the Chinese minorities, portraying the latter as an exploitative element. This policy of divide-and-rule is typical of any occupier aspiring to entrench his rule in the areas he has captured.

As for the some 350,000 European civilians and members of the military, several guidelines were determined. Nationals of Japan's allies—Germans, Austrians, Italians, and even Frenchmen—would not be harmed in any way. But that did not include *refugees* from Germany and Austria, meaning specifically Jews. It was also decided not to harm Russian citizens or even stateless persons of Russian origin in any way, so as to avoid damaging the fragile non-aggression pact between Japan and the Soviet Union signed in April 1941. Further, it was determined that citizens of enemy countries—the United States, Britain, Australia, New Zealand, Canada, and the Netherlands—would be put in internment camps. This category included most of the Jews who fell under Japanese control in the early months of 1942. For some reason Iraq was proclaimed in 1942 a "friendly enemy" territory—a territory that was a colony of an enemy nation but not itself an enemy, and therefore Jews of Iraqi origins, also known as Baghdadi Jews, were treated with some consideration.

As noted, the Jews who fell captive to the Japanese in the early months of 1942 were considered to belong mainly to the group of Western nationals of enemy countries. But there were also Jewish refugees from Germany, Austria, and even Italy. The need to determine a clear-cut policy became more obvious when Japan captured the large cities of Hong Kong, Manila, Singapore, Batavia, and Rangoon, all of which contained Jewish communities. Most of these Jews held British, American, or Dutch passports. Among the first actions taken against the Jews in those places were the confiscations of homes, estates, and other real estate property, the freezing of bank accounts and other liquid assets, and the seizure of gold and jewels. All this was done even before specific guidelines were determined in Tokyo. The need to decide how to deal with the Jews was now urgent. On the one hand, Japanese authorities may have thought that any action designed to harm the Jews would be welcomed by their German allies and would be seen as expressing Japan's desire to become part of the German strategy. Great benefits would be obtained for the small price of hurting the Jews. But there were those who feared that harsh treatment of Jews would further exacerbate Japan's already tarnished image in the West and might also jeapordize future ties with the United States after the war.

In order to find a golden rule between the two opposing views, and in order to decide on a binding policy toward the Jews, it was decided that an Imperial Liaison Conference was required. This conference was probably Japan's supreme institution during the war, and consisted of the most senior military and civilian leaders charged with conducting the war. The discussion regarding the newly captured Jewish populations was held in Tokyo on March 11, 1942.[1] The subject was presented by War Minister General Sugiyama Hajime (1880-1945). He did not deny the principles determined by the Five Ministers Committee in December 1938, which had stated that Japan would not adopt a discriminatory policy against the Jews. However, he argued that since then a dramatic change has taken place: Japan was now part of the Axis Alliance and was in the midst of fighting a war against the Western democracies alongside Nazi Germany and Fascist Italy. Therefore, "It is incumbent on us to check matters regarding the Jews, especially in view of our ties with other nations." He also issued a veiled threat: "If we do not undertake at once appropriate measures toward the Jews and their racial traits, it should not be ruled out that there will be undesirable incidents in the occupied areas." For this reason Sugiyama called for the adoption of something in the vein of the anti-Jewish laws enacted by Nazi Germany, but did not suggest going so far as to turn the persecution of Jews into the declared policy of Japan. That would furnish additional propaganda grist to the British and Americans, and would also be in stark contradiction to the Japanese "Eight Roofs" policy, under which members of all races and people can live in peace, harmony, and security under Japan's beneficent roof.

At the conclusion of the discussion, the Japanese government adopted a series of policies regarding the treatment of Jews in the Japanese-occupied areas. Apart from special cases, additional Jews would not be allowed to migrate to the areas of the Japanese Empire. As far as those Jews already residing in the territories were concerned, the Japanese authorities would treat them as citizens of the places where they lived, but due to their racial traits there would be constant surveillance of their persons and their businesses, and any pro-enemy activity on their part would be suppressed. It was also decided that Jews who could be of value to the emperor, among them those who could be of assistance to the Axis Alliance and those who did not oppose the national policy of Japan, would be carefully selected and would receive the same treatment they were accorded before the war. German Jews would be considered stateless (as were White Russian émigrés), but would also be under close surveillance. The results of the conference were dispatched to all Japanese legations, embassies, and consulates in East Asia and to the Army and Navy headquarters. Their implementation was entrusted to local commanders, starting with corps commanders and ending with the most junior officers.

A broad examination of these important decisions shows that there had been no dramatic change in the Japanese perception of how the Jews should be dealt with. Moreover, the new policies also contain an element reflecting Japan's determination to adhere to their already-stated policy of maintaining racial harmony in the areas under their control, the policy that was the foundation on which they wanted to base the Greater East Asia Co-Prosperity Sphere so dear to the hearts of their wartime leaders. A crude antisemitic policy would not be in step with the idea of social and racial harmony, which was seen as a vital national interest. The concrete result of the directives issued in March 1942 would be to make Jews in the occupied areas something akin to a "tolerated" or "protected" minority. Their protectors would be the military authorities, who would translate the guidelines they had received into concrete measures on the ground. The treatment of the Jews was in its essence not much different from the treatment of other European enemy aliens. In some cases the local attitude toward the Jews was determined by Japanese special police units, some of whose officers had once served in Manchuria and Shanghai and knew about the "Jewish Question" from their service there. A few local commanders tended to see the Jews as fully or partly responsible for Japan's reversals in the war that had begun with the defeat of the Japanese task force in the battle of Midway in June 1942, and those few did occasionally incite local antisemitic activity aimed at turning the Jews into scapegoats for Japan's growing hardships.

Most interesting is the fact that in the final analysis Germany had no visible influence on Japan's attitude toward and treatment of the Jews. Even if the Japanese may have sought to impress their wartime allies, they never adopted Germany's genocidal policies. This is made clear by a telegram sent to Japan in May 1942, two months after the Imperial Liaison Conference decisions were made and then intercepted by the Allies. In the telegram, Alfred Rosenberg, the chief ideologist of the Nazi party regarding Jewish matters, who was also serving at the time as the minister responsible for the German-occupied areas in the East, demanded that Japan take harsh measures against the Jews under its control, and specifically that it create severe limitations on the movements of Jews in southeast Asia, before the Jews became a problem. The Japanese government ignored this and other similar demands. Perhaps Japan no longer considered Rosenberg a major figure, since he had time to focus his attention on limiting the movements of Jews. It is likely that by this time the Germans understood that there was no hope that Japanese policy, determined at the highest levels of government, would shift toward persecuting Jews in the Japanese Empire, let alone considering their extermination, as Germany would have liked them to do.

Another possible reason for Japan's relatively mild treatment of Jews during the war is the fact that in its colonies Jews did not play any role in the emerging national liberation movements or in the existing and emerging communist parties. Similarly, Jews did not stand out in the local media or in the academic world. They were mostly middle-class and engaged in business or government service.

B. The Jewish Communities in the Japanese Empire, 1941-1945

The Singapore Community[2]

The first Jewish settlers in Singapore arrived in the 1820's, after the local sultan allocated Britain space for the construction of a port in his territory in 1824. By the end of that same year, the Jews had already built a forty-seat synagogue and purchased land for a Jewish cemetery, and the tiny community began to prosper. Some of its members became involved in local politics. By 1856, four Jews were serving on the Board of Municipal Commissioners (along with 8 Arabs, 9 Armenians, and 79 Europeans). The majority of the Jewish community's members were of Iraqi, Iranian, and even Afghan origin, and they controlled some fifty percent of the colony's real estate and trade. At the time ownership of half of Singapore's lands was in the hands of a very wealthy Jewish family headed by Sir Menashe Meyer, which had settled in the colony in the early nineteenth century. In 1878, an ornate synagogue called *Magen Avot* (Shield of the Fathers) was founded, and that synagogue functions to this very day. According to the 1931 local census, some 832 Jews lived on the island at that time. The community was known for its highly efficient communal structure and the strong bonds of solidarity among its members, in addition to the thorough Jewish education given to its children. It also had ties with and raised funds for the World Zionist Organization in Jerusalem.

In the late 1930's, stories of Jewish persecution in Nazi Germany reached Singapore, brought by several German Jewish refugees who had managed to reach the colony, but the tales seemed to the local community to be of another world, although it did raise funds to help those refugees who found haven in Shanghai. The Jewish community of Singapore, like the non-Jewish one, believed the British propaganda that the island was impregnable, easily defensible, and impossible to capture. Their confidence was shattered when Japan attacked Pearl Harbor, and two days later Japanese planes sunk two British dreadnaughts, *The Prince of Wales* and *Repulse*. The victories over these warships, the pride of the British navy, shocked Singapore, whose population now felt unprotected and exposed to Japanese onslaught. When Japanese forces landed in Malaya in the second week of December 1941, panic began to spread.

As Malaya fell to the Japanese a very small number of Malayan Jews, estimated at some thirty souls from Penang and Kuala Lumpur, were evacuated by the British authorities to Singapore, which appeared to be a safer haven. However, as the Japanese troops marched unopposed southward toward Singapore, fear spread among the European settlers there. Like many others, Jews sought ways to escape the island as fast as possible. Those with means and British passports either escaped by sea to Burma and from there to India or boarded the few ships that still sailed directly to nearby safe ports, chiefly Calcutta and Bombay. Some even headed to Australia. By mid-1942 some 250 Singaporean Jews had settled in Bombay, where they were aided by the local government and Jewish community.

Several Jews attempted to volunteer for the British army defending the island, but were turned down because of a law that banned the recruitment of local Asians to the British army. A few did manage to volunteer for the local auxiliary forces, among them David Marshal (born Mishal in 1908), a successful lawyer and a leading figure in the Jewish community who even participated in local politics.

During the ten weeks between the beginning of the fighting in Malaya in December 1941 and the surrender of Singapore on February 15, 1942, some thousand Jews—two thirds of the community—escaped the island. Much of their property was destroyed by Japanese bombardments. Some deposited their money and valuables in the hands of their local neighbors before escaping. Those who remained now had to live under the new occupation regulations dictated by the Japanese military authorities. The attitude of the Japanese to members of the local population was determined according to nationality, country of origin, and whether the individual was a civilian or a soldier. While the Japanese placed some 135,000 British, Australian, New Zealander, Indian and local soldiers in prisoner-of-war camps, two days after the fall of Singapore 1,279 Europeans belonging to enemy nations were put in detention camps. The fate of the local Chinese minority was worse: it is estimated that during the four years of their rule the Japanese murdered some 5,000 to 25,000 Chinese residents of Singapore.

The Jewish community now dwindled to between 600-700 souls. The Japanese policy toward its members was similar to that toward the general population. However, on March 15, 1942, a month after the fall of the island, its remaining Jews were ordered to present themselves at police headquarters where they were instructed to wear on their arms a band on which was written in Japanese the word "Yudaya." The few German Jews present were exempt because they were considered nationals of a friendly country, but the other Jews, including the wealthy, had to wear the band. Apart from that, they were allowed to carry on with their lives unmolested and were able to observe their religious rites and practices. By the end of the first year of the Japanese occupation of Singapore, the local Jewish community was virtually unharmed, partly due to the sympathetic attitude of their local non-Jewish neighbors. The only true indications of trouble were the few cases of Japanese occupiers stealing Jewish property, claiming that rich Jews in America would send their brethren financial aid.

All this changed on April 5, 1943, when Japanese soldiers arrested a hundred Jewish men, giving them less than twenty minutes to collect their belongings. They were interned in the infamous Changi Camp near Singapore (today the site of the international airport). The treatment they received there was no different than that meted out to the other 3,500 detainees in Changi. It seems that they enjoyed certain privileges, as they were allocated a special place in the camp and allowed to practice their religion, but like others imprisoned there, they suffered from lack of food, diseases, the terrible heat and humidity, and the absence of anything to keep them busy. Their main effort went simply to surviving the ordeal.

It is not clear why the Japanese decided at that point to arrest a sixth of the members of the Singapore Jewish community and imprison them. Nor is the basis of the list of names from which they were operating clear. It it known that at the time of the arrest, a German ship was anchored in the port and German officers on board it wanted the Japanese to take certain measures against the Jews. Nonetheless, it is hard to believe that the Japanese authorities acted simply on the basis of such a request. It can be assumed that by making the arrests they wanted to appease the Germans, given the fact that this took place at the same time as the Jewish ghetto of Hongkew was set up in Shanghai. It should also be recalled that the broad policy outlines toward the Jews were determined in Tokyo, but their implementation was left to local military commanders, who acted as they saw fit taking into account the changing conditions and the progress of the war—and their own personal idiosyncrasies.

As the fortunes of war turned against Japan, so did the attitude of Singapore's Japanese rulers turn against the local Jews. On October 10, 1943, forty of the hundred Jews arrested in April were removed from Changi and sent to a special camp of the Kempeitai, the Japanese special police units, where they were tortured and accused of passing intelligence to enemy forces. The other Jewish prisoners who remained in Changi were moved on May 1, 1944, to a camp that had once been the headquarters of the Royal Air Force in Singapore. The conditions there were no better than those prevailing in Changi, and the prisoners were kept busy maintaining the camp and building additional quarters for other prisoners. On March 22, 1945, five months before Japan surrendered, the remaining Jews of Singapore, consisting of 222 men, 200 women, and 50 children, were all placed in this camp. The men and women were separated; the children under ten stayed with their mothers, and those over ten stayed with their fathers. In this camp they huddled together with over 3,000 other prisoners, mainly British and Australian. In the four years of Japanese occupation some fifty Jews died, most of them from old age, illness or Japanese bombardment at the beginning of the war. Eight disappeared and presumably were tortured to death. But most of the community survived the war and returned home after Japan surrendered. Although much of their property had been stolen and local squatters had taken over their homes, they were able to rehabilitate their lives with the assistance of the British authorities. Soon those who had spent the war years in India also retuned, and the community arose from the ashes.

David Marshal had been one of the Jewish men interned in a prisoner-of-war camp. In April 1942 he was sent to Japan as a forced laborer and assigned to work in mines in the northern Japanese home island of Hokkaido, where he survived the war. After returning home he became once again involved in local politics, and in 1955 was appointed as the first chief minister of the colony on the eve of its gaining independence. He held that post for less than two years and was later appointed Singapore's ambassador to France and other European nations. He retired in 1993 and died two years later.

The Community in Burma[3]

A small Jewish community existed in Burma from the beginning of the mid-nineteenth century, consisting mostly of Jews who made their way east from Iran via India. The first Jew known to have settled in Burma was Solomon Gabirol, who was also a commissioner in the army of a local king called Alaungpaya in 1755. The existence of a permanent Jewish community in Rangoon dates back to the middle of the nineteenth century. Most of its members were Baghdadi Jews who had arrived in Burma on their way to destinations further east. The British government was apparently interested in attracting Baghdadi Jews, thinking they would bring capital and enrich the colony. Some members of the growing community were engaged in the opium trade. The first synagogue was built in 1857 and was named *Matsmiah Yeshua* (Nurturing Redemption). The synagogue post-dated the appearance of the community, and so there was already a congregation that could support it. By 1881 the community numbered 172 souls; in 1891 the number rose to 219, and by 1901 it was 506. In the early decades of the 1900's, there were a number of Jewish organizations in Rangoon and Mandalay. A second synagogue, called *Beth El* (House of God), was opened in Rangoon in 1932. Most of the Burmese Jews who held British passports (or Burmese passports) were traders. A few worked for the British colonial administration because of their language skills.

On the eve of the Pacific War the Burmese Jewish community numbered some two thousand souls, most of them residing in Rangoon. Thirty-two Jewish refugees from Lithuania who had escaped the Nazis thanks to the Sugihara visas came to Rangoon in 1941, aided by the American Joint Distribution Committee. They found conditions there almost unbearable and requested that the American organization help them get to other places. But before anything could be done, war broke out.

The Burmese Jews hoped that the British army would be able to halt the Japanese advance, but once Malaya, Singapore, and Indonesia had fallen to the Japanese it was clear that this was a forlorn hope, and that it was a matter of time before Burma would also be overtaken. On March 9, 1942, Rangoon surrendered. In the weeks preceding the surrender, some 1500 Jews, the majority of the community, fled west to Calcutta ahead of the invading Japanese army. Most of them took trains, some drove by car until they ran out of petrol, and several travelled by ship. A number of Jews married to local Burmese women found shelter with their spouses' families in the countryside. Over the course of the war several scores of Jews died, mainly of illnesses and malnutrition.

Some two hundred Jews remained in Rangoon. There is no evidence that those Jews who remained in Burma were in any way harmed, and they were treated according to their nationality. Since many of them were Iraqi, and Iraq was seen by the Japanese authorities as a "friendly enemy" nation, they were spared harsh treatment. Those holding British passports were jailed, along with other enemy aliens. During the Japanese occupation virtually no antisemitic articles appeared in the local press, and non-Jews were not required to hand over Jews to the Japanese military authorities. Apart from the execution of one Jew charged with spreading anti-Japanese rumors, and the looting of some Jewish property by Japanese occupiers, the Jews of Burma survived the war undiscriminated against by the Japanese. At the end of the war some 500 Jews returned to Rangoon, mainly from India. After Burma gained its independence in 1947, the majority of its Jewish community migrated to Australia and the United States.

The Jewish Community in the Philippines[4]

The existence of a tiny Jewish community in the Philippines goes back to the end of the sixteenth century. There are tales of two Converso Jews from Spain who were seized in the Philippines and tried in 1593 by an Inquisition court in Mexico because there were no Inquisition courts on the islands. It is not clear what the two were charged with. By the end of the seventeenth century, eight more Philippine Converso Jews were tried in Mexico. Three wealthy Jewish jewelers from Alsace, the Levy brothers, arrived in 1870 in the wake of the Franco-Prussian War and set up a flourishing business in Manila known as Levy Hermanos, Inc. The opening of the Suez Canal in 1869 made it easy for Jews living in countries along the coast of the Mediterranean Sea to settle in East Asia. Several Jews from Egypt, Syria, and other parts of the Ottoman Empire arrived thereafter.

Following the American occupation of the Philippines in the Spanish-American War of 1898, a number of Jews who arrived with the American army decided to remain there. More Jews arrived from the United States and set up businesses that traded with mainland Asia. They were joined at the beginning of the twentieth century by several Russian and Polish Jews escaping from persecution and pogroms in their home countries. The best-known among the Russian émigrés was Emil Bachrach, who arrived in 1901 via the United States and soon became involved in the furniture, banking, and transport businesses. Fifty additional Russian Jews arrived after the 1917 Bolshevik Revolution. At the end of the First World War, the local Jewish community numbered some 150 souls but did not have the means to maintain communal institutions such as a synagogue, schools, and a cemetery. The first synagogue was built in Manila in 1924, financed by the wealthy Emil Bachrach and his family. Religious services were provided by rabbis, circumcisers, and slaughterers who came especially for that purpose from Shanghai.

In the early 1930's there existed in Manila a Jewish community consisting of some five hundred souls, mostly European Jews, Sephardi Jews, and some American Jews. There was significant growth in the community during the 1930's, attributable to the rise of Hitler to power in Germany in 1933 and the independence granted to the Philippines by the United States in 1934. The first president of the Commonwealth of the Philippines, Manuel Quezon (1878-1944), was interested in the immigration of a large number of Jews to his country, believing (like some Japanese officials believed would be the case in Japan) that Jews with capital and skills would be able to speed the economic growth of the young republic. He brought before the Philippine congress a proposal that the country absorb some ten thousand Jewish refugees from Germany and settle them in the southern island of Mindanao. The Philippines' immigration laws, different and much more lenient than the American ones, did not pose an obstacle to bringing many Jews to the island nation, but the entire project failed for bureaucratic reasons.

The Philippines as an independent country did not yet have its own Foreign Service, let alone overseas diplomatic and consular offices, and so for consular services they had to rely on local American consuls. Those operated according to the severely restrictive American immigration laws, and showed no interest in granting Philippine visas to Jews, despite the interest of the Philippine government and the willingness of the local Jewish community to help absorb the newcomers. The result was that between 1937 and the outbreak of the Pacific War, only 1,300 Jewish refugees arrived, many of them fleeing from Germany and Austria and arriving via Manchuria, Shanghai, and Hong Kong. On the eve of the Pacific War there were some 1500 Jews in the Philippines, most of them living in Manila. Some of them were stranded in Manila trying to escape to Australia. The Jewish Refugee Committee of Manila was created to help absorb the arriving refugees from Shanghai after the outbreak of the Second Sino-Japanese War in July 1937. This body was permitted by President Quezon and the American High Commissioner Paul McNuttt (1891-1955) to select the refugees to whom Philippine visas would be granted. In this manner 28 German Jews arrived from Shanghai in September 1937. Most of the funds needed to care for the refugees were supplied by the American Joint Distribution Committee.

When the 14th Army of Japan, commanded by Lieutenant-General Homma Masaharu (1887-1946), occupied Manila on January 2, 1942, martial law was proclaimed and enemy aliens were required to register. Their future depended heavily on the passports in their possession. Enemy aliens whose countries were now at war with Japan, including the United States, Britain, Holland, and the British Commonwealth of Nations, were interned in two detention camps: one on the campus of Santo Tomas University and the other in Los Bagnos near Manila. Among the detainees were 250 Jews. Others not arrested were 1,300 German Jewish refugees (even though they lost their nationality in late 1941) and Jews who held passports belonging to Germany's allies, such as Austria, Italy, Vichy France, Romania, Hungary, Slovakia, Croatia, and Iraq.

The third group of Jews living in the Philippines consisted of Russian Jews who held a variety of passports issued in the 1920's by the Committee for International Refugees (the so-called Nansen passports) or by the Far Eastern Republic that existed briefly in Siberia and later by the Soviet Union.

The Japanese military authorities did not intervene in the running of the detention camps and allowed the prisoners to run their own affairs. They did not prevent the Jews who were not interned from helping those detained by sending them kosher food and fulfilling their religious needs. The Manila synagogue and school functioned throughout the war, and services were held regularly. In the Philippines, like in other Japanese-occupied areas, there were some cases of looting of property and money. In 1943 a number of antisemitic articles appeared in the local press, and some antisemitic broadcasts were aired on the local radio station. Still, the Japanese authorities did not go out of their way to discriminate against the Jews, mainly because the local Jewish leadership was able to persuade them not to. While the Japanese authorities did threaten the Jews to discourage them from engaging in black market acitivities, no steps were taken to molest Jews as a people or to curtail the existence of the communal institutions. While some people lost their homes and businesses and a number were abused, beaten, or on occasion imprisoned, the main physical harm suffered by the Jews as a group was illness and starvation. As in other places, a great deal depended on the local Japanese commanders. Some of them, particularly those who had trained in Germany, were somewhat hostile to Jews, but rarely were they aggressive. The leaders of the German Jewish community of the Philippines were able to persuade the Japanese occupation forces to abandon rumored plans of creating a ghetto in Manila. The rumors had spread following the visit to Manila in February 1943 of the German Ambassador to Tokyo Heinrich von Stahmer (1892-1978).

However, if there had been any truth to the rumor, the plan was prevented by the intercession of the leaders of the local German Jewish community.

The main attack on Jewish property occurred during the fighting between invading American forces led by General Douglas MacArthur (1880-1964) and the Japanese army at the end of 1944 and early 1945. In the battle for the liberation of Manila in February 1945, Japanese soldiers committed atrocities in which some 100,000 civilians were killed, among them seventy Jews. Some of the victims were murdered by Japanese soldiers in a massacre committed in the Red Cross hospital in Manila. But this massacre was carried out against all foreigners, not just on Jews. The local synagogue that was used as an ammunition depot by the Japanese was destroyed during the fighting. The majority of the Jews in the Philippines survived the war and reported that during the occupation they rarely encountered antisemitic expressions on the part of either the Japanese occupying forces or the local Philippine community.

The war took a toll on the community, and the majority of its members did not have the financial means and emotional stamina to remain and rebuild their community the way the Jews of Singapore, Hong Kong, and even Shanghai did. The majority opted to move to the United States, Australia, or (after 1948) to Israel, and a few even went back to Germany. By late 1948, fewer than 300 Jews remained in the Philippines.

In November 1947 the newly independent Philippines voted in the United Nations General Assembly for the partition of Palestine and the creation of a Jewish state there. It was the only Asian country to do so, and the vote was the result of American pressure and the feeling of some Philippine leaders that the Jews deserved their own state. The Philippines was among the first Asian nations to recognize Israel and establish diplomatic relations with it.

The Jewish Community in the Dutch East Indies (Indonesia)[5]

The first Jews who came to the Dutch East Indies (hereafter referred to by its modern name, Indonesia) were most likely Iraqi and Iranian Jews who joined Arab traders in their expeditions to the islands during the Portuguese rule there (1619-1641). In a later period, mostly after the expulsion of the Jews from Spain in 1492, some Spanish Jews also made their way to Holland and from there to Indonesia. A number of the new arrivals spoke Arabic and Portuguese and became middlemen and interpreters between foreigners and the local population. Jews were formally allowed to settle in Indonesia and work for the Dutch East Indies Company beginning in 1782. A few engaged in the spice trade, as well as in the sale of precious stones. The number of Jews on the islands grew steadily after the Dutch government, which had captured Indonesia in 1815, permitted Jews to settle in its Asian colony in 1882.

Indonesian Jews tended not to flaunt their religious affiliation, and some even tried to conceal it. This may explain why a strong, well-organized community didn't emerge until the 1930's. In 1930 the Dutch authorities conducted a population census in which 1,095 people identified themselves as Jews. On the eve of the Pacific War, Indonesian Jews numbered between 2,500-3,000, or two percent of the foreigners in that colony. They were divided between Iraqi Jews and the Ashkenazi community. The Iraqis concentrated mainly in Surabaya and were involved in import and export, small artisan shops, and peddling. The Ashkenazis lived mainly on the island of Java, concentrating in Batavia (today's Jakarta) and Bandung. The beginning of some communal organization can be discerned in the early 1930's, when Indonesian Jews began to assist several hundred Jews who had escaped from Nazi Germany. At the same time, a local newspaper called *The Land of Israel* appeared. A large proportion of the Jews of Indonesia worked for the East India Company, for the Shell oil company, or for the Dutch colonial administration. Others were professionals such as doctors, accountants, and lawyers. On the whole, they enjoyed a high standard of living, had virtually no ties with the local, predominantly Muslim population, and preferred to link their fates to that of the Dutch rulers.

Even before the Japanese attacked Pearl Harbor on December 7, 1941, the Dutch authorities proclaimed that they had no intention of supplying Japan with resources that would aid its war effort: mainly oil, rubber, and bauxite. After the fall of Holland to the Nazis in May 1940, the Dutch administration in Indonesia remained loyal to the Dutch government-in-exile in London. The Indonesian Jews were encouraged by the American promise to the Dutch government in November 1941 to send troops to help protect the islands in case of a Japanese invasion. After the fall of Holland, the American Joint Distriubution Committee assisted some 90 Dutch Jews to find shelter in Indonesia. Shortly after the outbreak of the Pacific War, Japanese forces quickly invaded Indonesia from Borneo and Malaya. On March 8, 1942, the Dutch colonial administration surrendered the islands. One of the first acts of the new conquerors was to release the Japanese civilians who had been interned by the Dutch. They then turned to dealing with the European population. The 1930 census was a convenient basis for determining who the foreigners were. At first the Japanese placed all those who had served in the Dutch army (including some Jews) in prisoner-of-war camps. This was followed by a decision to intern all of the 160,000 Dutch citizens in the islands, including women and children. The attitude of the Japanese occupation authorities toward the local Jews was no different than their attitude toward the other internees. The Japanese did not ask the Dutch or the native Indonesians to hand over the Jews. Those Jews who were Dutch nationals were imprisoned with the others. Those who held Russian or German documents were exempt. Iraqi Jews were also unmolested, as the Japanese treated them as Iraqi, nationals of a country not considered as an enemy of Japan.

In that first wave of arrests, only half of the Jews in Indonesia were interned. The rest were allowed to remain in their homes and carry on with their lives. But as the war situation worsened for Japan, in August 1943 the Japanese issued an order for the internment of all Jews, including Iraqi and German Jews. The change in policy can be partially explained by the growing resentment of the Jews that was developing in Japan, in the form of a large number of antisemitic articles in the Japanese media. In Indonesia itself, a number of antisemitic articles appeared, probably at the behest of the local Kempeitai commander, Murase Mitsuo.

Another major reason for the change of policy can be ascribed to growing German pressure on the Japanese authorities to undertake harsh measures against the Jews and to harm them. In July 1943, a German official by the name of Dr. Helmuth Wohlthat (1893-1973), arrived in Indonesia. He was a former senior aide to Reichsmarshall Herman Goering (1893-1946), and had taken part in discussions in 1940 on settling German and European Jews in Madagascar, where they would be exterminated in phases. He was sent to Tokyo before Pearl Harbor as the head of a German economic delegation to discuss with the Japanese government the possibility of Japan providing Germany with raw materials from territories Japan would capture, and how to transfer those materials to Germany. In the early stages of the Pacific War, Wohlthat remained in Tokyo and participated in joint German-Japanese discussions on military cooperation and coordination. Japan agreed to allow the Germans the use of Batavia as an operational naval base, and the use of the ports of Singapore and Surabaya for submarines. Having secured that agreement, Wohlthat demanded that the Japanese undertake severe measures against the Jews. This may have been the main cause for the change of the Japanese attitude toward the Jews of Indonesia Jews.

The new policy has to be seen in a broader context, namely the development of the war situation. The actions against the Jews were some of many steps in a broader policy that became increasingly harsh as it became obvious that Japan was not winning the war. The main victims of the new policy were first and foremost the local population, from whom the Japanese demanded a supply of laborers and essential raw materials during this time of rampant inflation, hunger, and a drastic fall in the standard of living. Additional victims were the local Chinese minority, which was accused of secretly supporting the Chinese nationalists. A quarter of a million Indonesians were sent to Japan or to other parts of its empire as forced laborers, and few returned home at the end of the war. The Japanese military authorities in Indonesia feared local uprisings and allied bombing of the sea lanes through which oil was sent to Japan. The senior Japanese commander was head of the 16th army, General Harada Komichi, and he allowed the detention of anyone accused of inciting revolt, including Jews and members of the Freemason Society. Harada, who had some experience in Jewish affairs from the time he served in the Special Branch section of the Japanese army in Manchuria, consulted his experts, Yasue and Inuzuka, and it seems that they advised him to ignore the Jews and focus on the local Muslim population. As a result, the Jews arrested were not subjected to harsher treatment than the other prisoners. There were cases when several non-Jewish Dutch people requested that the Jews be imprisoned in separate sections of the camps. The conditions of those who were imprisoned were in general harsh. While no one was allowed to leave the detention camps, they were permitted to observe the Sabbath, eat kosher meat, bake matzot for Passover, and observe Jewish holidays. A few were sent to forced labor camps, and some even helped build the bridge on the River Kwai. Their lot was later described by Rabbi Chaim Nussbaum, a graduate of the Telshe Yeshiva.

In comparison with the fate of Jewish communities in other areas of Japan's wartime empire, that of the Indonesian Jews was much harsher. This can be explained by the Japanese military authorities' stern treatment of the entire foreign population in those islands, and the worsening shortage of food and medicine. Post-war figures mention the deaths of scores of Jews during the war due to lack of medical attention, maknutrition, starvation, and old age. There were cases of looting, rape, and beatings, but there is no documentation of deliberate murder of Jews by the Japanese.

The imprisoned foreigners did not know of the end of the war and the surrender of Japan, or of Indonesia's declaration of independence on August

14, 1945. Several days later, the doors of the camps were opened and the majority of the internees went home, but in view of the war of independence against the Dutch waged until 1949, the majority of the Jewish internees departed and went mostly to Holland. There they met Dutch Jews who had survived the Nazi death camps in Poland and other places, and realized how fortunate they had been despite the harsh conditions in the Indonesian camps. Some eventually travelled to Israel and the United States. The last remaining Jews in Surabaya left that city in 2014.

The Hong Kong Jewish Community[6]

Jews were among the early foreign settlers who came to Hong Kong in the 1840's. Most of them were Iraqi Jews (known there as Baghdadis), who arrived from India under British protection and started trading in the newly opened treaty ports of China. Prominent among them were the Sassoon, Kadoorie, Gubbai, Elias, Somech, Soffer, Ezra, Raymond, Hardoon, and Solomon families, several of whom we have already mentioned. The first prominent Jew to settle in Hong Kong was Elias Sassoon, who arrived in 1844. Soon David Sassoon & Sons became one of Hong Kong's more prosperous foreign trading companies, dealing in opium and incenses. From this modest beginning they expanded into shipping, banking, insurance, real estate, and cotton. The Sassoons and the other families laid the foundations for the organized Jewish community that came to be in the late nineteenth century. In 1882 there were some 60 Jews on the island, a Jewish cemetery was consecrated in 1857 and in 1902 the *Ohel Leah* (Leah's Tent) synagogue was inaugurated. It continues to be active to this day. A year later, the community's wealthy families created a communal fund to finance its expenses. In 1905 the Kadoorie family built a Jewish club in the style of the British clubs so common in Hong Kong and other parts of the British Empire. In the early part of the twentieth century, Jews controlled some 30% of the island's trade. A Jewish man, Sir Matthew Nathan (1862-1939), served as the governor general of Hong Kong from 1904 to 1907.

As the port of Hong Kong grew busier and the colony prospered, so did the fortunes of the local Jewish community. Jewish families were involved in the establishment of the Hong Kong-Shanghai Banking Corporation and served on its board of directors. By 1911 there were 231 Jews in Hong Kong or some 50 families. The rapid growth of Shanghai as a major commercial and shipping hub drove a number of Hong Kong Jews to that flourishing port city in China. Therefore on the eve of World War II there were fewer than 75 Jewish families on the island. They were an integral part of the local British society and held British passports. Some became peers of the realm, and above all there is no reason to believe that they were on the receiving end of animosity or antisemitism from either the members of the British community or the Chinese locals.

In the late 1930's, several Jewish refugees arrived from Europe, and the community looked after their needs. Most had to leave soon after, because the British colonial administration refused to grant them permanent residence permits. When the Pacific War broke out, a number of Jews volunteered to serve in the Hong Kong Volunteer Defence Corps. Japanese troops invaded the island shortly after the attack on Pearl Harbor and occupied it after a four-day struggle that ended with the British governor surrendering on Christmas Day 1941 to avoid further carnage and destruction. As most of the Jews were British nationals, they were imprisoned in the civilian prisoner-of-war camp on Stanley Peninsula, together with the 7,000 other British and American nationals who had been caught in Hong Kong. Those who were in the army or served in volunteer organizations were imprisoned in a military camp at Sham Shui Po. The Japanese did not take into account the fact that many of the Hong Kong Jews were of Iraqi origin rather than British, and in contrast to how things worked in other parts of Japan's wartime empire they too were imprisoned. The conditions in both camps were harsh: the daily food ration amounted to 250 calories. Jewish communal organizations ceased to function. The Japanese army confiscated property and turned the synagogue into a military area. Banks, the media, and power plants also ceased to function, and hyper-inflation prevailed. This inevitably led to the collapse of the local economy. However, the Japanese authorities did allow the Jews to use prayer books and observe the Jewish holidays.

Nineteen Jews lost their lives in the fighting and during the three and a half years of Japanese occupation. Among them was Sir Eli Kadoorie, who died of illness in 1944. By the time Japan surrendered in August of 1945, Hong Kong's population, which had numbered some 1.6 million in 1941, had dwindled to 600,000. Jews were not singled out for worse treatment than others, apart from the looting of their money, gold, jewels, and household furniture and the closing of their bank accounts. Very soon after Japan surrendered, members of the Jewish community were back and rebuilding their businesses. After the collapse of the Nationalist regime on the Chinese mainland and the proclamation of the People's Republic of China in October 1949, Hong Kong once again became the most important business hub of East Asia, replacing Shanghai and Yokohama. In that situation the Jewish families prospered once again.

The Jewish Community in French Indo-China[7]

The first Jews to settle in French Indo-China, which comprised of modern Vietnam, Cambodia, and Laos, arrived during the French colonization of that part of Asia beginning in the 1840's. A mention of a Jewish presence in Indo-China appeared in the *London Jewish Chronicle* and later in the *Universal Jewish Encyclopedia*. Among the best-known Jews in Indo-China at the time was Jules Rueff. There is a brief entry on him in the *Dictionaire National des Contemporaines* (Paris, 1901) and another entry in the *1916 Jewish Encyclopedia* published in New York. He was born in Paris in 1854, went to Indo-China in 1872 to seek his fortune, and became one of the leading French pioneers in that colony. He was the originator of the plan to build a railway from Saigon to Mytho in Cochin-Chine and was a founder and director of *Messageries Fluviales des Cochine-Chine*, a shipping company operating mainly along the Mekong River. He was also involved in organizing various trade fairs in France and advocating for Indo-China's needs to various French governments. Another well-known French Jew, Sylvain Levi (1863-1935), one of France's leading scholars of the Orient in the late nineteenth and early twentieth centuries, was involved in establishing the Hanoi branch of the *Ecole francaise d'Éxtreme Orient* in 1902. There are no reports of the existence of any Jewish communal organizations or facilities, or of the existence of a synagogue or Jewish cemetery in Hanoi, Haiphong, or Saigon.

Information on the number of Jews in French Indo-China on the eve of the Second World War was supplied by the American Jewish Committee in 1940. They claimed that of a total population of some 15 million people, there were about a thousand Jews living in Hanoi, Saigon, Tourane, and Haiphong. Most of them were engaged in trade, free professions, school teaching, or banking and finance. Some were officials of the French colonial administration, and a few served in the French army. Apart from this report, there is virtually no knowledge about this community, including whether there was intermarriage and to what extent the Jews were integrated into French colonial society. There is no reference to Jews being involved in the local media or academia (apart from one case), and no suggestion as to whether they took part in the growing local nationalist movement. Apparently few bothered to learn the local language, and for the most part they kept to themselves, trying to maintain a very low profile in a society that resembled French society, which was somewhat tinged with antisemitism. There is no evidence of overt antisemitism in Indo-China before the outbreak of the war in 1939.

All this changed when French Indo-China continued to be governed by the French colonial administration after the collapse of France in June 1940. Unlike Indonesia, whose governor general chose to accept the authority of the Dutch government-in-exile in London, the French colonial administration was responsible to the Vichy regime, headed by Marshall Philippe Petain (1856-1951). The governor general, Rear Admiral Jean Decoux (1884-1963), negotiated an agreement with the Japanese government which permitted Japan to station troops in Tonkin, use its naval and air facilities, and stop the supply of weapons flowing from Indo-China to nationalist China. Otherwise the Japanese did not interfere with the running of the colony and left it to the French administration. Indo-China became, in fact, a Japanese protectorate where the Japanese army was supreme.

Following the collapse of France, Field Marshal Phillippe Petain emerged as chef d'etat and heralded a new National Revolution that made antisemitism one of its main pillars. One of the first manifestations of the new anti-Jewish policy was the revocation of the Cremieux Decree of 1870, which had allowed French Jews to become French citizens. On October 8, 1940, the Vichy government in France issued a series of anti-Jewish laws known as the "statute des Juifs," which applied to all Jews living in France and in territories under French rule. These statutes defined who would be considered Jewish (any person who had two or three grandparents of the Jewish race), and included in that category Jews who had converted to Catholicism. According to official French colonial documents, there were 140 Jews living in Indo-China at the time, including 18 children. It can be assumed that this 140 referred to families, which brings the probable number of individuals closer to the American Jewish Committee figures. A decree issued on October 18, 1940, banned Jews from working in the civil service, the army, or the diplomatic corps, and prevented them from holding teaching positions, editing newspapers, and directing films and plays. They were later forbidden to work for commercial companies that had contracts from public bodies. Jews were forbidden to work in the media, theater, radio, films, and public relations and were required to fill out detailed questionnaires regarding their origins, nationality, civil status, religion, financial assets and property. In a statute dated June 24, 1941, Jews were excluded from working in banks and insurance companies, and banned from involvement in stock trading and real estate. The number of Jewish university students was limited to three percent of the total student population, and the number of Jewish school children was limited to 2% of the population. The Jews of Indo-China were effectively being barred from almost all of the positions they had held for decades. As a rule, the local administration headed since the end of June 1940 by Governor General Admiral Jean Decoux tried to implement the new rules to the letter.

To judge from the existing colonial-era documents in both Vietnam and France, it seems that Admiral Decoux, like many other senior French naval officers, had a tendency toward antisemitism. He was determined to implement the anti-Jewish decrees to the letter, without questioning the need to follow them in a remote area of Asia where there was no German presence. Those decrees were dissimilar to the anti-Jewish laws that were fully implemented against Jews in French North Africa until late 1942, which included internment in camps and forced labor. In some instances the *Commission General aux Questions Juives* in Vichy was asked by the governor general not to insist that Jews be removed from the army, because of growing tension and border incidents with Thailand that required French military intervention. Decoux raised another issue: how would the local population view the anti-Jewish measures, which of course involved European people? In some cases, local officials decided to ignore the new statutes. While the Jewish secretary of the Buddhist Institute in Phnom Penh, Suzanne Karpeles, was dismissed, the director of the *Ecole Francaise d'Extreme Orient*, George Cosedes, remained at his post. Some Jews were able to continue running their businesses after "contributing" money to the colonial administration. In other cases, Jewish properety was seized, as were bank accounts.

Apart from these troubles, the Jews were not interned or otherwise molested. What was done to them took place without any Japanese involvement, and was due to orders that came directly from the Vichy regime. There is no evidence that the Japanese military authorities in any way interfered in the manner in which the French administration dealt with the Jewish population. The Japanese simply demanded that the French keep an eye on the Jews and prohibited them from admitting additional Jews to the colony. They did not insist on any specific acts of discrimination, and the local Jewish community survived the war virtually intact. There are no reports of Jewish refugees from Europe or occupied China seeking refuge in Indo-China. There is also virtually no evidence that Jews living in Indo-China on the eve of or during the war who attempted to escape to other locations.

The Vichy anti-Jewish laws were not automatically rescinded in the summer of 1944 when France was liberated from the Germans. Although the entire colony was seized by the Japanese in March 1945, the French civil servants did not want to annul the anti-Jewish statutes overnight, lest they be seen by the local population as having pursued a wrong policy. But in effect the anti-Jewish laws were no longer implemented. Much depended on the attitude of the local French colonial administrators. When the war in Europe ended in May 1945 and the Pacific War ended in August of the same year, most of the Jews of Indo-China emigrated to France. Admiral Decoux returned to France, where he was tried and sentenced to two years in prison for collaborating with the Vichy regime. He insisted that Japan was totally uninvolved in the policies he had pursued against the Jews of Indo-China. The remaing Jews left that country when it was divided in 1954 and the French presence ended.

The Jewish Community of Penang[8]

The early Jewish settlers in Malaya (or the Straits Colony) arrived from Baghdad at the beginning of the nineenth century and settled in the port of Georgetown or Penang. At the time, that port was second in importance only to Singapore. A number of Baghdadi Jews had left Iraq during the reign of Governor Daoud Pasha (1817-1831), who was responsible for persecuting Jews. The leading families who arrived in Malaya were the Mordechai, David, Grand, Menasseh, Akirev, Baruch, Yaacov, and Flinters families. They became involved in real estate and the incense and diamond trades. Apparently some became rich, opened a synagogue in a shop, and prayed under the guidance of a cantor, as they did not have a permanent rabbi. By 1881 there were 32 Jews in Penang, and ten years later their number swelled to 155. At its peak, in 1899, the community numbered 172 souls. They maintained ties with friends and relatives from Iraq who lived in India, Singapore, and Burma. There are no reports of a substantial communal organization. The synagogue operated from 1929 to 1976, and the Jewish cemetery established in 1805 contains 106 graves of Jews buried there from 1835 to 1978.

Like the members of other East Asian Jewish communities, the Penang Jews were not involved in local poilitics, culture, or media. There are no indications that any of them even worked for the British colonial administration (as some members of the Indonesian, Indo-China and Burmese Jewish communities did for the French, Dutch and British colonial administrations respectively). When the Japanese army launched its invasion of Malaya in December 1941, some 30 Jews were evacuated by the British army to Singapore, from where several managed to escape to India and Australia. Those who remained in Penang were forced to wear the Star of David, with the word "Jew" written on it in Japanese. The Japanese military authorities apparently made use of the technical skills of some Jews, who ended up working in Japanese military installations. Penang was used by German submarines in 1943, and the presence of German sailors in that port city caused problems: the German seamen attacked some Jews. The Japanese military commander was determined to prevent this, as he needed the Jews' skills, and informed the Germans that he would not tolerate any attack on Jews, whom he considered protected aliens. As a result, the Jews were not further molested or interned. After the war, most of the Jews left Penang and by 1969 only three Jewish families remained in that city.

The Jewish Community in Bangkok[9]

The earliest reference to a Jewish presence in what was then called Siam (and is now known as Thailand) appears in the memoirs of a Converso Portuguese Jew by the name of Fernando Mendes Pinto (1509-1583). He mentions the fact that among the traders who came from Europe to Siam there were a number of Jews, probably also Conversos. There is also mention of Jews in that country in letters and journals of Catholic missionaries dating to the second half of the sixteenth century. The Cairo Genizah, which contained many documents about Jews, raises the possibility that a number of Jews from Egypt and Syria were also trading in Siam. There are also documents describing the presence in Siam in 1683 of one Avraham Navarro, who worked as an interpreter for the London-based British East India Company.

While a growing number of Jews settled in various ports in South East Asia in the mid-nineteenth century, there is virtually no mention of Jews residing in what is now known as Thailand. This is due partly to the ruling Chakri dynasty's policy of preventing Europeans from settling in their kingdom. Aware of the fate of Burma, which had become a British colony, and Indo-China, which had fallen under French rule, Thailand made a successful attempt to remain neutral. It achieved this feat partly by not allowing foreigners to settle there in large numbers. By the early twentieth century, there were only 1,500 foreigners living in Thailand. Some of them were Jews, as evidenced by a number of Jewish names on graves in the

Bangkok Protestant cemetery. A growing number of Jews arrived and settled in Bangkok during the reign of Rama V (1853-1910). Known as King Chulalongkron, he slowly began to open Thailand's gates to Westerners, among them several Jews who came from Germany. Among these new Jewish arrivals were physicians, lawyers, and accountants, and a few were also involved in the hotel business. Two synagogues functioned in Bangkok in the early years of the twentieth century, one Ashkenazi and the other Sephardi, populated by the growing population of Middle Eastern Jews, who dealt mainly in precious stones.

Following the 1917 October Revolution in Russia, a number of Russian Jewish refugees arrived in Bangkok and remained there. They raised the Jewish population to around 200 individuals in 58 households. The most prominent among them was the Gerson family, which has led the community since the early 1920's and are still very active there. There is no record of persecution, antisemitism, or other acts or measures against Jews. This is due largely to the tolerant nature of the population and the peaceful nature of Thai Buddhism. Thailand was the first Asian nation that publicly supported the Balfour Declaration, through the representative of King Rama VI in London, Joseph Hochman, who was also a rabbi and one-time editor of *The Jewish Review*.

In 1932, Luang Philbunsongkhram (known as Philbun) led a military coup and took over power in Thailand. The new leader was determined to make Thailand a powerful nation in South East Asia, and his regime was styled partly on German Nazism and Italian Fascism, both doctrines he seems to have admired. If he was interested in the political side of these totalitarian doctrines, he did not borrow—let alone adopt and implement—their racial attitude toward Jews, although he did target Thailand's large Chinese minority, banning its members from certain professions. The Thai government even employed some Jewish merchants as its honorary consuls in various European capitals.

The rise of Nazism in Germany inevitably led to a growing effort of German Jews to seek haven in Asia. Shanghai was their preferred destination, but a number of them looked at Thailand and were told by Thai consular agents that in order to be admitted they would need to prove financial ability or employment. In 1937, some 150 Jewish refugees from Germany and Austria managed to obtain asylum in Thailand, aided by the charitable association of the local Jewish community. In spite of German attempts to persuade the Thai government not to admit Jews, the latter continued to issue visas to them as late as 1941. Bangkok Jews did encounter some antisemitism, mainly on the part of Germans living there. They were denied membership in the German socials clubs, but they never encountered official state-sponsored antisemitism. Since their number never exceeded 200, the Thai government basically ignored them. The newly arrived German Jews soon integrated into the Jewish and non-Jewish communities, and while they arrived virtually penniless, they were well-educated and -trained, and soon found positions mainly in the professions. The undeclared leader of the community was the ophthalmologist Franz Jacobsohn, who spoke fluent Thai and provided free medical care in the Bangkok School for the Blind. In 1948, he became the first Honorary Consul of Israel.

Thailand figured prominently in Japan's war strategy as a conduit leading to rubber-rich Malaya and oil-rich Indonesia. The Philbun regime was openly sympathetic to Japan's colonial aspirations, mainly out of sheer necessity. The day Pearl Harbor was bombed, a Japanese force of 10,000 soldiers landed south of Bangkok. A day later, the Thai cabinet decided not to resist Japan's demands for permission to station troops in its territory and signed an alliance with Japan. As an ally of Japan, Thailand declared war on the Western Allies on December 9, 1941, and began to arrest nationals of now-enemy countries. Japan took over responsibility for the Thai prisoner-of-war camps and later established its own prisoner-of-war camps within Thailand's borders. Jews holding British and American passports were among the 450 prisoners interned. Most of the other Thai Jews, especially those who held German and Austrian passports, were not molested. Dr. Jacobsohn was considered a German national and was not harmed. A number of antisemitic articles did appear in the *Bangkok Times*, whose editorial line favored Nazi Germany. The sources of most of the articles dealing with Jews were German news reports emanating from Berlin. Apart from this, the almost-200 Jews in Bangkok escaped unscathed, although technically some of them were considered prisoners of war. Those prisoners in the Thai prisoner-of-war camps did not lack food or medicine, and were allowed to continue to work in their professions.

This was not the case for those who ended up in the infamous Japanese prisoner-of-war camp in Kanchanburi on the River Kwai, which served as the base for the slave laborers who were building a railway line connecting Thailand with Burma. The story of this camp and the building of the bridge on the Kwai River has been amply told in books and made into an Oscar-winning movie. The Jewish side was related by one of the inmates, Rabbi Chaim Nussbaum, whom the Japanese captured in Batavia where he was serving as the rabbi of the local Jewish community. Since he was a

Dutch national—although born in Poland—he was arrested as an enemy combatant in May 1942 and later taken to Camp Changi in Singapore. In 1943 he was sent to Camp Kanchanburi, where in addition to being a slave worker he also served as the camp's chaplain to the several Jewish inmates. In his memoirs he describes in detail his own experiences and those of the score of Jewish prisoners who served in the Dutch, British, Australian, and American armies. At least ten of them died during the war.

Sephardic Jews who held Iraqi or Syrian passports were not harmed by either the Japanese or the Thai regime, and the Jews of Bangkok survived the war with minimal Japanese involvement in their fate. Toward the end of the Pacific War, when it was obvious that Japan was doomed, Thailand joined the Allies, declared war on Japan, and was among the founding members of the United Nations.

Jewish Refugees in India[10]

India was not occupied by the Japanese army, and had a large native Jewish population, centered mainly in the cities known at the time as Bombay, Calcutta, and Kerala. It provided shelter to thousands of Western Jewish refugees fleeing from both the Nazis in Europe and the Japanese in South East Asia. Even before the outbreak of the war in Europe on September 1, 1939, there were already 1,520 German individuals registered by the British authorities in India. When war was declared, 550 of them were interned as enemy aliens, among them 317 Jewish men. The Jewish Relief Association of Bombay was able to secure the release of most of these Jewish prisoners. This association was headed by some of the wealthier Jews of Bombay and Calcutta, who had connections with the British administration. On November 25, 1941, when a German ordinance deprived all German Jews of their nationality, the British colonial administration in India decided not to grant British papers to these refugees for the duration of the war, leaving the German Jewish refugees in effect stateless.

According to British figures, between September 8, 1940, and the end of 1943, some 400,000 Asian British subjects arrived in India, among them 986 Jews. After the fall of Singapore, Malaya, and Burma, additional Jews arrived, bringing the total number of Jewish refugees to 1,120. They were put up in government-financed hostels in Calcutta and later in Bombay as well. The task of supporting them fell to the Jewish Relief Associations in those cities. The same associations also raised funds to help the Jewish community of Shanghai. Early in 1943, 1,227 Jewish refugees from Poland, including 900 orphaned children, arrived in Karachi on their way to Palestine. The breakdown of the Jewish refugees in India in July 1943 was: 350 women and children, 147 in internment camps, 225 employed in commerce and banking, 127 doctors and dentists, 110 technicians and professionals, 58 merchants and businessmen, 25 elderly persons who were unemployed, 20 manufacturers and 18 unemployed inmates in the hostels, for a total of 983 refugees. Many refugees found employment in manufacturing for the war effort and in government service. The presence of so many Jews in India did arouse some antisemitic commentary, mainly from Moslem quarters, which forced the British government to limit the entry of additional Jews.

C. Intended Policy or Haphazard Measures

An overall examination of the fate of the small Jewish communities in the empire the Japanese created beginning in 1931, numbering a total of some thirty-five to forty thousand Jews who were lucky compared to their brethren who were exterminated in Europe, raises several questions as to the nature of Japan's policy regarding the Jews in the areas under its occupation. Among the questions are: did Japan have a clear-cut policy towards the Jews, and if so, why did Japan display a relatively tolerant and lenient attitude toward most of the Jews under its control rather than cave in to Nazi demands? Did Nazi Germany press Japan to take sterner measures against the Jews under its control, and if so, what were those measures and why did Japan basically ignore them? Why didn't the Japanese occupation authorities as a rule separate the Jews from the rest of the Western population who fell to them?

Documentary evidence and the testimonies of some Japanese officers involved in occupation policies show that Japan's policy toward the Jews in general and their attitude toward the Jewish communities in the areas under their occupation in specific were not haphazard but rather the result of a well thought-out policy stating that Japan must avoid being dragged into following the German path of antisemitism and must ignore Nazi demands regarding the Jews. The motives that influenced this policy were rooted in the broad spectrum of Japan's wartime strategy and its world outlook, which was based occasionally on prejudices and biases—some of them racist.

One fact that may help explain why Japan did not pursue the Nazi policy of the Final Solution is the absence of political, economic, or military cooperation between Imperial Japan and Nazi Germany during the war. The September 1940 Axis Pact spoke in broad terms of dividing the world into two spheres of interest: Germany would have a free hand in Europe while Japan would have the same in the Eastern and South East Asia. In late 1940 and early 1941, Germany began to press Japan to attack British possessions in South East Asia, mainly Singapore, to relieve the pressure on Germany in North Africa and the Middle East. Japan declined. Germany's repeated demands after Hitler attacked the Soviet Union on June 22, 1941, to attack the Soviet Union in Siberia were ignored. Japan also refused to enter the war against the Soviet Union in 1943, when German forces were already in a massive retreat after their defeat in Stalingrad. Instead, Japan sought to mediate between the Soviet Union and Nazi Germany to end the war on the eastern front. Probably one direct consequence of the Japan-Soviet Union Non-Aggression Pact of April 1941 was the Japanese policy of refraining from harming Russian Jews, whether they were Soviet citizens or stateless, in any way. The absence of close cooperation between Japan and Germany on the critical issue of opening a second front against the Soviet Union in Siberia turned the Axis Alliance into a purely declarative arrangement. This fact influenced very much the freedom of action Japan had on an issue far less important from their point of view: what to do with the Jews in the areas under their control.

Another matter was the fact that Jews did not play any role in local politics or the media or academia in the former Western colonies. There was also hardly any anti-Japanese underground in these colonies, or guerilla warfare waged against the Japanese. This was quite different from the situation in Europe, where Jews were involved in the various underground and partisan movements against the Nazi occupation, especially in France, Poland, and Yugoslavia, where a number of Jews held leadership positions in underground communist parties. In Asia, apart from David Marshall in Singapore, Jews played no role in the emerging national liberation movements in India, Indonesia, Indo-China, Burma, Malaya, the Philippines, and the Dutch East Indies. They were involved in trade, and a few were very wealthy, mainly in Hong Kong, Singapore, and Shanghai. Jews were not involved at all in the communist movements in China or South East Asia. The majority of them were prepared to cooperate with the Japanese occupation authorities not because of any sympathy toward Japan, but simply in order to survive. They also saw that the Western colonial powers were not prepared to defend themselves with force against the invading Japanese and surrendered their colonies to Japan in the early stages of the war, and may have wondered why the Jews should be the only ones in the European population to fight the Japanese.

On those occasions that Jews under Japanese occupation did fall victim to antisemitism, it was often derived from other Europeans: British, French, Dutch, and mainly White Russian émigrés.

It is reasonable to believe that Japan's attitude toward the Jews during the war was the result of a great deal of ignorance regarding them. The majority of the Japanese troops and their officers did not have any knowledge about the Jews, and few were tainted by antisemitism. There are testimonies that some Japanese commandants of internment camps on occasion humiliated Jews, claiming that Churchill and Roosevelt were Jewish. There were also cases of torture, flogging, and incarceration in isolation cells, but it appears that as a rule Japan's attitude toward the Jews was no different from its attitude toward other Europeans. There were no specific directives from Tokyo on how to deal with the Jews apart from the February 1942 guidelines, which as we discussed stated that Jews were to be treated like other enemy aliens, although special attention and surveillance would be applied to them. This directive did not smack of antisemitic bias.

Furthermore, in the territories occupied by Japan during the war, there was no visible or influential German or Nazi presence—apart from in Shanghai, as was already mentioned. It seems that the German communities in East and South East Asia were not that interested in the fate of the Jews. The absence of such a presence and pressures meant that the German government, in the form of its diplomatic representatives in various cities in Asia could not make demands on the Japanese concerning their treatment of Jews. True, several demands were made in Tokyo, but Japan basically chose to ignore them, and the Germans had no ability to enforce them. Perhaps someone in Tokyo was concerned over what would happen if they heeded the German demands and handed over Jews to them. This would cause a major logistical problem. It would mean concentrating the Jews in certain areas, separated from other Europeans, in order to transport them to German merchant vessels, necessary since Japan was already short of ships. Beginning in the latter part of 1942, the United States navy began to wage a very successful submarine war against the Japanese merchant marine, and the Japanese government could not spare ships to send thousands of Jews to Germany. Using the Trans-Siberian Railway was, of course, out of the question.

It is likely that from the end of 1942, the idea that Japan was going to lose the war began to permeate the mind of key Japanese leaders, both civilians and military. Many started wondering how they would clear their names in case they were put on trial as war criminals. If they weren't careful, they would be accused of ill-treatment of civilians and of persecuting the Jews in addition to committing crimes against prisoners of war. Since the idea that Jews controlled the world, particularly the Western democracies, was quite prevalent in Japan before and during the war, some may have thought it would be foolish to add to their list of crimes that of harming the Jews.

As we shall see, the general atmosphere in the Japanese home islands during the war, despite the several hundred antisemitic articles and other publications that appeared, was such that the "Jewish Question" was almost non-existent in the agenda and thought of the average Japanese person. They were increasingly concerned with surviving the war, a factor that became critical after the fall of Saipan in July 1944. What to do with the Jews, therefore, was at best a marginal issue, never a central one in Japan.

Could the Jews under Japanese occupation have been rescued from their misery had they been sent to other countries? The answer to this question is probably no. America, Britain, and the British Commonwealth of Nations were at war against Japan and could not spare the means and funds to transport several thousand Jews from East and South East Asia to safe places. Even if they had considered doing so, how would they do it, and where would they send the Jews? Even before the outbreak of the Pacific War, Britain informed the government of Japan that it should not issue transit visas to Japan for Jews who claimed they were traveling to Palestine. This was in line with the May 1939 White Paper regulations, which in effect closed Palestine to Jewish immigration. If the Western allies were not prepared to open their gates to fleeing Jews, let alone to bomb Auschwitz or the railway lines leading there or to other death camps, how could anyone expect the Japanese to do anything to save Jews in Asia? Russia could not offer any help, either—and in any case, would Russian Jews under Japanese control be ready to return to the country from which they escaped?

The only neutral countries that could have done anything were Sweden, Portugal, Spain, and Mexico. Even if we assume that they would be ready to help, how could Jews under Japanese control travel to any of them during the war?

It is important to keep in mind that many Japanese felt, and some continue to feel, that Jews control the world and especially the United States, and that their international contacts can produce miracles. This can be demonstrated particularly by the fact that in January 1945, the leaders of the Tianjin Jewish community, mostly Russian Jews, were invited to Beijing for a meeting with a senior Japanese officer, Colonel Hidaka Tomoki. After discussing with them the horrors of the war and the huge number of Japanese, Jewish, and American casualties, he added that it was well known that the Jews had enormous influence on the American government. Therefore, he requested that the Jewish leaders of Tianjin ask their American counterparts to persuade their government to end the war on honorable terms. He also reminded them of Japan's decent treatment of the Jews in its territories. One of the Jewish leaders came up with an interesting argument. He said that he was prepared to do so, but warned the Japanese officer that if word of this project got out and Japan's desperate situation became known, it would only intensify America's efforts to defeat Japan.

It is not clear whether the request was a personal initiative of Colonel Hidaka or whether he carried out orders from above. Those were the days when Japanese diplomats and some military officers were desperately trying to seek mainly Soviet, but also Swedish, and Swiss mediation to end the war. It is interesting that Hidaka's request, based on the historically correct fact that Japan did not go out of its way to harm the forty thousand Jews in its territories, was also based on an almost naïve assumption about the power and influence of international Jewry, a classic antisemitic motive.

Chapter 10

A Japanese Righteous Gentile: The Sugihara Case[1]

In the Avenue of the Righteous Gentiles in the Yad Vashem Holocaust memorial in Jerusalem, Japan is represented by one individual deemed worthy to be included: a man who helped some 6,000 Jews escape from Lithuania in the summer of 1940. His name was Vice Consul Sugihara Chiune (or Sugihara Sempo), who granted transit visas to Japan to some two thousand, six hundred Polish and Lithuanian Jewish families, thus saving them from either probable extermination by the Germans or prolonged incarceration or Siberian exile by the Soviets. Sugihara would have remained a footnote in history were it not for his efforts, made—as it was later claimed—without the prior approval of, and at times without the knowledge of, his superiors in Tokyo.

It is hard to determine what led Sugihara to help Jews, and to what extent he was aware that he would earn a place in Jewish history. Apart from him and Vice Consul Shibata in Shanghai, who alerted the Jewish community in that city to the Meisinger scheme, Japanese civilian or military officials did not go out of their ways to help Jews, probably because there was no need to. We have already noted that the Japanese government and military had no intention of liquidating the Jews in the territories under their control and consistently rejected German requests that they do so. What led Japan to act the way it did was not the result of any concern for the Jews but rather the result of cool and calculated considerations.

Myths abound regarding the personality and actions of Sugihara. Some originate with statements made by himself and his children during his later life, and some come from his wife Sachiko, who produced a biography of him after the war. According to the leading myth, he decided to help Jews on a hot July 1940 day when he saw hundreds of people waiting patiently outside the gates of the Japanese Consulate in Kaunas, Lithuania, where he served as vice consul, to obtain Japanese visas. He took pity on the waiting people and after hearing their plans, which will be discussed in greater detail later, decided to grant them transit visas to Japan. After his superiors in Tokyo refused to approve his decision to issue the visas, he decided to do so without their authorization, and was subsequently punished after the war by being expelled from the Japanese Foreign Service and doomed to a life of abject poverty. The true story of Sugihara is more complex than that, and even though it does not change the respect Jews and Israel have for this man and his humane behavior, the facts are somewhat different.

Sugihara Chiune was born in 1900 in a small town called Yaotsu (Gifu Prefecture) near Nagoya. He grew up in Korea, to which his family relocated after Japan annexed that peninsula in 1910. The family barely eked out a living, but had enough to give Sugihara a decent education. After graduating from high school in 1918, he enrolled at the prestigious Waseda University in Tokyo. A year later he answered a newspaper advertisement placed by the Japanese foreign ministry seeking candidates to study the Russian language. He was accepted to the program and was sent to study Russian and German in Harbin, in a school run jointly by the Southern Manchurian Railway and the Japanese Foreign Ministry and designed to train Russian specialists. Over the course of his studies, he was asked by one of the heads of the Japanese Intelligence Branch in Manchuria, Colonel Hashimoto Kingoro (1890-1957), to obtain intelligence on the Soviet Union from Jewish refugees who had gathered in the border town of Manchuli. This was the first time Sugihara had come in contact with Jews. In 1925, he married the daughter of a family of White Russian exiles, whose mother apparently held antisemitic views. In an interview he granted shortly before his death, Sugihara stated that until his appointment to the Japanese Consulate in Kaunas in 1940 he knew little about Jews or Judaism, and basically understood only that they were not wanted in Europe. This does not fit the facts: as part of his work for the foreign ministry and the Japanese army, he made contact with Jews in Manchuria in the early 1920's.

Sugihara remained in Harbin and taught Russian there until 1932, when he found a position in the newly established Manchurian affairs office. In 1935, he divorced his Russian wife and married a Japanese woman. In 1938 he returned to Tokyo and served in the Japanese foreign ministry as an expert on Soviet affairs. The ministry planned to attach him to the Japanese embassy in Moscow, but the Soviet government refused to confirm his appointment, no doubt realizing that he was an intelligence officer and fluent in Russian. He was instead sent to the Japanese embassy in Helsinki, Finland. Soon he caught the eye of Japan's ambassador to Berlin, General Oshima Hiroshi (1886-1975), who suggested to the Ministry that

Sugihara be sent to Kaunas, Lithuania, and devote most of his time to gathering intelligence on Poland, Russia, and Germany, predominantly to determine the intentions of the Soviet government vis-à-vis Germany and whether Germany would carry out its threats and invade the Soviet Union in spite of the August 1939 Molotov-Ribbentrop Pact. In Kaunas, Sugihara befriended a number of Jewish families and even visited their homes.

September 1939-June 1940

When Germany invaded that part of Poland allotted to it under the Russo-German pact of August 1939, and occupied it in a blitz campaign in September and October of that year, some 15,000 Jews escaped from Poland to Lithuania, which was formally independent but in reality was under Soviet domination following the Molotov-Ribbentrop Pact, which had given the Soviet Union effective control of the eastern part of Poland and the three Baltic states. Among the better-known Jews who fled from Poland to Lithuania were future Irgun commander (1943-1948) and later Israeli Prime Minister Menachem Begin (1914-1992), future Haganah (Jewish underground in Palestine) commander Moshe Sneh (1909-1972), and Zerach Warhaftig (1906-2002), then a central figure in the Polish Zionist organization and later a signer of Israel's declaration of independence and a minister in various Israel cabinets.

June-September 1940

On June 15, 1940, Soviet troops entered Lithuania, and seven weeks later, on August 3, 1940, it was annexed by the Soviet Union. Even before that, on July 1, 1940, the Soviet authorities banned all political activities and organizations apart from those supporting the Communist party. Local Jews as well as Jewish refugees from Poland began seeking ways to escape from that country, given the fact that the Soviet authorities immediately began to round up Jewish leaders of the Socialist, Bundist, and Zionist movements. Some of those arrested, including Begin, were deported to camps in Siberia. Sugihara befriended a Jewish family in Kaunas and even attended a Hannukah party in their home in December of 1939. Over the course of that event Sugihara was asked, in his capacity as vice consul of Japan in Kaunas, about the possibility of obtaining transit visas to Japan on the way to other countries, mainly the United States. Perhaps it was after that conversation that he began to mull over ideas of how to help Jewish refugees who had fled from the Nazis and now wanted to escape the Communists. However, Sugihara's reports to the foreign ministry in Tokyo consist mostly of intelligence reports on Germany's intention to attack the Soviet Union and contain little comment on the condition of the Jews.

Vast number of Jews living in Lithuania now sought ways to leave as the Russians began to persecute them, accusing them of "bourgeois leanings" and of being hostile to the Soviet Union. In the summer of 1940, rumors began to circulate among Jewish refugees in Kaunas that the Japanese vice consul was prepared to grant Japanese transit visas. Hundreds of people began to gather outside the gates of the Japanese consulate seeking the precious documents. In August 1940, Sugihara sought Tokyo's permission to grant such visas, which would be valid for a two-week stay in Japan for persons bearing Czech and Polish passports. By August 14, 1940, he had already issued 1,711 transit visas. However, he was ordered by Tokyo to stop issuing visas except to those who possessed a valid entry visa to their destination and could prove that they had the financial means to pay for their passage and their stay in Japan. In a cable sent to him from Tokyo on August 16, 1940, Sugihara was told that many refugees arriving in the Japanese port of Tsuruga had not complied with the regulations and that he was to stop issuing visas. By August 25, he had managed to issue 2,135 transit visas, and justified his actions to Tokyo by saying that there were no consular officers in Kaunas from other countries who could issue visas to refugees. Perhaps because of the large number of visas he issued to Jewish refugees, or because of the dearth of intelligence he was supplying, but above all because the Soviets demanded that all foreign consulates in Lithuania be shut down, the Japanese government decided to close the consulate in Kaunas, and Sugihara was ordered to make arrangements to close it no later than August 25. By the 30th, he had moved to a hotel and continued to stamp passports in his hotel room, and when he left Kaunas altogether he proceeded to do so in the railway station and even from the railway car which carried him to his next destination. Eyewitnesses say that as the train left the station, Sugihara tossed the stamp he used to issue visas out of the window, leading some Jewish refugees to stamp fake visas. By the time he left Kaunas, he informed Tokyo that he had stamped some 2,132 transit visas, minimizing the numbers perhaps deliberately. Some of the visas issued were for individuals, and others meant for entire households. Not all of the visas were used, and this makes it difficult to substantiate the claim that Sugihara was instrumental in helping between 6,000 and 7,000 Jews leave Lithuania. He also told Tokyo that he advised those to whom he issued the visas that they would have to satisfy the Japanese authorities in Tsuruga that they had the necessary means to keep them going in Japan. He asked the Japanese authorities to make sure that even before they left Soviet ports in Siberia, holders of transit visas to Japan were checked to make sure they had the required funds.

The Jews who reached Vladivostok on the Trans-Siberian Railway paid for the journey with funds provided by the American Joint Distribution Committee and HIAS. Those who did not have enough funds on them to pay for the sea voyage relied on money transferred to the head office of the Japan Tourist Bureau in Tokyo by HIAS via the New York branch of the Thomas Cook Travel Agency. Tokyo transferred the money to its representatives in Tsuruga. Another issue had to be resolved: where would the Jewish refugees stay in Japan while there? One answer was Kobe.

The Jewish community of Kobe, which before the war consisted of about a hundred families, some of Middle Eastern origins and the others Ashkenazim, became involved in making sure the Jews arriving in Tsuruga could demonstrate to the authorities that they had enough funds to satisfy the regulations that would allow them to land. Part of this task was undertaken by the Trigoboff family, a leading Russian Jewish family in Kobe, and others, who together used the assistance of Japanese Bureau of Tourism officials to help the Jews who entered the country via Tsuruga. This led to another unique phenomenon: the Japanese government assigned a number of officials as escorts for the Jews. They boarded the ships in Siberia and handed the money given to them by the Kobe Jewish Community and by HIAS through Thomas Cook and the head office of the Japan Tourist Bureau to the refugees, so they could demonstrate that they had the necessary funds and thus were allowed to land in Tsuruga.

In June 2011, Kitade Akira, a former official of the Japan National Tourist Organization, the affiliate entity of the Japan Tourist Bureau, published an article in which he related the story of a Tourist Bureau official by the name of Osako Tatsuo, who was assigned to make travel arrangements for some 2,000 Jewish refugees aboard vessels sailing from the Siberian port of Vladivostok to Tsuruga. Osaku was Kitade's superior officer in JTB, and many years after the event told him the story of taking care of the Jewish refugees on board the 2600-ton vessel *Amakusa Maru*, which made weekly trips from Siberia to Japan. Osaku had a list of names provided by the Thomas Cook Travel Agency, and he commented that he had a difficult time identifying the Jewish refugees who were entitled to get funds, as they had foreign-sounding names and the sea was usually choppy and many passengers were seasick and not paying much attention to his requests to speak with them. Those who could not be identified on board were given the money by Osaku's colleagues in Tsuruga as they disembarked before proceeding to the Japanese immigration officials. His colleagues in Tsuruga also helped the Jewish refugees to board trains that would take them to Yokohama and from there to Kobe.

Other elements in the Japanese government were involved in helping the Jewish refugees find temporary shelter in Kobe. An official named Kotsuji Tetsuzo (1899-1973), who held a doctorate in Semitic studies from the Pacific School of Religion in Berkeley, California, worked for a while for Foreign Minister Matsuoka. He was able to obtain Matsuoka's agreement to have the Jewish refugees remain in Kobe for a while, although Matsuoka conditioned his agreement on the approval of the Kobe police chief and added the requirement that the Jews renew their visas on a weekly basis. The Jewish refugees who lived in Kobe in 1941 were able to do so due to the positive attitudes of the authorities. Those who had some contact with ordinary Japanese people viewed Japan as a country free of the antisemitism to which they were accustomed in Eastern Europe. Those few local Japanese people whom they met were friendly and curious about their religious practices and rituals. The community held a Passover Seder in April 1941, with matzot imported from the United States. Two synagogues were active in Kobe, and the refugees established their own schools.

In this manner about 4,000 Jewish refugees had arrived in Japan by September 1941. Some of them proceeded to other destinations. They were aided by the Polish ambassador in Tokyo, Tadeusz Romer (1894-1978), who helped arrange entry visas for them to the United States, Canada, and other countries willing to admit them. On the strength of these visas, the Jews could obtain transit to Japan.

When war broke out on December 7, 1941, the funds remitted to Japan's Jewish refugees by HIAS and the Joint Distribution Committee ceased arriving. The burden of caring for the Jewish refugees who were still in Kobe now fell on the Kobe Jewish community, which could not cope with it. The Japanese authorities did not want to have several thousand Jewish refugees in Kobe, and decided that all those who came before the attack on Pearl Harbor—over a thousand individuals—had to relocate to Shanghai. That included the students and teachers of the Mir Yeshiva. During the war Kobe was often bombed by American bombers, and the *Ohel Shlomo* synagogue was destroyed. Several Jewish families remained in Kobe after Japan surrendered and rebuilt the synagogue.

We now return to the key question: on the basis of what was Sugihara able to issue transit visas to Japan? In his cables to Tokyo, he mentioned Curacao and Dutch Guinea as excuses to justify the granting of transit visas. Many of the people to whom he issued his visas had in their possession official papers signed by a Dutch consular official certifying that they were proceeding to the tiny Caribbean island of Curacao or to Dutch Guinea (later Surinam), both colonies that were under the control of the Dutch government-in-exile in London. The Curacao idea originated when Nathan Guttwirth and Leon Sternheim, two Jewish Dutch nationals who were studying at the Mir Yeshiva, applied for a Japanese transit visa, saying that they were proceeding to Curacao. The Dutch ambassador to the Baltic States, L.P.J de Decker, who was based in Riga, and the honorary Dutch consul in Kaunas, Jan Zwartendijk, had approved their application to travel to Curacao, and Guttwirth and Sternheim were seeking ways to travel via the Soviet Union and Japan on their way to Curacao. The main point was that there was no need to obtain an entry visa to Curacao; permission to land there was granted individually by the local governor. Ambassador de Decker did not specify this condition when he stamped the passports of the Mir Yeshiva students with the notation that no visa was required to live in Curacao. This document enabled Sugihara, based on this notation in the passports, to issue transit visas through Japan to their destination.

The next problem was how to travel to Japan while theoretically on the way to Curacao. Given the war situation, there remained only one way: by rail across the Soviet Union and by sea from Siberia to Japan. Soviet transit visas were obtained through the intercession of Warhaftig, who spoke with the Lithuanian Deputy Prime Minister Pius Globacki. The Russians were ready to grant Jewish refugees transit through their territories to elsewhere, as they did not want additional Jews after the two million they inherited as a result of their annexation of Eastern Poland and the Baltic states. There was also a financial consideration: the Jews paid for their rail fare with cash money—in American dollars. The funds, two hundred dollars for each passage, were provided by the American Joint Distribution Committee and HIAS. The flow started. Between October 1940 and August 1941, 3,489 Jewish refugees arrived in Japan, among them 2,178 Polish Jews, including three hundred rabbis and Mir Yeshiva students. The rest were Jewish refugees from Germany who had visas to the United States and or to any of a number of countries in Latin America.

The position of the Japanese government in regard to these developments was inconsistent and at best confused. On the one hand, Sugihara had acted according to the broad outlines of the policy of the Japanese government, but on the other hand, he had also acted on his own, driven probably by humanitarian considerations and the lack of specific directives from his government in Tokyo. The government had not realized how many transit visas he was issuing, and would probably have made greater efforts to stop him had they known the magnitude of his operation. Japanese foreign ministers such as Arita Hachiro and later Togo Shigenori did not want Jewish refugees in Japan, fearing that their presence could harm their relations with Nazi Germany and perhaps even with the Soviet Union. They noted that Britain had not only closed her own gates to Jewish refugees after allowing several hundred Jewish children from Germany and Austria to come to Britain in what became known as the Kinder Transport, but had also closed the gates of Palestine. If the British and the Americans turned their backs on the Jews, why should Japan become involved in helping them? Staff members of the Japanese embassy in London reported that in May 1940 the British government interned some 26,000 refugees from Austria and Germany, many of them Jews, suspecting them of being sympathetic to Nazi Germany. The reports did not comment on the fact that this excuse was at best preposterous: had they been sympathetic to the Nazis, they would have stayed in Germany. Several Japanese ambassadors reported to Tokyo that they tried to prevent Jews from going to Japan, among them Shigemitsu Mamoru (1887-1957), Japan's ambassador to Britain, and Togo Shigenori (1882-1950), the ambassador in Moscow. The Japanese foreign minister between July 1940 and July 1941 was Matsuoka Yosuke, the man who pushed Japan to join the Axis pact with Germany and Italy. He claimed in a conversation with Lev Zykman, the Harbin Jewish communal leader, that while it was true that he had concluded the Axis Pact, he was certain that there was no antisemitism in Japan and that this view was not his personal one but part of the exalted ideology of Japan since the dawn of the empire.

Those Jews who were lucky enough to obtain the Sugihara visas were thus saved from an uncertain fate, either to be killed by Lithuanian collaborators who were glad to get rid of the Jews or by the Germans, or to languish in Soviet prisons.

After Kaunas

Years later, it became known that in his efforts to obtain intelligence on both the Germans and the Russians, Sugihara established close working relations with members of the Polish underground intelligence, who supplied him with a great deal of information that he used in his cables to Tokyo. Two such Poles were on his staff at the Kaunas consulate, and he even allowed them the use of his official car. Later he maintained close ties with Polish intelligence officers working out of Stockholm. The German government apparently knew of his activities and kept an eye on him. After the closure of the Japanese consulate in Kaunas on August 30, 1940, Sugihara was transferred to Berlin and served under the new Japanese ambassador there, Kurusu Saburo (1886-1954). Even during his brief stay in Berlin, which totaled less than three months, Sugihara issued 69 transit visas to German Jews. It is not clear whether Ambassador Kurusu was aware of the visas Sugihara issued in Kaunas and Berlin. If he was, he made no issue of the matter. In a cable to Tokyo, however, Kurusu wrote that there was no need to grant asylum in Asia to refugees expelled from Germany, Italy, Hungary, and the Baltic states, and nor would granting such asylum be of benefit to Japan. If we do not stem the tide now, he wrote, the refugees will be the source of much trouble in the future.

From Berlin Sugihara was transferred to Prague, where he served as acting consul general until February 1941. When the Japanese legation in Prague closed in March 1941, Sugihara was transferred briefly to Koenigsberg in Eastern Prussia. The German authorities, knowing of his connections with Polish intelligence, asked Japan to remove him from that city, and he was transferred to the Japanese legation in Bucharest where he served until the arrival of the Red Army in Romania. In all of these posts his expertise in Russian affairs proved useful. It is no wonder that the Russians, who knew he was a Japanese intelligence officer, captured him when the Soviet Army entered Romania in the summer of 1944 and sent him to Siberia. When he was repatriated to Japan in 1947, he along with hundreds of other former Japanese diplomats was dismissed from the Japanese Foreign Service, as Japan was now under American occupation and there was no need for an independent foreign ministry. Those dismissed were given severance pay for their previous service in the Japanese foreign ministry. Many of them were reinstated after Japan regained its independce in April 1952. Years later, Sugihara's wife claimed that he was dismissed for issuing visas to Jews in Kaunas without authorization, but this claim cannot be substantiated. In the late 1940's, Sugihara worked for a Jewish merchant in Tokyo. Later, again because of his fluency in Russian, he represented a Japanese firm in Moscow for fifteen years. This would give rise to the allegation that he was also a Soviet agent all those years, surely the Soviets knew exactly who he was before giving him a visa to work in Moscow. But there is definitely no proof to back this allegation.

Sugihara's actions in saving Jews were well known to many people in Israel. One of them, who served as commercial attaché in the Israeli embassy in Tokyo and had been granted a visa by Sugihara, tracked him down and in 1968, at the behest of then-Israeli Minister for Religious Affairs Zerach Warhaftig, also the beneficiary of a Sugihara visa, Sugihara was invited to visit Israel. While there, he was received by Prime Minister Levy Eshkol (1894-1969), who awarded him a plaque commemorating his exploits in helping saved Jews and arranged for a scholarship for his son to study at the Hebrew University of Jerusalem. It was only in 1985, a year before he died, that Yad Vashem decided to recognize Sugihara as Righteous Gentile. Many to whom he had given visas worked together to plant a tree bearing his name plate in Jerusalem. He was too old and frail to travel to Jerusalem, and received the associated certificate from Amnon Ben Yochanan, Israel's ambassador to Japan. Toward the end of his life, the Japanese government reinstated his pension.

Why Sugihara Chiune was granted the title of a Righteous Gentile, even though he did not fulfill the key requirements set by Yad Vashem for this distinction? He did not risk his own life or those of his family members, and he did not knowingly rescue Jews from imminent death, for in the summer of 1940, few considered the total extermination of Jews possible. The pressure to grant Sugihara this honor was exerted by Minister Warhaftig, and it was probably politically expedient for both the Israeli and Japanese governments to have at least one Japanese official among the Righteous Gentiles and to demonstrate that not all Japanese people disliked Jews or were antisemitic in those dark days. Unlike Spain under Franco, which took credit for rescue operations carried out by Spanish diplomats who helped save some 40,000 Jews during the war, the Japanese government never took credit for Sugihara's activities. In 2006, the Japanese composer Ichiyanagi Toshi wrote an opera called *White Nights of Love: Visas for 6,000 Jewish Refugees*, which was staged in Tokyo and won much acclaim. Many articles and books have been written in Japanese and English on this unique man.

Why did Sugihara become one of the very few Japanese people (a group that included Higuchi and Yasue) who bothered to help Jews, even though he may have risked his career by disobeying orders? In the end, his career was not damaged: after Kaunas, he was promoted and sent to Berlin, to Prague, and later to Bucharest. It must be noted that other

Japanese diplomats in Berlin and Vienna granted 1,200 visas to Jewish refugees. Between October 1940 and August 1941, some 3,500 Jewish refugees arrived in Japan, the majority in possession of visas to the United States or to various South American countries. Sugihara issued his visas in the summer of 1940, a year and a half before the Wansee Conference of January 1942, at which the plan to exterminate the Jews was approved and put into operation. The Japan option was by that point virtually non-existent for European Jews, since Japanese consular and diplomatic representatives in various European cities were issued a general directive not to admit Jews to Japan. This was done partly to appease Germany, partly because very few Jews bothered to apply for Japanese visas because it never occurred to them as a real alternative, and partly because the Japanese Foreign Service officials understood the general policies of their superiors. By effectively barring Jewish refugees from Japan, the Japanese foreign ministry ignored its own previous belief about the enormous influence that world Jewry wielded over Western governments. Japan could have won much praise from Jews (who, as we discussed, were believed by many Japanese officials to control international public opinion) if they had made the slightest effort to rescue Jews. It would certainly have won them points in the United States prior to Pearl Harbor.

Most of those who have been awarded the title Righteous Gentiles were involved in hiding Jews during the Holocaust or preventing them from being handed over to the Germans and their collaborators. There was no need to hide Jews from the Japanese. They did not build death camps or hand over Jews to the Nazis, and the Jews in territories under Japanese occupation did not face the danger of being liquidated. Besides, it was impossible to hide Jews in Asia because of their obviously different appearance.

What happened to the Japanese officers who were known as Jewish affairs specialists? Captain Inuzuka, who helped Jews in Manchuria and later in Shanghai, was transferred by the Japanese navy to the Philippines in 1943. Two years later he was captured by American forces, who wanted to try him as a war criminal. He was spared because he had in his possession a cigarette box he'd received in March 1941 from Rabbi Frank Newman on behalf of the American Union of Orthodox Rabbis, in gratitude for the services he had rendered to the Jewish people. The box's dedication matched Inuzuka's explanation, and he was safe. He returned to Japan and was active in the Israel-Japan Friendship Association until his death in 1965. Colonel Yasue was captured by the Soviet army in Manchuria and was probably sent to Siberia, where his trail goes cold. One report indicates that he died in Siberia in 1950. These two men shared an interesting trait. They were both antisemites who translated and circulated the *Protocols of the Elders of Zion*, but their behavior toward the Jews of Manchuria and Shanghai was humane and pragmatic. Goya Kano, who as was mentioned earlier was the official responsible for the Hongkew Ghetto, was beaten up by some Shanghai Jews when he was interned in that city shortly after the end of the war and returned to Japan.

Why were there no other known Japanese individuals who were prepared to rescue Jews? The answer seems to be quite plain. Most Japanese people, whether civilians or soldiers, had no clue about Jews, their religion, or why they should be treated in any way differently than other foreigners. It is also important to note that the Japanese have historically been a highly disciplined people whose culture encourages them to act according to the book and carry out orders scrupulously. There were few cases during the era in question of people disobeying orders or following a personal initiative; in fact, even Sugihara Chiune was not one of those rare exceptions. Most of the time he, like other Japanese diplomatic and consular officials, obeyed orders without asking superfluous questions. And since they were not asked to carry out violent acts against Jews, the officials did not ask questions about them. There was also a practical issue, however. Assuming that some people would have wanted to help Jews, they would have had to know something about Japan's policy regarding the treatment of the Jews, and above all would have needed an idea of how could they help them. Perhaps some guards could have been more humane in the camps where Jews were interned with non-Jews, but helping Jews or other Westerners escape from prisoner-of-war or internment camps was a totally different matter. There would be a need to hide the Jews, or to help them reach a neutral country, both impossible tasks. No Japanese patriot would consider attempting such acts. Sugihara stands out mainly because Israel decided to make him an example and as such highlighted the fact that he deserved the gratitude of thousands of Jews.

Chapter 11

The Japanese Policy toward the Jews in Japan's Home Islands

Before the outbreak of the Second World War, several hundred Jews lived in Japan, mostly in Tokyo and Kobe. To them were added the few thousand Jewish refugees who arrived before Japan attacked Pearl Harbor. The Japanese policy toward the Jews in the home islands was important not only for the Jews who resided there, but also because it reflected what Japan's attitude to the Jews in the territories it occupied in the first half of 1942 would be. Even before 1939, it was evident that Japan sought to distance itself from the Nazi racist policies toward the Jews, perhaps because there were still a number of Japanese cabinet ministers who thought that Jewish power and influence could be utilized to reduce the mounting tensions between Japan and America. Their assessment, as we have discussed, was that if the government of Japan decided on a policy of appeasing the Jews, that could help them in their contacts with Washington and other capitals in the West, and American Jewish leaders could be persuaded to assist them in mobilizing resources to develop Manchuria.

We noted earlier that this idea was discussed at the highest levels of the Japanese government at the suggestion of War Minister General Kotaro Nakajima. The key meeting was held in Tokyo on December 6, 1938, with the participation of Prime Minister Konoye Fumimaro, Foreign Minister Arita Hachiro, Finance Minister Ikeda Seihin (1867-1950), War Minister General Nakamura Kotaro (1881-1947), and Navy Minister Admiral Yonai Mitsumasa. At the conclusion of the discussion, a statement containing a number of principles was issued: "Our diplomatic ties with Germany and Italy compel us to avoid adopting the Jewish people, in view of their rejection by our allies. But we must not reject members of this people for what they are because of our declared policy of racial equality, and because their rejection is contrary to our spirit. That is true especially in view of Japan's need for foreign capital and our desire not to alienate America." Therefore, the five ministers decided that at that stage of the war, "We shall not disqualify or reject the Jews currently residing in Japan, Manchuria, and China, and they shall be treated like any other foreigner. Those who want to enter Japan in the future, we shall treat in the same manner as other foreigners. We shall not undertake any initiative or issue special invitations for Jews to enter our territories, but capitalists and engineers will be recognized as desirable." This statement allowed for the rescue of thousands of Jews who arrived not only in Japan but also and in greater numbers in Manchuria and the territories Japan occupied in China. The policy was reconfirmed several weeks later in a statement to the House of Peers in early 1939 by Foreign Minister Arita Hachiro that Japan would not discriminate against the Jews and would treat them like other foreigners residing in her territories.

After Japan's attack on Pearl Harbor, which was followed by Japan's declaration of war against the United States, and a few days later by similar declarations by Germany and Italy, the Japanese government faced a dilemma: how ought it to deal with the few hundred Jews already residing in the home islands? For those Jews holding British or American passports, the solution was easy: they were sent to internment camps in the resort areas of Karuizawa and Gora (Hakone) near Tokyo as enemy aliens. Some would later be repatriated to America or Britain together with foreign diplomats, in exchange for Japanese diplomats and other Japanese nationals serving and living in the two Western countriess. Those Jews who remained in Japan were not physically or otherwise molested.

Jewish Musicians and International Politics[1]

The main difficulty arose regarding Jewish refugees from Europe, who came to Japan in a quest for shelter from Nazi persecution. Japan was committed to seeking an alliance with Germany, but the Axis alliance made no reference to Jews, and therefore each case was dealt with on an individual basis. As most of the Jewish refugees who made their way to Japan and Shanghai arrived before that pact was signed on September 28, 1940, the government of Japan decided to adopt a pragmatic, flexible, and non-dogmatic policy toward Jews, although the German embassy in Tokyo and German foreign ministry officials in Berlin often requested that they deal harshly with Jews. One example of Japan's refusal to go along with the German attitude to Jews was its granting approval to the Nippon-Columbia Records Company, an offshoot of the American Columbia Records, which wished to retain the long list of Jewish performers on its record label. The German embassy in Tokyo presented the Japanese government with a list that included leading Jewish musicians such as violinists Mischa Elman, Bronislav Huberman, Yehudi Menuhin, Szimon Goldberg, Yasha Heifetz, Fritz Kreisler, Joseph Szigeti, and Efrem Zimbalist and requested that they be dropped from the circulation list, and that their records not be sold in Japan. Another demand Nazi Germany made of Japan was that Jewish musicians should not be employed by Japanese orchestras. The demand related specifically to the Krakow-born conductor Joseph Rosenstock (1895-1985) and Klaus Pringsheim, the Jewish brother-in-law of the famous author Thomas Mann. Rosenstock was a well-known conductor in Berlin until he was dismissed by the Nazis shortly after they came to power in 1933. He was appointed conductor of the Tokyo Symphony Orchestra in 1936, and told journalists that the Nazis were lowering the level of music in Germany. This assertion resulted in a complaint by the German embassy in Tokyo, which led the Japanese government to formulate the following reply quoted by Professor Ben-Ami Shillony in his book on Japan and the Jews: "It is well known that the attitude of the Japanese public to Jews totally differs from the official German position, and there are even groups in Japan which sympathize with Jewish refugees. Our government cannot do anything that might be interpreted as supporting racial discrimination or taking a position against the Jews."[2]

When the issue of establishing a new orchestra, founded by the Victor Record Company and supported by a leading Japanese company called Tokyo Electric, arose, Rosenstock and Pringsheim were both considered for the post of conductor. Neither received the position; the orchestra founders eventually settled on Manfred Gorlitt, a German musician of Jewish origins—although he was able to get a confirmation that only his great-grandfather had been Jewish and Gorlitt himself had even been baptized. Gorlitt left Germany in the late 1930's because he could not find a position despite being a member of the Nazi party. He began to conduct the new orchestra in Tokyo in January 1940. Three years later he was removed due to pressure from radical Japanese groups who demanded the position be given to a Japanese musician and not to a foreigner, even if he was German.

Klaus Pringsheim fared better, despite the fact that he was an admitted Jew. He had studied music in Vienna under Gustav Mahler and was a conductor, composer, and teacher. He was lucky enough to have left Germany in 1931, and between 1941 and 1946 was the conductor of the Japan Chamber

Orchestra. He was only interned—in a camp called Tokyo-Koishikawa near the resort town of Karuizawa—during the final months of the war, along with another Jewish musician, the Russian-born pianist Leonid Kreutzer, who had taught at the Tokyo Music Academy. Other Jewish teachers in this academy included violinist Alexander Mogilevsky and pianist Leo Sirotta (1885-1965). The Ukranian-born Sirota arrived in Japan in 1929 for a six-month visit, during which he taught in the Tokyo Academy of Music and was asked to stay on. He remained in Japan until after the end of the war, and continued to be a very popular piano teacher. In 1939 he sent his daughter Beate to Mills College in California. She returned in 1945, and as she spoke fluent Japanese she soon joined the government section of the occupation authorities and was very influential in the drafting of the paragraphs dealing with women's equality in the 1947 MacArthur Constitution. Another well-known Jewish musician in Japan was singer Margaret Netzke-Lowe.

Part of the reason Japan allowed these people to continue with their activities had to do with the love of many influential Japanese people for European classical music, the absence of other well-known foreign musicians who were ready to work in Japan, and most of all the high artistic level of these musicians. The Japanese authorities did not pay much attention to musicians' origins or religious affiliations, and in any case the Jewish musicians did not advertise their religion or openly practice it. The Japanese interior ministry officials were apparently satisfied that these musicians, some of whom held German, Austrian, or even Russian passports, were nationals of friendly countries. They ignored the German government's cancellation of the citizenship of its Jews in 1941 and the fact that this rendered the German-Jewish musicians stateless. During the war, the German embassy in Tokyo sent a note to the Japanese foreign ministry listing German musicians active in Japan. They were divided into three categories: German musicians who were German citizens resident in Japan; German musicians resident in Japan who had lost their German nationality; and musicians who were German citizens, but in whom the embassy had no interest. The last category included the Jews. The Japanese government apparently preferred to ignore the list.

Most of the Jewish refugees who made it to Japan ended up in Kobe, where the local Jewish community made a commitment to the Japanese authorities that it would be responsible for the new arrivals' wellbeing and that the refugees would not be a burden on Japan. However, being a tiny community, it did not have the necessary means to care for them all and appealed frequently to the Joint Distribution Committee in New York.

The archives of the JDC are replete with frantic cables from Jewcom (the cable name of the Kobe community) asking for funds, which were sent. At some point the Kobe Jews could no longer bear the burden, and suggested that the refugees be transferred to Shanghai. The Japanese government agreed, so did the Jewish refugees, and thus began the movement of thousands of Jews from Kobe to Shanghai even before Pearl Harbor.

Japan's Policy toward Jewish Refugees in the Empire: 1941-1945

Populist Antisemitism[3]

Over the course of the war, the emperor, the prime minister, or most of Japan's other government ministers never issued any statements referring specifically to Jews. Yet the authorities did allow some daily newspapers and important magazines to deal with the Jewish problem, and this was done in an antisemitic spirit that often resembled the notoriously antisemitic German publication *Der Sturmer*. The media's approach was to stress the dominant position of the Jews in Western democracies in order to intensify the anti-American and anti-British propaganda they were running. Like in Germany, the Jews were accused of running the governments of the two greatest western democracies, and now Japan was portrayed as fighting not only the two Western powers but also the destructive influence of world Jewry. In a publication called *A Citizen's Guide to Assured Victory*, the writer Tokutomi Ichiro (1863-1957) wrote that America had become a Jewish den. The American historian John Dower, whose monumental work *War Without Mercy* dealt with the demonization of America by the Japanese and vice versa, concluded that the anti-Jewish propaganda was not used to persecute the Jews but rather as part of the official propaganda intended to maintain high morale at home, to explain to the Japanese people why and against whom they were fighting, and to silence criticism by creating an artificial demonic enemy that all Japan must unite to fight. Other writers commented that while Germany was fighting against the Jews in Europe, Japan's role was to wipe out any Jewish influence on the Asian continent. It did not matter to the media figures writing on the topic that Jewish influence in Asia was virtually non-existent.

There is no evidence that Japan's wartime leaders, from the emperor down to the prime minister, cabinet members, the heads of the armed forces, were openly antisemitic, but it cannot be ignored that during the war years there were many expressions of antisemitic sentiments. Ben-Amy Shillony counted 170 antisemitic books and 472 articles in the same vein that appeared in Japan between 1936 and Japan's surrender in August 1945. They contained arguments, for example, that since there was a Jewish dictatorship in England and the United States, Japan was bound to fight the Jews as well as those countries in order to rescue all of humanity. The mass circulation dailies *Asahi Shimbun*, *Mainichi Shimbun*, and *Yomiuri Shimbun* devoted some editorials to the Jewish problem and accused the Jews of being responsible for, among other crimes, the outbreak of the war. *Mainichi* even organized a symposium on the Jewish problem, called "The Jewish Problem and the International Ideological War." The keynote speaker was General Shioden Nobutaka, the leading antisemite among the top echelons of Japanese establishment. In March 1943, he arranged a series of lectures and exhibitions on "The Jews and International Secret Societies," whose purpose was to prove that the Jews wielded vast control over Western democracies and that democracy itself was an ideological instrument in the hands of the Jews, assisting them in their aim of ruling the entire world. All the misfortunes of the universe, he insisted, were instigated by the crooked, devious, and venal Jews. Even the surrender of Italy in September 1943 was explained as part of a Jewish conspiracy. As the tide of war turned against Japan, antisemitism may have been used more to distract the public eye from the looming defeat than to express a true antisemitic ideology. Populism usually thrives at times of dire political, economic, social, and as was now the case in Japan, military crises. It is at such times that the public begins to lose confidence in its leaders and institutions. The need to find scapegoats becomes strong, and during the latter part of the war this populist antisemitism touched the raw nerves of some Japanese people, linked emotionally with fears of the loss of sovereignty, foreign occupation, termination of the imperial system and the loss of the exalted value of *kokutai* (the Japanese entity and national essence). Populist antisemitism was aimed in fact at the urban working and middle class, and not at the majority of the Japanese population, which lived in rural areas. It was intended to intensify the hatred of the "other" in order to justify the goals of the regime.

What was the impact of these articles and publications on the Japanese people? Since there were a mere several hundred Jews in Japan at the beginning of the war, and few were interned, anti-Jewish feelings and antisemitism had little meaning to the majority of the Japanese people, who began to sense in early 1943 that something had gone seriously wrong with the war. Since there were no visible Jews around, they could not vent their anger on them. The majority of the Japanese people began to be concerned with their own daily efforts to survive, and did not even accuse the Jews of playing a key role in the aerial bombardment of the home islands of Japan, which intensified in the summer of 1944 after the fall of Saipan and Tinian. Nonetheless, anti-Jewish propaganda reached every home in Japan either via daily newspapers or through school textbooks. In one such volume, it was written that Churchill, Roosevelt, and even Chiang Kai Shek were puppets in the hands of the Jews, and that their strategy was devised by international secret societies of gamblers, speculators, international businessmen, and industrialists. It stressed that Hitler and his associates were the saviors of humanity. Jews were also accused of causing the war between America and Japan. At this stage, Japan's great appreciation for Jacob Schiff and the assistance he had given Japan during the Russo-Japanese War was conveniently forgotten.

Few of Japan's wartime leaders shared these views. Standing out against them were two foreign ministers, Arita in 1939 and Matsuoka in 1940. They argued that at no time did the government of Japan make a commitment to Germany to enact its antisemitic policies in Japan or in territories occupied by Japan. In December of 1940, Matsuoka, who more than any one else among Japan's leaders had pushed for Japan's entry into the Axis alliance, told Lev Zykman, the Jewish businessman from Manchuria, that this neutrality on the subject of the Jews was the position of Japan, and that its government had no qualms stating so openly. Only twice during the war did the Japanese Diet discuss the matter of the appropriate attitude toward the Jews. In response to a question posed by the ultra-nationalist and leading antisemite General Shioden Nobutaka, who was re-elected to the Diet by an impressive majority in Tokyo in 1942, Education Minister Okabe Nagakage (1881-1970) replied that the policy of Japan toward the Jews was a matter of pragmatism and not ideology, and admitted that the government had not devoted sufficient time to studying the matter. The absence of official statements regarding the Jews could be seen as a signal to the Japanese people that the government was not party to populist antisemitism and that its policy at times contained elements of empathy towards the Jews.

Therefore, the Japanese government did not intern the approximately 900 Jews living in that country at the war's beginning in concentration camps or hand them over to the Germans. There were several reasons for that. The first has already been mentioned: fear that if Japan were to be defeated, the

Jews would wreak vengeance. Second, the military, political, and economic cooperation between Japan and Germany was at best very loose, and in reality was nearly non-existent. Japan did not see any reason to respond to Nazi demands to deal with the Jews the way they did. Third, the construction of concentration camps would have embroiled the Japanese government in a logistical nightmare. With rare exceptions, Japan did not even use Jews as forced laborers as the Nazis did, although they did use American prisoners of war, Koreans, Indonesians, and others from their occupied territories for that purpose. Despite the fact that the United States interned some 120,000 Japanese-Americans for almost the entire duration of the war, Japan never considered interning the 900 Jews as a retaliatory act. At one point the idea of exchanging Shanghai Jews for Japanese Americans interned in America was mentioned, but it never got off the ground. There likely would have been some trouble with it: the Shanghai Jews would no doubt have loved to go to America, whereas the Japanese-Americans considered themselves entirely American, and few would have gone to Japan.

Even those few Jews, mainly musicians, whose removal the Germans did insist upon were too important for Japan to part with, and so its officials ignored the demands. Only in Shanghai did the Japanese government cave in to German ideas when they transferred some 5,000 Jews into a Jewish ghetto, but still neither handed them over to the Germans nor physically molested them. The Jewish community of Kobe continued to exist. The majority of the Jews in Tokyo and Yokohama survived the war and were alive and safe when Japan surrendered on August 14, 1945. It seems that Japan's leaders did not want to appear to accept German dictates on the matter of race, particularly as Germany's views of the Japanese race were not highly complimentary of them. They felt that they did not in any way owe Germany assistance in this matter. The easiest way to handle the awkwardness was to simply ignore the repeated German government requests transmitted through the German Embassy in Tokyo, and those of the German foreign ministry to the Japanese ambassador in Berlin, Lieutenant General Oshima Hiroshi. The German government never admitted to Japan the nature of its Final Solution, or admit to Japanese diplomats the existence of the death camps and gas chambers. As already mentioned, no Jew in Japan was associated with the communist or socialist movement or belonged to any opposition group. The Japanese leadership was very careful not to engage in radical measures when it came to Jews, and preferred to treat them like other enemy aliens captured in the course of the war. To sum it up, it can be argued that during the war ultra-nationalism, anti-communism, and Pan-Asianism were far more important than antisemitism. To the extent that there were some Japanese antisemites, most of them viewed the Jews as communists. There was nothing in Shinto or Buddhist texts that dealt with Jews, let alone encouraged antisemitism, and there were no anti-Jewish pogroms in Japan or in the territories it controlled.

Chapter 12

The "Jewish Question" in Japanese-German Relations, 1936-1945[1]

German-Japanese relations have known ups and downs since the middle of the nineteenth century. Germany was not among the Western nations which imposed unequal treaties on Japan, and therefore the attitude of the Japanese people toward imperial Germany was not one of animosity. It was devoid of the residual tension that characterized Japan's ties with other European powers. Germany became the model for Japan's new army, while Britain was the model for the Japanese navy. Japan's new leaders adopted some of the ideas that were the foundations for the 1889 Meiji constitution (which was in force until it was replaced by the MacArthur constitution in 1947) from the German Reich, created by Bismarck in 1870. At the constitution's base was the decision to place the armed forces directly under the control of the emperor, and not to have them answer to the civilian government or parliament. There was a very limited measure of civil rights offered under the 1889 constitution, and they were seen as bestowed by the benevolent sovereign emperor as a gift to his grateful citizens.

During the First World War, Japan and Germany fought on opposite sides, but apart from brief battles in the Shandong Peninsula in September-October 1914, Japanese forces were not sent to the Western front in France to fight German troops. Under the Versailles treaty, Japan inherited Germany's Asian and Pacific territories and were awarded with mandates over the Marshall, Carolina, and Marian Islands in the Pacific.

In the 1920's, the German Weimar Constitution served as a model for the very few Japanese who wanted to introduce a more liberal, enlightened, and democratic regime in their country. Beginning in 1919, Japan, Germany and even Italy, were in the same camp of dissatisfied and resentful nations that were convinced that the Treaty of Versailles had robbed them of what belonged to them by right, and that the Western powers were determined to keep them as third-rate powers. To many Japanese politicians and senior military officers, this suspicion was confirmed in the 1922 Washington Conference, which limited naval armaments and gave Shandong back to China. As long as the economies of both countries functioned properly, however, there was little fear that ultra-nationalist right-wing extremists would rise to power and seek to undermine the Versailles and Washington systems.

The Japanese media did not go out of its way to greet the new Nazi regime in Germany after 1933 mainly because of Hitler's racial doctrines, which relegated the "Yellow" race to, at best, a position of cultural transmitters rather than creators (though this was better than being classed as destroyers, like the Jews were). Clearly such a definition was unpalatable to many Japanese people, who viewed themselves as the bearers of a magnificent imperial culture under whose wings people of various races, among them Korean and Chinese, lived in peace and harmony. The attitude of some Japanese writers and commentators toward the rise of Nazi antisemitism was at best tepid. The so-called "Jewish Question" was never at the top of the Japanese agenda. Both countries, in any case, had other and more urgent matters to attend to. Germany became involved in renewed rearmament and sought ways to undo the Versailles arrangements, while Japan desperately tried to rehabilitate its economy from the ravages of the Great Depression and the creation of Manchukuo. Japan was the first power to secede from the League of Nations. It would soon be followed by Nazi Germany and Fascist Italy, thus undermining the European collective security arrangements of the 1920's. Both nations openly discussed the need for *lebensraum* and the need to in effect undo the Versailles and Washington arrangements, Germany in Europe and Japan in Asia and the Pacific. In 1936, Japan and Germany signed the Anti-Comintern Pact, which was basically a declarative pact aimed at increasing the political coordination between the two powers and designed to align their policies against international communism and the Soviet Union. Although this pact did not mention Jews, some Japanese writers began to identify Bolshevism with world Jewry after this point.

"Japan Is Not Dependent on Germany"

The new Nazi measures against Jews, notably the Nuremberg Laws, did create some backlash in Japan and they were criticized in some newspapers. But as more and more Jews were fleeing Nazi Germany, and as the United States, Canada, Australia, and Britain, followed in 1939 by Palestine, effectively closed themselves to large-scale Jewish immigration, more Jews began looking at East Asia as a temporary and or even permanent haven. Japan and Manchukuo required entry visas, but there was no such documentation needed for travel to Shanghai or other parts of China. Starting in late 1938, Japanese diplomatic and consular officials reported to Tokyo a growing number of Jews from Germany, then later Austria and Czechoslovakia, who were making their way to East Asia either by rail across the Soviet Union or more frequently by sea from Italian and French ports on board Italian, French, and Japanese passenger vessels sailing to Shanghai. The Japanese government now had to formulate a policy on how to deal with these Jews: should they allow, even encourage, large-scale Jewish immigration to East Asia? If so what conditions would be attached to that? The other option was to totally prevent the immigration whatever circumstances prevailed.

There were two schools of thought where this matter was concerned. The first included those who thought that this was an opportunity to utilize the enterprising spirit, financial strength, and managerial and technical know-how and skills of European Jews for the development of the Manchurian and may be even the Japanese economies. Perhaps a liberal immigration policy toward the Jews would help alleviate the growing anti-Japanese feelings in the United States, especially after the outbreak of the second Sino-Japanese War and the atrocities committed by the Japanese army in Nanjing in December 1937. The second camp argued that Japan should follow the Nazi approach and totally bar the entry of Jews to Japan, Manchukuo, and the occupied areas of China. Their argument was based on the claim that Jews were rootless people and would do their utmost to undermine the foundations of the Japanese polity as they had elsewhere, according to the pseudo-scientific theories of Alfred Rosenberg.

Among those who espoused the "open door" policy regarding the Jewish refugees were senior Japanese officers who had been dealing with Jews in Manchuria and in those areas of China occupied by Japan, and their attitude was dictated by urgent pragmatic needs and the economic conditions that Japan faced in the new territories. The policy that was eventually agreed upon was pragmatic: each case would be judged according to its merits, and there would be no blind following of German antisemitism. Under no circumstances was there ever any thought given to expelling the Jews already living in Japan, China, and Manchukuo, regardless of whether they were permanent residents, nationals of other countries, or stateless.

A good example was the explanation given in 1938 by General Higuchi Kiichiro, the head of the Japanese Special Forces in Manchukuo, when he decided on his own authority to permit the entry into Manchurian territory of several thousand German-Jewish refugees stranded in the Soviet-Masnchurian border town of Manchuli. The German government presented a note of protest to the government of Japan, and the Chief of Staff of the Kwantung Army, General Tojo Hideki, asked Higuchi to explain his actions. Higuchi explained, "As long as the German policy is applicable only to its own territories, I have no criticism of it and to do so would be inappropriate. However, when the Germans are unable to solve a problem within their own frontiers and force it upon others, they have to be prepared to accept criticism from those upon whom they impose it … and I support German-Japanese friendship … but Japan is not dependent on Germany and I seriously ponder the attitude of the Germans, the Japanese Foreign Ministry, and the Japanese War Ministry, who expressed their wonderment over the legitimate foreign policy of the government of Manchukuo which was done in coordination with me and according to my advice…." In spite of the convoluted language, it was clear that General Higuchi was very critical of the German intervention into what he considered purely domestic Japanese affairs, and that he was angry over what he considered the fawning behavior of the Japanese bureaucrats who did not defend Japan's honor and sovereignty properly, certainly in deciding who to admit to its territories. Apparently his stand did make an impression in Tokyo, and Tojo upheld his position, as did the Japanese government. Most of these refugees ended up in Shanghai, where they spent the war years. A few were able to make it to the United States.

From the Axis Pact (September 1940) to Pearl Harbor (December 1941)

The ties between Germany and Japan were further tightened when Japan signed the Axis Pact with Nazi Germany and Fascist Italy. While the agreement said that in the coming decade the parties would support each other with all available means at their disposal it one of them was attacked by a third party not involved in the pact, it did not require the signatories to join the war already in progress. At Japan's request, the Soviet Union was not included among possible enemies. The pact was basically a vague military alliance. It also omitted any mention of the Jews and what Japan and Italy were expected to do about them. That absence, though, is still a moot point, as the Japanese government by signing this pact indicated its tacit acquiescence to the antisemitic policies of Nazi Germany. Foreign Minister Matsuoka Yosuke, the man who propelled Japan into this pact against the views of some of his colleagues, chief among them Prime Minister Konoe Fumimaro, should have known from his vast experience with the United States that America would not tolerate Japan's signing a pact with racist, antisemitic Nazi Germany. If there had ever been a slim chance of reducing American-Japanese tensions, the Axis pact buried it forever.

After Japan's defeat by the allies, several Japanese historians claimed that one of the reasons for America's decision to use the atomic weapon against Japan (and not against Germany) was Japan's decision to join the Axis pact. These Japanese writers ignored the fact that the bomb had not been tested until July 16, 1945, two months after Germany had surrendered. Some Japanese people saw the destruction of Hiroshima and Nagasaki by atomic bombs as a Jewish plot or an act of revenge, and a few seemed to be aware of the facts that a large number of the scientists employed in the development of the weapon were Jews and that some of the leading experts were themselves refugees from Nazi Germany or fleeing other European countries for fear of persecution. For some reason, the name of Albert Einstein, whose letter to President Roosevelt in December 1939 had led to the development of the bomb, is still revered in Japan.

Even after Japan signed the Axis pact, her policy toward the Jews did not undergo any major change. We have noted that even before the outbreak of the Pacific War Japan permitted the entry into Manchukuo of several thousand Jewish refugees, and the entry into the home islands of several hundred Jews, including those with transit visas—some of them stamped by Sugihara Chiune. Many of them willingly went on to Shanghai, or were sent to that city after Pearl Harbor, but their lives were saved. This policy was implemented by Japan in spite of German demands that Japan be strict with these Jews. These demands were related to Germany's decisions about the citizenship of the Jews of Germany, Austria, and Czechoslovakia. In November 1941, Germany decided to revoke their passports, and they became stateless. It was then that the Germans began making demands for special and humiliating treatments of these stateless Jews, which the Japanese government usually ignored. On several occasions Japan told the Germans that they were not bound by treaty or any other reason to accept Germany's antisemitic doctrines. One of the few German demands which Japan did accede to was the dissolving of the Far Eastern Jewish Congress, a body that had in fact been set up by the Japanese army in 1937 to control the Jews of Manchuria and China. The dissolution of the Congress did nothing to worsen the situation of the Jews under Japanese control, as it was created solely to serve as an instrument of the Japanese army in controlling the Jews of East Asia. In any case, upon the outbreak of the war in Europe in September 1939, the occupation of Western Poland by Germany, and even more so after the German attack on the Soviet Union in June 1941, the last escape routes for Jewish refugees from Europe to East Asia were sealed, and the Japanese government was no longer bound to deal with the matter intensively. Italian and German ships stopped sailing through the Suez Canal in 1939, and beginning in June 1941, the Trans-Siberian Railway was also blocked.

From Pearl Harbor (December 1941) to Japan's Surrender (August 1945)

Even after Japan declared war on the Western powers, there was no discernible change in its policy toward the Jews. Japan and Germany formalized their alliance by signing a military agreement in Berlin on January 18, 1942, a month and a half after Japan's surprise attack on Pearl Harbor. The agreement called for the division of the world into spheres of interest: Germany would be the dominant power in Europe, and Japan would be dominant in East and South East Asia, including the Dutch East Indies, Australia, and even New Zealand. Some mention was made of military coordination and cooperation. Since this was a strictly military agreement, the "Jewish Question" was not mentioned. In the course of the war it became evident that military, diplomatic, economic, technical, or any other type of cooperation was virtually non-existent between Japan and Germany, due to geographic distance, poor communications, mutual suspicions regarding the goals of the others, operational and logistical difficulties, and different types of weapons. Language barriers and cultural differences did not make collaboration any easier.

Japan's strategy was basically regional, and once it attained its limited objectives by May 1942, it did not see any need to divert forces to help the Germans in the Middle East or North Africa, where the Germans would have found them useful. Germany, for its part, did not operate in the Indian Ocean, where collaboration between the two Axis nations could have been dangerous for the Allies. Japan's leaders basically hoped that at that point the Allies, chiefly the United States, would see no point in extending the war and would seek a negotiated peace since Japan was holding many territorial cards for bargaining purposes. After the war, the military attaché in the German embassy in Tokyo, a man by the name of Kretchmer, testified that the two general staffs decided to wage the war separately, each according to its own plans and strategic aims.

The main problem that hung over German-Japanese relations during the war was what to do about the Soviet Union. From the day Hitler launched his attack on the Soviet Union, Germany pleaded incessantly that Japan launch an attack on the Soviet army in Siberia in order to ease the pressure on the German forces fighting the Red Army in the European theater of operations. As early as July 1941, the Japanese government had already decided not to attack the Soviet Union unless it was already totally defeated by the Germans. Japan also decided that it would be forced to take measures against the Soviet Union if the latter permitted British and American aircraft to use its bases from which to attack Japan. It was assumed that only in such an event would Japan try to occupy parts of Siberia. Unless that happened, Japan had every intention of abiding by its April 1941 Non-Aggression Pact with the Soviet Union. There are records of meetings in Berlin between Foreign Minister Ribbentrop and Japan's Ambassador Oshima in which Ribbentrop repeatedly expressed the Nazi demand that Japan attack at least the Russian naval base in Vladivostok, thus pinning down hundreds of thousands of Soviet troops in Siberia so they couldn't be sent to defend Moscow and Leningrad or fight in Stalingrad. In July 1942, Oshima replied that while Japan had attained significant achievements, it was still engaged in a tough war against the United States and Nationalist China and could not make a diversionary attack.

The German defeat in Stalingrad in late 1942 and early 1943 and the defeat of the Africa Corpus in Egypt and Libya starting in October 1942 convinced Japan that under no circumstances should it attack the Russians. This position was confirmed on several occasions by the Japanese General Staff and transmitted to Germany. This policy was adopted because, among other reasons, the Soviets promised Japan that they would not attack Japan in Manchuria and China.

Beginning in late 1942, the Japanese government attempted to secure a cease-fire on the Russian front and to obtain a separate peace between Germany and Russia. Their explanation was that the emperor himself saw this as a first step toward the attainment of universal peace, a goal that he cherished, and that he had already spoken about it with Prime Minister Tojo. In an atmosphere in which Japan was thinking of mediating between the Germans and the Russians as part of a universal peace process, it was clear that Japan would not take any part in the Final Solution against the Jews or even appear to be in close collaboration with the Nazis on other matters.

There was another reason for the chill in German-Japanese relations during the war: there had never been any great enthusiasm in Japan for German racial doctrines. Japan's main war aims were the expulsion of the Western colonialists and imperialists from Asia and the prevention of a communist takeover of the new states to be created in Asia after the war under Japanese domination and guidance. While Hitler was apparently pleased with the defeat of the Western powers in Asia, he also saw the destruction of Western colonies in Asia as a setback for the doctrine of the superiority of the white race. Japan may have harbored fears that Germany would try to take control over certain Western colonies, such as the Dutch East Indies and Malaya, from Japan in order to supply its own needs.

Whatever the reasons, it is obvious that the so-called "Jewish Question" was a very minor matter on the German-Japanese agenda during the war, and if it was raised at all it was as a matter of routine in talks between Oshima and Ribbentrop in Berlin, or Ott (and later Von Stahmer) and his Japanese interlocutors in Tokyo. The most radical action against the Jews was that in Shanghai, where it will be recalled that Japan partly implemented a German proposal and created a Jewish ghetto. There is no evidence that this was done in full coordination with the Germans. Even in Shanghai, the Jews ordered to move to Hongkew were Central European stateless Jews; Russian Jews were exempt, so as to avoid provoking the Soviet Union. Japan's efforts to bring about a separate Soviet-German peace were rejected by Hitler, who would have had to announce that attacking the Soviet Union in June 1941 was a colossal error.

In late October 1943, Stalin promised the American secretary of state, Cordell Hull, that soon after Germany's surrender the Soviet Union would enter the war against Japan. Although unknown to the Japanese at the time, Stalin's offer in fact ruined Tokyo's hopes that the Soviet Union could play a mediator's role to end the Pacific War. It also dashed any hopes some Japanese leaders still harbored that the Soviet government would accept their mediation for the attainment of a Soviet-German peace. It was in August 1944 that Hitler gave his final negative reply to this suggestion. The Russians, too, turned down the offer.

On the Jewish issue, both governments faced another difficulty: in Germany there were specific individuals and organizations responsible for the implementation of the Final Solution, headed by Heinrich Himmler and Adolph Eichmann. The key decision regarding the Final Solution was made at the Wansee conference near Berlin in January of 1942. In Japan there was no civilian ministerial level, or even a lower-level official body, that dealt specifically with Jews. Treatment of the Jews was on an individual basis, and the responsibility of dealing with issues that arose regarding them fell to local military commanders in the occupied territories and the ministry of the interior in the home islands. These decision-makers wanted above all law and order, stability and calm in the areas under their control, and therefore did not take genocidal measures against the Europeans or Americans who now came under Japanese occupation. True, they tortured, starved, and humiliated thousands, and used some of them as forced laborers to build fortifications, roads, and railways, but there was never any consideration given to a plan of systematic extermination of Europeans in general and Jews in particular. In the Japanese-occupied territories in Asia there were a few thousand Germans. There were Nazi party branches in various Asian cities, to which some of the German settlers belonged, but there is no evidence that they espoused antisemitic violence. At most they inserted some antisemitic material in the local media, but that had little if any effect on the Japanese. Consequently, there were no massive pressures on the Japanese government or military authorities to single out the Jews for special treatment, let alone annihilation.

An example of Japan's unwillingness to hitch its horses to the German antisemitic cart was the response to an invitation extended to Ambassador Oshima by the German foreign ministry to attend an international conference titled "The Role of the Jews in the Current International Situation," due to be held in Kracow in June 1944. Oshima suggested to Tokyo that he attend the conference only as an observer and not as an active participant, in order, he claimed, to avoid providing propaganda grist to Japan's enemies' mills. Others invited to participate in the conference were the prime minister of Slovakia, the interior minister of Hungary, and the mufti of Jerusalem, Haj Amin el Husseini. Since the allies landed in Normandy on June 6, 1944, the conference never took place: Germany was busy with more important matters.

We have seen that general policy guidelines were formulated in March 1942 stating that Jews would be treated like other aliens, but that special attention would be given them in view of their origins and race. Early in 1943, the possibility of losing the war started to penetrate the minds of a number of senior German and Japanese officers, and they realized that it was only a matter of time before the Allies would launch a second front in Europe and bring their long-range bombers closer to the home islands of Japan. In such an atmosphere, it was evident, at least to the Japanese, that the several tens of thousands of Jews under the Japanese government's control was not their greatest problem. In Japanese diplomatic documents of the time, there are few references to a drastic solution of the Jewish "problem."

Since the Japanese people and government were totally unaware of the extermination of the Jews in Europe, they were not in a position to even warn neutral nations with whom they had ties about the Holocaust. Even those in the so-called Japanese "peace camp," which consisted mainly of former prime ministers, a number of diplomats, and officials of the finance ministry, were unable to alert Western powers about the Holocaust or to state clearly that Japan had no involvement in the Final Solution. They simply did not know about the systematic extermination of European Jewry. Thus Japan deserves a few merit points. Even if some Japanese leaders assumed that Germany was exterminating the Jews, they may have wondered if there was any strategic connection between the planned extermination of the Jews and winning the war against the Allies.

After the war, Japan's leaders made no attempt to put the blame for the Holocaust exclusively on the Nazis. They preferred not to deal with the issue at all, and it was rarely mentioned in the trial of Japanese war criminals that opened in Tokyo in late 1945 and ended in December 1948. By contrast, the Holocaust was, of course, a central issue in the trial of the Nazi war criminals in Nuremberg. Among the Nazi war criminals on trial was Alfred Rosenberg, who had provided the so-called scientific dimensions of the Nazi racist doctrines that seeped into Japan in the 1930's. The Japanese war criminals did not even use the fact that the lives of tens of thousands of Jews were preserved as an excuse to soften their guilt for their crimes against other peoples. Unlike Germany, after the war Japan did not include the Holocaust as a subject in its school history textbooks. True, maintaining the proper attitude in regard to the Pacific War is a highly charged matter in Japan to this very day, and there is an effort to downgrade and minimize the discussion of this painful era in modern Japanese history. This is exactly the opposite of what has taken place in Germany, where the Holocaust remains a major subject in history textbooks. In Germany, Austria, and some other nations, Holocaust denial is considered a crime punishable by law, whereas in Japan Holocaust denial does not come under criminal law. On the contrary, attempts to charge Holocaust deniers in Japan have been met with opposition from those who fear that lawsuits on the subject would stifle freedom of speech and criticism, and violate media and academic freedom of expression.

In conclusion, the Jewish issue in German-Japanese relations from 1933 until the defeat of both countries in 1945 was at best marginal and not of major consequence. This may be one reason why Japanese historians did not tend to study it in depth until the early 1960s. Yet it is amazing that today there exist over 150 studies in Japanese on the "Jewish Question" and the policy of Japan toward its Jews in the 1930's and 1940's. Perhaps they are intended to demonstrate to American Jews that while Japan cannot deny its ties with Nazi Germany, unlike the Germans the Japanese were humane and fair to the Jews. And indeed, the Japanese did not hand over Jews to the Germans as did the French, Dutch, Belgian, Polish, Ukranian, and other peoples in Nazi-occupied Europe. From a purely historic perspective, they are right.

Chapter 13

The Japanese, the Holocaust of European Jewry, and Israel

A. Did the Japanese know about the Holocaust as it was taking place?[1]

At several points in this study, it has been noted that in spite of Japan's adherence to the Axis Pact, there was never any meaningful strategic cooperation between Germany and Japan over the course of the war. Each party conducted the war on its own. Furthermore, beyond the fact that there was no visible military coordination and cooperation, even on the diplomatic arena, the two had serious disagreements on a number of issues. One disagreement was regarding Japan's relations with the Soviet Union, due to Japan's persistent refusal to launch an attack against the Russians in East Asia. Another was an earlier Japanese refusal to launch an attack on Singapore in 1940 and 1941. A third was the refusal of the Japanese government to treat the Jews in a violent and murderous manner, as the Nazis did. Naturally, under these circumstances, the Nazi leaders did not see any reason to inform the Japanese, in general terms or in detail, of their plans to exterminate European Jewry. However, due to the fact that Japan and Germany were allies, Japan did have a number of sources of information regarding what was happening in Germany and its occupied areas. The questions that have never been fully or even partially answered in a satisfactory manner were: who were these sources; what was their access to those in Germany directly or even indirectly involved in the extermination of the Jews; and could the government and military of Japan be aware of the mass murder of European Jewry taking place and the magnitude of the Nazi death machine?

Overt and Covert Sources

From the Japanese side, potential sources for providing information about the fate of European Jewry were first and foremost Japanese diplomats and officials stationed in various European capitals and major cities, such as ambassadors, minister plenipotentiaries, military and naval attachés, other attachés, and members of the consular staff and intelligence officers such as Sugihara Chiune. They were posted mainly to Berlin, Rome, Bern, Stockholm, Lisbon, Madrid, Bucharest, and Moscow. The diplomats reported to the foreign ministry in Tokyo. The military and naval attachés reported directly to their respective headquarters in Tokyo. Their natural sources for information about European Jewry would be German government officials, mainly officials in the foreign ministry under Joachim Von Ribbentrop who dealt with East Asia.

Other sources would be the German military and the *Abwehr*, the German intelligence service. The Japanese ambassador to Berlin during the war, General Oshima Hiroshi, was an ardent admirer of Hitler and of the German culture and language. He maintained constant contact with Foreign Minister Ribbentrop, and on a number of occasions he received hints that Germany was determined to solve the Jewish problem once and for all. But he was never explicitly told by what means this problem would be solved, under what timetable, and how many people it would involve.

Another question is to what extent the heads of the German foreign ministry and the supreme command of the German armed forces were in the picture regarding the Final Solution. There are some six thousand documents from that period that have survived in the archives of the Japanese foreign ministry, in addition to 60,000 pages of the protocols of the Japanese war trials (IMTFE), reports of Japanese diplomats to the foreign ministry in Tokyo, reports of the military and naval attachés to the Japanese army and navy, and reports from Japanese consular officials to the consular division of the Japanese foreign ministry. The documents indicate a lack of detailed knowledge of the Nazi plans to exterminate the Jews that had been decided upon at the Wansee conference in January 1942. There were virtually no Japanese reports of the mass killings of Jews that began soon after the German invasion of the Soviet Union on June 22, 1941. Most the Japanese diplomatic and consular documents that mentioned the "Jewish Question" dealt with issuing entry or transit visas or other matters pertaining to Jewish migration to Japan or travel through Japanese-held territories.

Other Japanese nationals who could have been aware of the killings of Jews were Japanese business representatives in Germany, some countries occupied by Germany, and neutral countries such as Switzerland, Sweden, and Turkey. They of course had no contacts with Jewish businessmen, who no longer existed in the Reich or the occupied nations—and barely existed in the neutral states. Many Japanese businessmen residing in Britain and in the United States were repatriated over the course of 1942 and returned to Japan, so they too could not have heard anything.

A third group that could have heard something were Japanese journalists, who after Pearl Harbor wrote and broadcast mainly from Berlin and Rome, but also traveled in German-occupied areas in Europe. Until the signing of the Axis Alliance in September 1940, there were regular reports in the Japanese media about anti-Jewish measures, mainly originating from Germany. There were reports of the Nuremberg Laws and the "*Kristallnacht*" pogroms of November 9, 1938. The Japanese government made no effort to censor such news items. Once Japan became part of the Axis, however, a tight censorship was imposed on news that could harm Germany or present it in an unfavorable light. Mentioning the persecution of Jews was seen as reporting on Germany in a negative way.

Another body that dealt with Jewish affairs on the eve of and during the Pacific War was the second section of the research department of the Japanese foreign ministry, which was responsible for the so-called "Jewish Question." This body activated the ostensibly unofficial Association for Political and Economic Studies, which was established in the mid-1930's and was a cover for collecting material on Jews and mainly for spreading antisemitic material in Japan. Over the course of the war, this association published a magazine called *Jewish Studies*. The contact person between the Association and the Japanese foreign ministry was Shiratori Toshio (1887-1949), who served as Japan's ambassador to Italy from the end of 1938 to the end of 1940. He was one of those Japanese diplomats who fervently supported and advocated for Japan's entry into the Axis Alliance. There is evidence that the *Jewish Studies* publication was also used by the German Embassy in Tokyo as a conduit to spread antisemitic material, although the German ambassador, Eugen Von Ott, was not known to be an avid Nazi. Nevertheless, the embassy did support the antisemitic activities of General Shioden Nobutaka and helped him organize a series of symposiums and conferences dealing with the "Jewish Question." Even in this case, though, nothing was said about the annihilation of the Jews as a whole.

Another source which could have provided information to the Japanese people and government about the German policy toward the Jews was Western media, mostly those of Britain and the United States. While in the general Western media there were a number of stories dealing with the systematic killing of Jews that began to take place in the summer of 1941 and intensified in 1942, none of this was ever reported in the Japanese media. Similarly, when by the end of 1941, more stories appeared in the Jewish media in Britain and the United States describing the mass murder of Jews in Eastern Europe, and similar mention was made on the British Broadcasting Corporation, but these stories had little impact on the public's knowledge in the West, let alone in Japan or its occupied territories. It must be remembered that Japanese media gatekeepers were ordered never to cite from enemy sources and that the Japanese citizenry were forbidden to listen to foreign news broadcasts—mainly British and American radio stations. Even if some Japanese people were exposed to these broadcasts, the stories describing the killing of Jews were always accompanied by the caveat that such stories had to be treated very carefully, as they could not be verified. Thus, foreign media were not a credible source for the Japanese. The first confirmation of the mass killing of Jews by gas reached the World Jewish Congress representative in Geneva in late 1942, and that too was greeted with much skepticism by the Western media.

After the war, the American media devoted a great deal of space to describing the atrocities committed by the Japanese army in Nanjing in December 1937 and in the Philippines during the first five months of 1942. Much mention was made of the experiments on human beings carried out by the secret Japanese unit 731, which operated in Manchuria over the course of the war. It devoted less space to atrocities committed by the Germans in Europe. Many Japanese people saw in this a manifestation of racism: why were the Americans more lenient toward the Germans and more critical toward the Japanese?

After the war, Japanese scholars and officials made many attempts to compare the detention camps built in the United States to house more than 120,000 Americans of Japanese descent to the Nazi concentration camps. Few of them paid attention to the fact that the American camps were called "Relocation Centers," and that while they demonstrated a regrettable racist tendency on the part of the United States government, under no stretch of the imagination could they be compared to the concentration camps—and certainly not to the death camps—of Nazi-occupied Europe. Some Japanese apologists of the time preferred to conveniently forget that Japan launched the war, and that the Japanese-American internees were not used as forced laborers.

The only source that could have shed light for Japan on the policy of the Final Solution was the German government itself. Obviously, it had no interest in explaining, even to its Japanese allies, its intentions toward the Jews and the true meaning of the Final Solution. The German ambassadors to Japan during the war, General Von Ott and Heinrich Von Stahmer, met regularly with officials in the Japanese foreign ministry. Records of conversations were kept, but they do not make any mention of the fate of European Jewry, nor did the Japanese raise such unpleasant subjects. It is unlikely that the German ambassadors in Tokyo were themselves ever briefed by Berlin on the extermination of European Jewry.

The main efforts of the Germans ambassadors from June 1941 at least until 1943 focused on convincing the Japanese to abandon the Non-Aggression Pact Japan had signed with the Soviet Union in April 1941 and to attack the Russians in Siberia in order to reduce the pressure on the retreating German forces in Eastern Europe. The arguments became more intense after the German defeat in Stalingrad in January 1943. They resembled Stalin's incessant demands on his Western allies to open a second front in Europe as early as possible for similar reasons.

Among the staff members of the German embassy in Tokyo were some Gestapo personnel. Colonel Meisinger, a Gestapo officer, served in Tokyo for a brief period prior to being transferred to Shanghai. Apparently part of the task of Gestapo personnel in the embassy was to spread fear in Japan over the existence of Jewish spies and fifth-columnists. As it turned out, however, the most senior foreign spy ever caught in Japan was Richrad Sorge, a German whose mother was Russian. An ardent communist, he had spied for the Soviet Union and had very close ties with the German ambassador and his senior staff members, including Meisinger, one of his drinking companions. Sorge was the one who informed Stalin in the fall of 1941 that Japan had no intention of expanding the war to the Soviet Union. This information finally convinced Stalin that he could move some 600,000 soldiers from Siberia to the European front, a move credited with stopping the German army at the gates of Moscow. Sorge was captured, along with his Japanese collaborators (one of whom had ties to the office of Prime Minister Konoye), in late 1941 by the Japanese police. They were executed in 1944. None of them were Jewish.

The information department of the German Embassy in Tokyo was involved in disseminating antisemitic literature to the Japanese media. Some of this material was used by Japanese writers to pen articles against Jews, but most of the material was not even used. This department also disseminated the *Protocols of the Elders of Zion* and other antisemitic literature to the Japanese public. In the material there was never any mention of the Final Solution or the existence of death camps. The impact of this propaganda is hard to evaluate. Since most Japanese people had never seen a Jew in their lives, the material probably didn't mean much to them, unless it was in connection with the leaders of the Western allies who, the Japanese were told, were under the control of international Jewry (whatever that was).

In Japan and the territories under its control there were a number of Nazi and pro-Nazi organizations, some consisting of German nationals, others consisting of local people who for various reasons thought it useful to join them. Their influence was very limited. In January 1943, the German embassy in Tokyo helped put together an exhibition in a large Tokyo department store on the theme "The Freemasons: The Secret International Organization of the Jews." It was also instrumental in helping General Shioden's Association for the Study of the Jewish Question arrange for its 1943 conference, and a year later helped the League for the Implementation of the Imperial Education Rescript to organize a symposium on Jewish plots against Japan. In those gatherings there was absolutely no mention of what was taking place at that very moment in Auschwitz, Birkenau, Treblinka, and other Nazi death camps in Europe. Thus the average Japanese newspaper reader could not have had any inkling about the mass murder of Jews that was taking place far away from Japan. The "Jewish Question" was a matter of which he had little knowledge, about a people of whom he knew virtually nothing.

The Japanese policy toward the Jews was determined in the March 11, 1942, meeting, some six weeks after the Wansee conference (January 20, 1942) that had sealed the fate of European Jewry. It is unlikely that Japanese leaders were informed of the decisions made during the Wansee gathering. The Japanese policy, as we have discussed, was the diametric opposite of the Final Solution. There is no clear-cut evidence that Nazi Germany ever demanded that Japan hand over Jews in areas under its control to be included in the Final Solution.

After the war, a number of Japanese intellectuals and academics stated that they'd had no idea what the Nazis were doing to European Jewry. In this they were no different than millions of people in Western, Central, and even more so Eastern Europe, who claimed they knew nothing of the systematic killing of Jews. Perhaps the first intimation of what the Final Solution meant came to many Japanese people in the form of reports on the Nazi war trials in Nuremberg between the summer of 1945 and late 1946. These trials were reported on extensively in the Japanese media at the demand of the American occupation authorities, who wanted to demonstrate to the Japanese how evil their war-time allies were. It can be safely argued that the majority of the Japanese people had no interest in what had happened to European Jewry. They were busy battling for sheer physical survival after the devastation of their homeland by American bombers. Even if they had shown some interest, it would have been hard for them to imagine how their war-time allies could have master-minded the killing of some six million people. In this they were not the only ones. To this very day, it seems impossible to comprehend.

Perhaps one of the reasons the Japanese government ignored the German requests regarding the Jews was rooted in the almost total absence of any military, naval, or even political cooperation between the two. But apart from that, the concept of genocide was not known to the Japanese. Even the Rape of Nanjing, horrific as it was, was not intended to be and did not amount to genocide. There has never been a Japanese Wansee conference to plan the extermination of the Chinese or Korean people.

As a result of this almost total absence of knowledge regarding the Holocaust, the Japanese people felt no obligation toward Jews or, since 1948, to the State of Israel as far as expressing contrition or paying reparations, compensation, or restitution. The property owned by Jews in the Japanese occupied areas which was confiscated by the occupation authorities was returned to its owners by the Allies shortly after Japan surrendered. Jewish property in China was nationalized by the communists after the establishment of the People's Republic of China in October 1949.

We have seen that the German government never considered the "Jewish Question" a matter of high priority in its dealings with Japan. There is no evidence that the German embassy in Tokyo was in touch with Japanese experts on Jewish affairs, such as Colonel Yasue or Captain Inuzuka, either in Tokyo or later in Shanghai. True, the German embassy was instrumental in terminating the existence of the Congress of Far Eastern Jews that had been sponsored by the Japanese military authorities in Manchuria, but this body had never possessed any importance or influence, and its total dependence on the Japanese army was obvious.

Japanese cabinet ministers made hardly any statements relating to Jews during the war. One rare example was the reply of the Japanese Home Minister Ando Kisaburo (1879-1954) on January 26, 1944, to a question posed in the Diet by General Shioden Nobutaka.in which he accused the Japanese government of ignoring the "Jewish Question." The minister replied that Japan's policy was to eradicate discrimination based on race, but that this did not mean full equality. Each person had the place he deserved, in which he could live in peace and prosperity. Japan's goals were to implement the policy of co-existence and economic well-being.

In the same debate, Education Minister Okabe Nagakage said that while the Jewish problem was important, the government had not yet paid enough attention to it, and that he wanted to study the matter in depth and discuss it later. The cabinet secretary said that Japan was doing all it could to study the ideological issues in depth and would react to any development as the needs arose. These replies show that while the Japanese government did not come out openly against antisemitism in Japan, it also went no further than that in supporting prejudice against the Jews. It never called for the annihilation of Jews or for taking special measures against them.

There is no evidence of overt anti-Jewish expressions in open or closed meetings by Emperor Hirohito, Prime Minister Tojo Hideki, Foreign Minister Togo Shigenori, the commanders of the army and navy, or the war and navy ministers—in other words, by the key decision-makers in Japan during the war. There is no evidence to indicate that the decision-makers knew of what was happening to Jews in Europe. The general assumption is that even had they been told, the magnitude of the crime was so mind-boggling that even they, who had few qualms about sacrificing millions of Japanese lives for the sake of Japan's victory in the war, could not have comprehended the meaning, dimensions, and magnitude of the Holocaust.

Japan's Attitude to the Arab World[2]

In the 1940 Axis Pact's division of the world into spheres of influence, the Middle East was to be in the German sphere of influence, and thus Japan did not pay much attention to it. Oil produced in Arab countries could not, in any case, be used by Japan, simply because there was no way of getting it there. To the extent that there was any mention of the Middle East in the Japanese media during the war, some newspapers supported the Arab position on Palestine, saying that Zionism was a tool in the hands of Western imperialists and was designed to help the West control the Arab oil fields. None of the Arab states explicitly declared war on Japan in December 1941, but then they were not yet independent and thus could not. Syria and Lebanon won their independence in 1943 and 1944, and along with Egypt and Saudi Arabia remained neutral for some time thereafter. Only toward the end of the war was it indicated to several Arab states that they would obtain membership in the newly created United Nations Organization only if they declared war on Germany (which in any case was about to surrender) and Japan. Therefore, in March 1945 Egypt, Syria, Lebanon, Iraq, and Saudi Arabia declared war on the Axis powers, including Japan. This declaration of war did not obligate the Arab states to take any action, military or otherwise. It was mainly declaratory.

In the future, Japanese historians would not hold this against the Arabs. If during the First World War and immediately after it successive Japanese governments had expressed sympathy and support for Zionism, during the Second World War Zionism was described as an instrument in the hands of Western colonialism and imperialism. It is interesting to note that after fleeing from Iraq following the failure of the Rashid Ali Al-Kilani uprising against the British in April 1941, the Grand Mufti of Jerusalem, Haj Amin el Husseini, who was expelled from Palestine by the British in 1937 and eventually found shelter in Iraq, escaped to Iran and with the help of an Italian diplomat and found refuge in the Japanese legation in Tehran where he resided from late August 1941 until October 1941. He eventually reached Germany via Turkey and Italy in late 1941. In February 1942, the Mufti was in Rome and proposed to the Japanese ambassador there that some of his radio broadcasts in Arabic produced by the Germans should be aired on Japanese radio channels to incite Muslims living in India, Malaya, and Indonesia against the British and Dutch. In his broadcasts from Berlin during the war, the Grand Mufti called on Arab and Muslim people, wherever they were, to support Japan. The broadcasts could have had some impact on Asian Muslims in India, Malaya, and Indonesia, but most of them had no short-wave radios, and thus never heard them. These broadcasts were not of much help to Japan, either. In 1942 a proposal that Japan join Germany and Italy in issuing a proclamation supporting independence for the Arabs and for India was opposed by Germany, which feared Japan's intentions regarding the oil-rich Middle East. Nothing came of the idea.

The American Occupation and the Blurring of Holocaust Awareness in Japan

During the nearly seven years of American occupation of Japan from September 1945 to April 1952, the Japanese people were busy rehabilitating their devastated country, coming to grips with the defeat of their empire, rebuilding their destroyed cities, and attempting to reconstruct their shattered economy. They also had to confront the integration of over five million Japanese citizens, both soldiers and civilians, who poured back into the home islands from the vast regions of the former Japanese empire. These newcomers had to be fed, housed, clothed, and employed. The country's moral and physical devastation did not leave the average Japanese citizen much time or peace of mind to wonder about the fate of European Jewry: they could barely come to grips with what their wartime leaders had done to their own country. For many years, the average Japanese person was unaware of what Japanese troops had done in Nanjing in December 1937, when anywhere from 100,000 to 300,000 innocent Chinese civilians were killed, wounded, raped, or tortured.

The Japanese war trials opened in Tokyo at the end of 1945 and lasted until late December 1948, much longer than the Nazi war trials in Nuremberg that lasted less than a year in 1945-1946. Unlike the Nazi war criminals, among them Alfred Rosenberg, the leading ideologist of the Nazis, who was executed in 1946, the Japanese war criminals were not charged with genocide. Perhaps this explains why the noted Japanese novelist Kenzaburo Oe (1935-), a Nobel Prize winner in literature, could later argue that Japan really never came to grips with the fact that it was a racist nation. It remains unclear even now whether the Japanese developed a guilt complex or guilt feelings, something that typified the Germans more than the Japanese.

In the early years after its defeat, Japan never considered paying reparations or restitution to the tens of thousands of Europeans whom it had victimized in the territories it had occupied, mainly in China and South East Asia. It is hard to find in the contemporary writings any sense of guilt, shame, or even embarrassment about anything connected to the "Great East Asia War" (*Dai Toa Senso*) or, as the Americans termed it, the Pacific War, or as many Japanese people put it, "that war." The key Japanese argument in both the war trials and the media was that any nation would have done what Japan did, given the circumstances Japan found itself in the late 1930's. As a rule, most Japanese people did not want to talk about the war, because they realized that there wasn't much sense in discussing a war that Japan had never had a remote chance of winning. Since the Holocaust was part of the legacy of World War II, they did not want to discuss it. On rare occasions, one can find the work of a Japanese scholar who attempted to make a clear distinction between Japan and Germany, its wartime ally. At least Japan had never carried out genocide, they argued, and therefore Japan had to be judged differently. As far as many Japanese people were concerned, the Holocaust was a European event, which did not take place in Asia and had no counterpart in Asia. Even the most brutal Japanese soldiers and officers, perhaps with the exception of some of those posted to China, never did to the people of the nations they occupied what the Nazis did to the Jews.

Later, when more Japanese scholars studied the Holocaust in greater depth, they were convinced that even the worst Japanese antisemites were never capable of doing to the Jews what the Germans did, and that even non-violent anti-Jewish sentiments were not as visceral of those that prevailed in Nazi Germany.

The American occupation authorities did everything they could to minimize publication in Japanese about the horrors of the war in Europe, and that included information on the Holocaust. The reason for the omissions may be quite simple—perhaps they were afraid that the Japanese would have asked them embarrassing questions: Why didn't you bomb Auschwitz? How about the rail lines leading there? Why didn't you stop the Holocaust once its dimensions became known? Why did you close the gates of your country to Jewish refugees fleeing Nazi Germany and the countries it occupied, while we Japanese enabled almost twenty thousand of these refugees to reach Shanghai and survive the war there?

It can be safely argued that the American occupation authorities did nothing to inculcate among the Japanese the lessons of the Holocaust or to teach them about the horrors committed by their wartime allies. Part of the occupation ideology was that it was necessary to uproot Japan's feudal past, and some American officers may have wondered—not illogically—whether mentioning the Holocaust and its dimensions would elicit a response reminding them of the two atomic bombs that were dropped on Hiroshima and Nagasaki in the closing days of the war, which caused the deaths and maiming of over 400,000 Japanese people over the following years. To their credit, Japanese historians refrained from stressing the Jewish origins of some of the key developers of the atomic bomb, key among them Robert Oppenheimer, Edward Teller, Isadore Rabi, Leo Szilard, Max Born, Emilio Segre, Eugene Wigner, Victor Weisskopf, Richard Feynman, and Eugene Rabinowitz. They did not mention Einstein's role at all, apart from his 1939 letter to President Roosevelt warning of the possibility that Germany was developing weapons of mass destruction and could thus win the war. Several years later, questions were being asked in Japan as to why the Americans had not used an atomic bomb against Germany. The questioners did not care to believe that the main reason was timing—the bomb had not yet been tested when Germany had surrendered in May 1945. Rather, they tended to believe that Japan, as an Asian nation, was the preferred target. They thus accused the Americans of racial motivations that led to the use of the two atomic bombs. It is no wonder, then, that the American occupation authorites never permitted the Japanese media to publish information on the atomic bombs dropped on Hiroshima and Nagasaki and their aftermath.

To their credit, those Japanese writers who did deal with the American occupation and its impact on Japan did not stress the role of a number of Jewish members of the military government who held key positions in the occupation and were instrumental in shaping its policies and above all in the writing of the MacArthur Constitution. Among them were Colonel Charles L. Kades (whose Hebrew name was Kadish), who coordinated the writing of the 1947 Constitution, and Beate Sirota-Gordon, who was mentioned earlier. Wolf Ladijinsky, a Columbia University graduate, was instrumental in shaping the land and agrarian reforms, which had a massive effect on Japan, ending tenancy, granting land to former tenants, and revolutionizing agriculture. Theodore Cohen was chief of the labor division in MacArthur's team and devised labor laws. Alfred Oppler dealt with legal and judicial reforms, and suggested that Japan create a family court system and civil rights office.

Another reason why the American occupation authorities rarely mentioned the Holocaust had to do with the new realities in East Asia. There was never an attempt to equate the Japanese with the Nazis. After 1947, the United States needed Japan's support because China was about to fall into the hands of the communists, and in June 1950 the United States became involved in the Korean War. The United States now urgently required the friendship and assistance of their World War II enemies Japan and Germany. The United States could argue that in both countries there had been a process of reforms and a transition to democratic regimes, but this would not be entirely accurate. While Germany did undergo a process of some de-Nazification between 1945 and 1949, there had barely been a start to a similar process in Japan, and those who were purged immediately after the war were back in business—and in government, politics, industry, and even education—barely two years after the war. In 1957, a leading politician, Nobosuke Kushi, a member of Tojo's wartime cabinet who was purged after the war, became Japan's prime minister.

Few Japanese people ever considered how Germany successfully rid itself of its Nazi past and became the democratic nation it is today. That achievement can mostly be credited to what was then the Western-oriented and -dominated Federal Republic of Germany, and not to the communist-controlled Democratic People's Republic of Germany. Germany made these changes by engaging in comprehensive nationwide educational programs which openly addressed and acknowledged Germany's responsibility for the Holocaust. Germany undertook to create a vast and generous restitution system for the Jewish victims of Nazism and in 1952 signed a Reparations agreement with Israel. These policies have helped bring Germany back to the family of nations and earned it much respect in the international community. It also paved the way for the reconciliation between Jews and Germany and Germany and the State of Israel that few thought possible in the immediate aftermath of the Second World War. The reconciliation culminated in 1970 with West Germany's Chancellor Willy Brandt asking forgiveness on his knees at the site of the Warsaw ghetto. No Japanese leader has ever perfomed an act of this magnitude regarding Japan's actions in China and Korea. Japanese leaders, by contrast, found it very difficult even to admit to their country's use of the so-called "comfort women," mainly Korean and Chinese slaves who served as sex objects for Japanese soldiers during the war.

When the occupation ended in April 1952 and Japan was about to win back its sovereignty the Japanese government initiated steps designed to establish diplomatic relations with Israel. This did not derive from a desire on Japan's part to atone for the sins of their wartime allies, but rather from a sober desire to bring about normalization of ties with all United Nations member states and to improve Japan's standing in the United States, where Jewish power was still perceived to be paramount. The establishment of diplomatic relations and the opening of an Israeli legation in Tokyo in December 1952 did not prevent Japan from observing almost to the letter the strictures of the Arab economic boycott against Israel. This boycott came to an end only in the 1990's, following the signing of the Israel-Egypt peace treaty and the Israel-Jordan peace treaty, and the beginning of negotiations between Israel and the Palestine Liberation Organization in the framework of what became known as the Oslo Peace Process. It is perhaps typical that during the first Gulf War (1991), when Israel was attacked by 39 Iraqi Scud missiles, there was no sense in Japan that it ought to help Israel, a victim of Iraqi aggression. A country that did aid Israel economically, politically, and morally was Germany, whose foreign minister even visited Israel in the midst of the war. Few wanted to remember that Germany had supplied Saddam Hussein with the chemicals used by Iraq to develop chemical warheads. Maybe the Scud attacks on Israel reminded some Germans of Auschwitz. Still, as far as Japan was concerned, while this was not just another war because it involved the flow of oil from Iraq to Japan, they could not yet publicly empathize with Israel.

A number of reasons can be considered for Japan's hesitance to align itself with Israel. Perhaps Israel was seen in Japan as an American ally. Then too, perhaps Japan, as a pacifist nation, did not view favorably the emergence of Israel as a major military power possessing a large army capable of defending itself and reportedly developing its own independent nuclear capability. During a visit to Israel after the Six-Day war, a Japanese academic was heard to comment that "for centuries we Japanese were samurai, now merchants. For centuries you Jews were merchants, now samurai." It is not clear if this was said in criticism or in appreciation. During the second Gulf War (2003), there were those in Japan who said that America was once again engaging in war in Iraq to appease Israel due to the huge Jewish influence on the administration of President George W. Bush. Once again we see the motif of Jews who control the world through their control of the economy and media of the only superpower left in the world after the end of the Cold War. Once again there were accusations that the Jews were homeless and rootless, materialistic by nature, cosmopolitan and dangerous to the body politic, and always happy to foment wars.

The Beginnings of Holocaust Awareness in Japan

Two events introduced the Japanese people to the horrors of the Holocaust. The first was the appearance of the Japanese translation of *The Diary of Anne Frank* in 1952, the same year that the American occupation ended. According to Haifa University scholar Rotem Kowner, the *Diary* sold several million copies, and it became a symbol of the horrors of war and man's inhumanity in general, though it did not become a source of identification with the plight of the Jewish people. Most importantly, *The Diary of Anne Frank* opened the gates for the publication of books and articles that dealt with the Jewish Holocaust. A new generation grew up in Japan that wanted to know more about why their country's leaders joined forces with Nazi Germany in the mid-1930's, when Japan became a party to the Anti-Comintern Pact and even more so in September 1940, when it signed the Axis Pact.

The second major event was the capture by Israeli agents in May 1960 of Adolph Eichmann in Buenos Aires, and later his trial in Jerusalem between April and December of 1961. The trial was covered widely by a number of Japanese correspondents who were dispatched to Jerusalem by their newspapers and who used their stay in Israel to describe the country, its people, Jewish history, antisemitism, and mainly the connection between the rise of modern Israel and the Holocaust. In the ensuing twenty years, many works dealing with the Holocaust were translated to Japanese, and some became best-sellers. Among these were the works of Elie Weisel, Primo Levy, and Paul Cellan. The timing of the end of the American occupation of Japan, the Eichmann trial, and the growth of pacifist sentiments in Japan, accompanied by radical anti-American sentiments, led to an attempt to equate Hiroshima with Auschwitz. The attempt was unsuccessful in the long run: it became evident to a number of Japanese writers and historians that there was a basic difference between what happened in Auschwitz and what occurred in Hiroshima and Nagasaki not only in terms of the number of casualties but in other aspects as well. Some Japanese writers argued that Auschwitz was a one-time event that was over, while Japanese civilians continued to die of wounds caused by the two atomic bombs dropped on Hiroshima and Nagasaki—in other words, it was still an ongoing event. Even so, no one ever accused the Americans of committing genocide against the Japanese. While the Japanese still recall the effect of the two atomic bombs on second- and third-generation victims (called *hibakusha*), they seem to ignore the long-term impact of the Holocaust on the huge number of Jews in Israel and elsewhere who survived that ordeal. Clearly, in spite of the fact that there is a Holocaust museum in Fukuyama near Hiroshima, it is impossible to draw any equation between what happened there and the Holocaust of European Jewry. A few Japanese also voiced the well-known argument that the Jews brought the Holocaust upon themselves because of their special character and inferior race.

Holocaust Denial in Japan[3]

From there the road to Holocaust denial was short. Some Japanese writers followed the path of Holocaust deniers in Europe. Among them, the schoolteacher-turned-writer Uno Masami (1942-), who published several best-selling books on the Jews and the Holocaust, stands out. The books sold millions of copies, and their titles are indicative of their content: *If You Understand the Jews You will Understand Japan* (1986), *The Economic Strategy of the Jews* (1992), and *The Hidden Empire* (1993). He claimed that the Holocaust was a fabrication invented by the Jews to justify the establishment of the State of Israel, the expulsion of the native Palestinian Arabs from their land, and the obtaining of reparations and restitution from Germany. On the basis of the same "myth," he stated, Israel later also received billions of dollars from the United States. Another claim he made was that it was impossible to kill five thousand people a day with Cyclon B gas, which was used in Auschwitz. In general, he argued, Jews wanted to harm Japan because it was Germany's ally during the war. He claimed that in Israel the Holocaust took on a religious stature, immune from criticism, and was offended by the idea that anyone who questioned its existence was accused of being antisemitic. Influenced by the *Protocols of the Elders of Zion*, he argued that Israel was established by Ashkenazi Jews whose origins were in Khazar and not in Palestine, and therefore they should return to their place of origin in Central Asia. He and others quoted extensively from the works of such known Holocaust deniers as former University of Lyon professor Robert Fourisson and the British historian David Irving. Some researchers attach the rise and later the fall of Holocaust denial in Japan to radical anti-American feelings in that country. Despite these negative feelings, it was easier to blame the Jews instead of the United States, Japan's major ally, with whom it had a defense treaty and which was its major export target. The way to do that was to malign the Jews and to conveniently forget the efforts of Jacob Schiff and other Jewish bankers who had helped Japan eighty years earlier, and to take a swipe at the heads of the American economy and banking world, many of whom were Jews. It is interesting to note, however, that Uno Masami and others were ardent admirers of Israel, and he even visited Jerusalem. In this respect he epitomizes those who are antisemites but at the same time great supporters of Israel.

Another affair that showed the extent of Holocaust denial in Japan was the publication of an article in the monthly magazine *Marco Polo*, fashionable among the new Japanese Yuppies. Published in January 1995, the article claimed that there was no evidence that Jews were murdered in the Auschwitz gas chambers, and stated that the Final Solution of Hitler was to settle Jews in Eastern Europe. The Holocaust, it argued, was an invention of the Allies. The article made use of the works of well-known European and even American Holocaust deniers. A storm broke out shortly after the appearance of the article, when a Tokyo Jewish community group monitoring antisemitic expressions in Japan decided to make this a test case but postponed action because of the Great Hanshin earthquake of 1995. Into the fray entered the B'nai B'rith Anti-Defamation League, the World Jewish Congress, and other international Jewish bodies. Their dilemma was not easy. If they threatened the magazine with the withholding of advertisements, they would only demonstrate the international Jewish organizations' vast control over the world's economy and their ability to gag those who disagreed with them and didn't accept their interpretation of the events of the Second World War. This, naturally, would enable Japanese antisemites to claim that they were right and that the rootless Jews now threatened their freedom of expression. After lengthy discussions, the organizations decided not to remain silent. Among those who stopped advertising in the magazine were the German car maker Volkswagen and a number of Japanese firms. The editor of *Marco Polo* was fired, the magazine ceased to appear, and ostensibly the affair died down, but that didn't last long. Several publications in Japan began to ponder why the Jews were so sensitive about the Holocaust, and they published a number of articles on Jewish history and the Holocaust. Inevitably there were attempts to equate Auschwitz with Hiroshima, but that did not succeed any better than it had in the past.

In that same year, 1995, the religious body *Soka Gakkai* mounted an exhibition called "The Courage to Remember: Anne Frank and the Holocaust." The exhibition was shown in Hiroshima and Nagasaki. Another matter of note was a series of articles in the popular weekly *Shukan Kinyobi*, in which two writers, one of Japanese origins and the other a Japanese man raised in Austria, attacked Japanese Holocaust denier Kimura Aiji (1937-) for a book he had written called *Disputed Points over Auschwitz*. He sued them for libel. A Tokyo district court initially determined that it was not competent to determine if indeed gas chambers had existed. Three years later, that very court published its final verdict, in which it rejected Kimura's claim for libel, saying that the International Tribunal at Nuremberg determined explicitly that Nazi Germany had indeed murdered vast number of Jews by gas in concentration camps. Japan recognizes this as a historic fact. This destruction of the Jewish people is known as the Holocaust, said the verdict.

Additional reasons for the negative portrayal of Jews in Japan in the 1990's had to do with the severe economic recession that Japan began to experience when the bubble economy collapsed in 1990. Japanese economists attempted to blame the United States for this development, and there were also references to the supposed secret unit 731, which was said to conduct biological tests on human beings in Manchuria, and whose commanders and scientists, at America's insistence, were never tried as war criminals. The Koreans raised once again the issue of the so-called "comfort women," Korean women who were forced to serve as prostitutes for Japanese troops during the war. This issue has finally been resolved in January 2016 reparations, wherein Japan committed itself to indemnifying those Korean "comfort women" still living. New revelations about the atrocities that had ben committed by Japanese troops in Nanjing in December 1937 also led to indirect charges that Japan was being subjected to an internationally orchestrated attack for its behavior during the war. The death of Emperor Hirohito in 1989 also raised anew the issue of war guilt and responsibility.

A few Japanese historians still maintain an interest in studying the Holocaust, but it is no longer a major issue in the broad public debate. A Holocaust museum called the Fukuyama Holocaust Education Center—the only such museum in Asia—was opened in Fukuyama, 50 kilometers east of Hiroshima, in 1995. Its founder and director, Pastor Otsuka Makoto, met with Anna Frank's father Otto when the latter visited Japan in 1965. The center was funded by Beit Shalom, a Kyoto-based Christian pro-Israel organization. It hosts mainly Japanese schoolchildren and overseas visitors. A growing number of publications in Japanese discuss the rescue of Jews by Japanese people during the war and make various attempts to distance Japan from Nazi Germany. Since the 1960s, there was ongoing interest in the Holocaust that may point to inner psychological needs of Japanese society. Japan still has trouble coming to terms with the atrocities its soldiers committed during the war. Perhaps one way of confronting these charges is to demonstrate that other nations—both Japan's allies and its enemies—also committed atrocities: the Germans in Auschwitz and elsewhere, the Americans in Hiroshima and Nagasaki, and the British in Dresden. There remains in Japan to this very day the dichotomy noted throughout this book: great admiration toward Jews (associated with the rescue and protection of many Jews during the war), and fear of Jewish power. That discussion is now limited to several professional historians, whose major efforts are toward distinguishing Japan from its wartime ally, certainly on all matters that pertain to Jews.

In 2014, a Japanese man burned a number of copies of the *Diary of Ann Frank* in various Tokyo public libraries. This led to a vast outcry on the part of the Japanese people and resulted in the replacement of the books, paid for by the Israeli Embassy, by Israelis, and by ordinary Japanese citizens who pooled money in a public fund for the purpose. It was generally opined that the criminal was deranged.

Japan's Relations with Israel[4]

A detailed discussion of Japan-Israel relations goes beyond the scope of this book, whose main theme, of course, is Japan and the Jews during the Holocaust. Nonetheless, certain key themes should be mentioned. The ties that slowly evolved between the two countries, were initially and only partly indirectly influenced by the Japanese attitude to the Jews during the war and the complete absence of any guilt feeling on the part of the Japanese people as far as the fate of European Jewry is concerned, or for that matter any guilt feelings for the atrocities committed by Japanese troops in China during the Pacific War or the evils committed upon the Korean "comfort women." Japan's policy toward Israel, unlike that of many countries, was not in any way influenced by the Holocaust, since Japan did not feel a need to atone for the crimes committed by Nazi Germany.

It was noted in earlier chapters that Japan supported Zionism after World War I partly because it was still allied with Britain and thought it both morally right and politically correct to support the Balfour Declaration and the establishment of a Jewish national homeland in and later awarding Britain the mandate over Palestine. However, as Japan pivoted closer to Nazi Germany, it abandoned its support for Zionism in order to avoid angering the Nazis or their Arab allies, such as the Grand Mufti of Jerusalem. The Japanese decision-makers also realized that Britain itself had turned against Zionism when it published the May 1939 White Paper which, if fully implemented, would have doomed the Zionist enterprise in Palestine. Now Zionism had become a tool of British imperialism. This change of attitude toward Zionism did not prevent Japan from helping thousands of Jewish refugees fleeing from Nazi Germany.

In September 1945, at the same time that the armed struggle of the Palestinian Jewish community against the British mandatory regime began, the American occupation of Japan got under way as well. Japan, devastated and defeated, was not in the mood to follow events in Palestine and think about the struggle of the Jewish community in Palestine to gain independence, or about the attempts of Holocaust survivors to make their ways across the Mediterranean Sea to that country. The Japanese people were engaged in another struggle—a physical one for sheer survival. Even the war trials of Japanese war criminals that opened in December 1945 and lasted until December 1948 barely mentioned the Holocaust or the Jews, let alone not deal with them in depth: someone counted and discovered that the word "Jews" appears exactly 164 times in the more than 60,000 pages of the IMTFE proceedings. The autumn 1947 discussions in the United Nations General Assembly on the proposed partition plan for Palestine elicited little interest from Japan. Japan was still occupied, and had no independent foreign relations; it bore almost no interest for the United Nations in general and less for its involvement in the Palestine question in particular.

The establishment of Israel on May 14, 1948, and the ensuing first Arab-Israel War were reported upon in the Japanese press, but there were no Japanese correspondents in Israel at the time and most of the reports came from news agencies.

Unlike the countries of Western and Eastern Europe, Latin America, the British Commonwealth of Nations, and the United States, which all supported the partition of Palestine and the creation of a Jewish state, Japan during the occupation was not a member of the United Nations. Therefore, it did not have to take a position on the very sensitive issue of the creation of a Jewish state in Palestine. And there was no reason for it to do so. Japan was not yet dependent on Arab oil. It was evident in 1947 that many countries that voted in favor of the establishment of a Jewish state did so out of guilt feelings for what some of their populations had done to Jews during the Holocaust, but this was hardly relevant to Japan. A number of countries, notably the United States, Canada, Australia, New Zealand, and even some Latin American nations, may have harbored guilt feelings over closing their gates to Jews fleeing Nazi Germany before and during the war, but again this was not relevant to Japan, considering what has been discussed in this study. Some governments may have felt that if they gave the Jews a state of their own, some of the Jews in their own countries would immigrate to the new state, thus diminishing Jewish presence in their country and thus reducing antisemitism. This may have been antisemitism in reverse: "Let the Jews go to Israel and leave us alone." Years later a Japanese diplomat told Arab leaders that their country had nothing to do with the partition of Palestine and the ensuing 1948 war. At the same time, Japan could honestly tell Israel that it did not participate in the extermination of Jews during the war. On the contrary, it indirectly helped save some 40,000 Jews who took shelter Japan and the territories under its occupation. As a result, the relationship between Israel and Japan was not loaded with memories of the Holocaust, unlike Israel's relations with many countries in Europe, especially Germany.

Recognizing Israel: Political and Economic Problems

In April of 1952, on the eve of the end of the occupation of Japan and the restoration of sovereignty, the Japanese foreign ministry dispatched letters to various countries, mainly United Nations members, in which it announced its impending restoration of sovereignty and expressed its desire to establish diplomatic relations. This was part of the process of bringing democratic Japan back to the family of nations. In Israel this overture aroused a debate within the foreign ministry as to whether it should proceed to establish ties with Japan, a member of the Axis Alliance. As the same time, it could not be denied that Israel was in the midst of negotiating with West Germany for reparations and had already established full diplomatic relations with Italy, another Axis partner. Since 1948, Israel had established full diplomatic relations with Austria and opened embassies in most Eastern European communist nations, some of which, like Romania and Hungary, had actively collaborated with Nazi Germany to exterminate their Jewish population during the war. The decision to establish diplomatic relations with Japan was made by Prime Minister David Ben-Gurion, and was in line with his policy of expanding Israel's presence on the Asian continent. An Israeli legation was opened in Tokyo in December 1952. It was the first Israeli diplomatic representation on the Asian continent. Israel did not even demand reciprocity, and was satisfied with Japan dispatching a non-resident minister – plenipotentiary to Tel Aviv. Several years later, Japan appointed a full-time minister to Tel Aviv and opened a legation. In 1963 the level of representation was raised to that of embassies. Like all other nations represented in Israel, the Japanese embassy is in Tel Aviv and not in Jerusalem, the capital of Israel.

We have noted that the Eichmann trial received vast coverage in the Japanese media. It was through that coverage that, for the first time, more Japanese people began to understand what had happened in the Holocaust and to acknowledge that Israel had the right to speak for the entire Jewish people and was the country that absorbed the greatest numbers of Holocaust survivors. The Eichmann trial reminded the Japanese people of the trials of their own wartime leaders. The Tokyo trials were and remain highly sensitive in Japan, partly because the emperor was never tried for war crimes even though he approved all of the major moves and key decisions that led to the war. There was some public discussion in Japan on whether Israel had the right to kidnap Eichmann from Argentina, bring him to Israel, and try him for crimes that had not been committed on its territory on people who were not its citizens, and which had been committed years before Israel had become an independent state. Most Japanese writers agreed that Israel had the right to try Eichmann in Jerusalem.

The central issue in Israel-Japan relations until the late 1980's was Japan's almost total surrender to the Arab economic boycott against Israel.

The reason was obvious: Japan's growing dependence on oil and predominantly on Arab oil, which soon accounted for some 70% of its energy imports. Israel did not wish to deal with the matter directly, as the Japanese government argued that it could not compel Japanese companies to trade with Israel. Israel decided to leave the handling of the matter to international and mostly American Jewish organizations, such as the B'nai B'rith Anti-Defamation League. This once again provoked the old canard about wealthy American Jews trying to dictate Japan's policy toward Israel and consequently to embroil Japan in serious tensions with the oil-producing Arab states. That, it was suggested, would endanger the country's economic development and could undermine its fragile democracy, pushing Japan back to the ultra-right-wing nationalism that had brought about its disastrous defeat in the Second World War.

Another issue that separated the two countries was their respective attitudes to nuclear weapons. These attitudes were shaped by the traumas experienced by both nations during the Second World War: the Holocaust for Israel and the bombing of Hiroshima and Nagasaki for Japan. The two drew totally distinct lessons. Japan replaced its militaristic regime with a liberal democracy, renounced the use of war as a tool of national policy, and made a strategic decision not to pursue nuclear weapons. It swore that under no circumstances would it ever resort to employing nuclear weapons. Israel drew the opposite lesson. It too said "Never again," but in Israel's case that meant pursuing a nuclear option to ensure its existence and survival. The alleged bomb, which Israel has never confirmed possessing, became known as Israel's "insurance policy" or "the bomb in the cellar." Many Japanese writers on the left criticized this Israeli policy and saw in it a dangerous precedent that would encourage other nations in the Middle East to adopt similar insurance policies.

On the eve of the Six-Day War, many Japanese correspondents arrived in Israel. Some of them wrote of the possibility of another Holocaust and the abandonment of Israel by the rest of the world, a feeling that many Israelis experienced at the time. The pacifist –leftists in Japan, meanwhile, were terrified of another war, regardless of its causes, and argued vehemently over Israel's decision to pursue it in this case. Some left-wing writers even claimed that Israel was in any case a tool of American imperialism designed to thwart Arab nationalism. The swift Israeli victory in the June 1967 war only deepened fears in Japan over what some writers called Israel's unbridled nationalism, and led them to claim that Israel was the root cause of all the problems in the Middle East. Some stressed the special ties between Israel and the United States and repeated the old conspiracy charge that presented Jews as bent on controlling the world. Only a few Japanese Christians were delighted with the unification of Jerusalem under Israel.

Relatively few Japanese people understood the connection between the Jews and their ancient capital Jerusalem and the Land of Israel, and few bothered themselves with the questions of why Jerusalem was a divided city between 1948 and 1967, and why one of the first acts of Israel after the Six-Day War was to effectively annex East Jerusalem and tear down the barriers that divided the city until then.

The next time Israel figured prominently in the Japanese consciousness was when three Japanese terrorists, members of the *Sekigunha* (the Japanese Red Army) carried out an attack at Lod International Airport near Tel Aviv in May 1972. The men arrived from Rome on board an Air France plane and retrieved automatic weapons from their luggage while it was still on the conveyer belt. They then opened fire and killed some twenty-three innocent civilians, most of them Christian pilgrims from Puerto Rico. One of the terrorists, Okamoto Kozo (1947-) from Kumamoto, was apprehended by the Israeli authorities. It turned out that he had trained in a terrorist camp in Lebanon run by the Palestine Liberation Organization. He was tried in Israel, and the trial was extensively covered by Japanese media. Some Japanese supporters even raised funds to help defray his defense costs. A few weeks later, the government of Japan dispatched a special emissary to Israel to express its apologies for the massacre and offer to compensate the families of the victims. Some Japanese leftists later criticized this humane act.

Several months later, in September of 1972, 11 members of the Israeli Olympic team were captured by Palestinian terrorists and murdered in the Munich Olympic Village following a failed attempt to rescue them. In a memorial service held in the Olympic stadium in their honor, Japan was represented by one athlete, while other countries were represented by their entire delegations. Japanese pacifists never ceased to remind the Japanese people that Israel was engaging in the development of nuclear capability, stressing that Japan was the only country that had ever been attacked by atomic bombs. A few mentioned the fact that the Japanese prime minister at the time of the attacks on Hiroshima and Nagasaki, Suzuki Kantaro (1868-1948), had rejected the July 26, 1945, Potsdam ultimatum calling for Japan's surrender before the bombs were dropped as unworthy of consideration. The two bombs forced the Japanese decision-makers to accept the

Potsdam Ultimatum and surrender before other Japanese cities were totally obliterated.

Japan came under massive pressure during the October 1973 Yom Kippur War, which was accompanied by an Arab oil embargo on countries that were deemed to either have diplomatic and economic ties to Israel or to support the Jewish state. The prevailing feeling in Japan at the time was that the United States, which two years earlier had established contact with the People's Republic of China without prior consultation with Japan, could never abandon Japan in favor of China. Now Japan was faced with a major problem: the Arab states demanded that Japan sever its diplomatic relations with Israel, as twenty-four African nations in fact did. Many in the Japanese government and business community were prepared to accede to the Arab demand, and Japan was on the verge of caving in. At the last moment it was deterred from doing so by U.S. Secretary of State Henry Kissinger (1923-), who feared that an isolated Israel would continue fighting even after a cease-fire was proclaimed between Israel, Egypt, and Syria. Continued fighting could undermine his new Middle East strategy, which called for a working cease-fire, the beginning of a partial Israeli withdrawal in the Suez Canal sector, and the lifting of the Arab states' oil embargo. Japan was torn, as it were, between Arab threats and American pressure. Kissinger explained that Japanese moves against Israel would harm sensitive American interests and could even damage Japanese-American relations. A face-saving formula was finally agreed upon: the Japanese Cabinet Secretary issued a statement in which Japan called for total Israeli withdrawal from territories captured in the Six-Day War, stating further that it did not recognize the Israeli occupation of these territories and did recognize the legitimate rights of the Palestinians on the basis of relevant United Nations resolutions. The only reference to Israeli rights was a call made to all parties to honor the territorial integrity of all nations in the Middle East.

As a result, Japan did not suspend its diplomatic ties with Israel. It now began to tread very carefully between the Arabs, Israel, and the United States. Japan-Israel relations were now seen as a function of Japanese-American relations. The policy of the Japanese government was supported by the industrialists, by the foreign and finance ministries, by MITI (Ministry for International Trade and Industry), by pro-Palestinian intellectuals and academics, and by anti-American elements. In 1976, the government of Japan permitted the opening of a Palestine Liberation Organization (PLO) office in Tokyo, and five years later Arafat was invited to Japan as a guest of the Parliamentary League for Japan-Palestine Friendship.

Relations after the Start of the Peace Process in the Middle East[5]

Since the late 1980's there has been a marked improvement in Israel-Japan relations. This is due to a number of major developments, among them the signing of the Israel-Egypt Peace Treaty of 1979, a slight decrease in the importation of Middle Eastern oil to Japan due to its increased use of nuclear reactors to generate electricity, and the growing importance of the Israeli market for Japanese products, mainly automobiles. In the fall of 1987, a Japanese foreign minister paid an official visit to Israel for the first time since the establishment of diplomatic relations between the two countries. In February of 1989, Israel reciprocated with President Chaim Herzog representing his country at the funeral of Emperor Hirohito and later attending the coronation ceremonies of Emperor Akihito. That same year, Israeli Foreign Minister Moshe Arens visited Japan, but in a balancing act, Yasser Arafat was also invited, to parallel his visit. In April 1991, the Japanese car manufacturer Toyota lifted its ban on the sale of its cars in Israel, possibly due to the impact of the First Gulf War and massive American pressure. More Japanese officials and opinion-makers realized that to continue caving in to the Arab demands for economic boycott of Israel would anger American Jews, but to abandon the boycott efforts would anger the Arabs. The First Gulf War, in which Israel was hit by 39 Scud missiles without responding in kind, provided Japan with another reason to change its official attitude to Israel.

The serious economic crisis in which Japan found itself beginning in the early 1990's, with the bursting of the "bubble economy" that foreshadowed what would happen in the United States and other parts of the world in 2008, once again led to an outpouring of antisemitic feelings in Japan. We have discussed briefly the popularity of Uno Masami's books, which achieved huge success in Japan and sold millions of copies. These books found an echo in Japan's traditional fear of foreigners and animosity against America, and since it was assumed that the Jews ruled America, this distaste led to increased anti-Jewish feelings. However, in the 1990's it was more difficult that it had once been to convince Japanese intellectuals, academics, and journalists that the Jews were the root of all evil and were the people primarily to blame for Japan's deepening economic crisis. The Jews had never filled, and still do not fill, any signifanct role in Japan's economy. They were never part of any major Japanese conglomerates, while many Jews play key roles in the American and global economies. When matters of economics arise in the Japanese media, mention is often made of the fact that during Bill Clinton's presidency (1993-2001) the American secretary of the treasury, its overseas trade commissioner, and chairman of the Federal Reserve Bank were all Jewish.

The 1990 economic crisis, however, was purely home–made, resulting from the collapse of the real estate market, the absence of regulation over banks that lent money to cover mortgages, and the corruption of some Japanese politicians. The connections between the large business conglomerates and the Japanese politicians who were funded by them was evident. It was also obvious that since Jews played no significant role in the Japanese media, universities, or political and cultural life, they could not be blamed for the current ills of Japan. The thrust of anti-foreignism was to to blame America, but since bashing America was not politically correct, the Jews were an easy, better-defined defined target.

Major events that took place in the Middle East following the First Gulf War had a vast influence on Japan-Israel relations. Among them were the Madrid Peace Conference of October 1991, the election of Yitzhak Rabin as prime minister of Israel in June 1992, the signing of the Israel-Palestine Declaration of Principles in September 1993, the evolution of what became known as the Oslo Peace Process, the signing of the Israel-Jordan Peace Treaty in October 1994, the restoration of diplomatic relations between Israel and now the Russian Federation, and the establishment of full diplomatic relations between Israel and India and between Israel and the People's Republic of China, both in January 1992. As part of the Oslo Peace Process, Japan became part of what was known as the Multilateral Negotiations Track, which was involved in discussing such issues as water, refugees, arms control and reduction, the environment, and economic development. Japan now wanted to play a growing role in international relations, partly because of its passive stand during the First Gulf War, to which its major contribution was 13 billion dollars to help cover the war's costs. This was referred to derisively in the West as "Checkbook Diplomacy," insulting Japan. The Western powers told Japan that if it wanted to play a more active role on the world stage and even be considered for a permanent seat in the Security Council, it would have to become more actively involved in international peace-keeping efforts and take a clear stand on the resolution of international conflicts, among them the Arab-Israel conflict.

The first Japanese prime minister to visit Israel was Muruyama Tomiichi, who was the official guest of Israeli Prime Minister Yitzhak Rabin in 1994. This milestone visit was followed by Japan's decision to participate in Middle East regional projects, including the development of the Jordan River Basin in cooperation with Israel, Jordan, and the Palestinian Authority. Foreign Minister (and future prime minister) Taro Aso (1940-) signed a number of agreements of that nature during his visit to Israel and the Palestinian territories in 2007. Japan's policy statement on Israel and the Palestinians issued on November 24, 2007, stated that it accepted the principle of two independent states living side by side whose borders would be along those of the pre-1967 Israel. The Palestinians, the policy statement said, must engage in face-to-face negotiations with Israel, while the latter was asked to freeze settlement-building in the occupied territories and to abide by United Nations resolutions on the matter. Japan also expressed support for the peace efforts of the Quartet (that is, the US, the UN, the EU, and Russia) and offered to assist the parties to the conflict in creating confidence-building measures. This statement reflected Japan's new Middle East policy, its attitude to Israel, and its constant attempt to steer a balanced course that did not exceed the framework determined mainly by the United States and accepted by the international community. Since then, Japan's relations with Israel have been on an even keel in spite of some shrill voices from the Japanese radical left and ultra-nationalist antisemitic right. Both countries have an interest in expanding their ties with cooperation in new spheres, particularly science and technology.

Another visible expression of Japan's warming relationship with Israel was the visit of Japanese prime ministers to Israel. Muruyama, as was mentioned, visited in 1994 as a guest of Yitzhak Rabin, and he was followed by Junichiro Koizumi in 2006 and Abe Shinzo in 2015. During his visit, Abe signed a series of agreements with Prime Minister Benjamin Netanyahu (1949-) dealing with scientific, economic, and cultural ties between the two countries. All of Israel's prime ministers since 1990 have visited Japan during their terms of office, including Prime Ministers Yitzhak Shamir (1914-2014), Yitzhak Rabin (1923-1995), Ariel Sharon (1928-2014), Ehud Olmert (1945-), Ehud Barak (1942-), and Benjamin Netanyahu. President Shimon Peres (1923-) was also a much-honored guest in Japan. By 2015, Israel-Japan relations were very cordial and the "forty wasted years" (1952-1992) were slowly forgotten.

Conclusion

And this brings us back to the central theme of this study: Japan and the Holocaust. Seventy years after the end of the Second World War, more and more Japanese people are beginning to understand what befell European Jewry, the magnitude of the disaster that was inflicted upon the Jews by Japan's wartime ally. Do the Japanese people make the link between Israel and the Holocaust? Do they agree with Israeli Prime Minister Benjamin Netanyahu's statement that "If the State of Israel is lost, the Jewish people are lost"? Do they understand that the existence of the Jewish people is conditioned upon the continued existence of the State of Israel?

Perhaps North Korea's growing nuclear development and nuclear weapons tests as well as its missile tests fired over Japanese territory, and the growing military might of the People's Republic of China might sensitize the Japanese people to Israel's fears of a nuclear-armed Iran, led by a Holocaust-denying regime, calling incessantly for the annihilation of Israel.

On the other hand, the global economic crisis that started in 2009 and hit Japan badly also spurred renewed theories about a global Jewish conspiracy that was aimed at either subjugating the entire world to Jewish rule or bringing about the collapses of rich countrys' economies, Japan's among them. While it was obvious that Israel could not be faulted for the economic slump of the end of the first decade of the twenty-first century, Jews, and especially American Jews who held senior positions in the Clinton, Bush, and Obama administrations or headed vast American financial conglomerates such as Goldman Sachs and Lehman Brothers, could once again become easy targets.

Did Japan learn anything from the Holocaust about the need for the Jewish people to have a state of their own? The response to this question seems to be positive. At a time when there are growing voices in the West calling for the de- legitimization and perhaps even for the dismantling of the State of Israel, arguing that its establishment was a historic mistake, few in Japan question the right of the State of Israel to exist as a separate, free, sovereign Jewish and Zionist entity. There is criticism of Israel's foreign policy on certain issues, such as settlements and the continued occupation of what are seen as Palestinian territories, but few people in Japan question Israel's right to exist.

Perhaps in the seven decades since the Second World War and the Holocaust, more people in Japan have come to understand what happens when an enlightened, progressive, and technologically and scientifically advanced people like the Germans of the 1930s falls victim to fanatic and even deranged leadership and allows it to carry out genocide. Japan cannot be immune to the almost daily calls emanating from Tehran calling for the destruction of Israel, stating that the country will be wiped off the map.

Increasing numbers of Japanese people are becoming aware that even an Israeli-Palestinian peace settlement will not necessarily solve all of the problems of the Middle East, which include such issues as poverty, lack of education, the rise of Islamism and Jihadism, and the absence of democracy and rule of law, to name a few. In 2015 Japan felt the wrath of extremist Islamic fundamentalism when two Japanese citizens were beheaded by ISIS (Islamic State in Iraq and Syria) fighters. Perhaps this more than any other event in recent years made more Japanese people understand that there are many other causes for the perennial unrest, tensions, and conflicts in the Middle East other than Israel.

Most Israelis hope that the decision-makers and shapers of public opinion in Japan will entirely disabuse themselves of the illusion that the resolution of the Israel-Palestinian conflict will automatically lead to the resolution of all other regional conflicts. Perhaps the Japanese people have now learned that what befell Japan in the Pacific War was the direct result of their own leaders' policies with virtually no resistance from the Japanese people, whereas the Jews were the victims of a regime that championed an ideology of virulent antisemitism that not only justified persecuting the Jews but in fact sanctioned genocide. It is hoped in Israel that there are more responsible leaders in Japan who understand Israel to be the quintessential and only haven for the Jews, even for those who do not reside in it, as many Jewish leaders and individuals do. Perhaps they will better understand why Israeli and Jewish leaders often pounce on any expression of antisemitism not only in Europe but throughout the world—and that includes Japan as well. Combatting antisemitism and Holocaust denial is not only the duty of Israel and world Jewry, but the duty of all peace-loving people in the world, and that certainly includes Japan.

Beyond the typical relations that exist between Israel and Japan, two nations on the fringes of the Asian continent, there stands one basic fact that cannot be denied, and that has an enormous moral lesson: at the time of the greatest disaster that ever befell the Jewish people, the attitude of the government and basically the people of Japan towards the persecuted Jews under their control was by and large fair and even humane. At that time this fact was hugely significant and even today it is an event that the Jewish people will not quickly forget.

Selected Bibliography

Documents

Archives of the American Joint Distribution Committee 1933-1944. New York and Jerusalem: Countries Collections, China folders, nos 456-464, 478-480, 482, 487-490, 501. Japan folders nos 723-727, Philippines folders nos 784-787a.

Bando, Hiroshi. *Nihon no Yudayajin seisaku 1931-1945* (Japan's Jewish Policy 1931-1945. Documents from the Foreign Ministry Diplomatic Record Office). Tokyo: Miraisha, 2002.

Documents of the German Foreign Ministry Dec. 1941-May 1945. Microfilms in the Department of State, Washington, DC.

Documents of German Foreign Policy 1918-1945. Series D, 1937-1945, Washington, DC.

Dull, Paul A. and Michael T. Umemura, eds. *The Tokyo Trials: A Functional Index to the Proceedings of the International Military Tribunal for the Far East.* Ann Arbor: University of Michigan Press, 1957.

Guide to German Records. Microfilms in the National Archives, Alexandria, VA.

International Military Tribunal Far East. Files deposited in the Federal Record Office, Alexandria, VA.

Japan Ministry of Foreign Affairs. *Nihon Gaikusho Jiten* (Diplomatic Record Office). Tokyo: Yamagawa Shuppansha, 1991.
   File Chosa 2-44 America ni Okeru Yudayajin Mondai.
   File J 2.3.0.
   File J 2/3/0 J/X 2-6
   File I 4/6/0/ 1-2 Minzoku Mondai Kankei Zakken: Yudayajin Mondai.

Lowenthal, Rudolph, ed. *Japanese and Chinese Materials Pertaining to the Jewish Catastrophe.* New York: YIVO.

Records of German Foreign Policy. National Archives, Washington, DC.

United States Department of State. *Records Relating to Internal Affairs of Japan 1930-1939.* File 894. National Archives, Washington, DC.

United States Government. *Records of Former German and Japanese Embassies and Consulates 1890-1945.* File T-179. National Archives, Washington, DC.

United States Department of State. *Papers Relating to the Far East: Relations with Japan 1931-1941.* Washington, DC: Government Printing Office, 1943.

United States Department of State. *Records Relating to Internal Affairs of Japan 1940-1941.* File 894. National Archives, Washington, DC.

Uyehara, Cecil. *Checklist of Archives in the Japanese Ministry of Foreign Affairs Tokyo 1868-1945*. Washington, DC: Library of Congress, 1954.

Newspapers
Bulletin of the Association of Former Residents of China, Tel Aviv
Evreiskaya Zhizhn (Jewish Life), Harbin
Israel Messenger, Shanghai
Japan Times Weekly and Transpacific, 1938-1941, Tokyo
Jewish Times Asia, Hong Kong

Primary and Secondary Sources
Adler, Cyrus, ed. *Jacob H. Schiff: His Life and Letters*. New York: Doubleday Doran, 1928.
Akabori Anne Hoshinko. *The Gift of Life: A Biographical Account of Japanese Diplomat Chiune Sugihara*. Sacramento: Edu-Comm Plus, 2005.
———. *Power and Culture: The Japanese American War, 1941-1945*. Cambridge, MA: Harvard University Press, 1981.
Altman, Avraham. "Controlling the Jews, Manchukuo Style." in *From Kaifeng to Shanghai: Jews in China*, edited by R. Malek, Sankt Augustin: Momumenta Serica Institute and the China Zentrum, 2000:279-317.
Altman, Avraham, and Irene Eber. "Flight to Shanghai, 1938-1940: The Larger Setting." *Yad Vashem Studies* 28 (2000): 65-82.
Archer, Bernice. *The Internment of Western Civilians under the Japanese, 1941-1945: A Patchwork of Internment*. Hong Kong: Hong Kong University Press, 2008.
Armbruster, Georg, Michael Kohlsrstruck, and Sonja Muhlberger, eds. *Exil Shanghai 1938-1947, Judisches Leben in der Emigration*. Berlin: Hentrich & Hentrich, 2000.
Banham, Tony. *We Shall Suffer There: Hong Kong's Defenders Imprisoned, 1942-1945*. Hong Kong: Hong Kong University Press, 2009.
Bauer, Yehuda. *American Jewry and the Holocaust: The American Joint Distribution Committee, 1939-1945*. Detroit: Wayne State University Press, 1981.
Ben-Canaan, Dan. *The Kaspe File: A Case Study of Harbin as an Intersection of Cultural and Ethnical Communities in Conflict*. Harbin: Heilongjang People's Publishing House, 2009.
———. "The Jews of Harbin: Nostalgia vs. Historic Reality." In *Mizrekh, Jewish Studies in the Far East*, edited by Boris Kotlerman. Frankfurt: Peter Lang, 2009.
Ben Dasan, Isaiah, *The Japanese and the Jews*. New York: Weatherhill, 1972.

Benda, Henry, J.K. Irikura, and K. Kishi, eds. *Japanese Military Administration in Indonesia: Selected Documents.* New Haven: Yale University Press, 1965.

Ben Dor, Benite. *The Ten Lost Tribes: A World History.* Oxford: Oxford University Press, 2009.

Ben-Eliezer, Judith. *Shanghai Lost, Jerusalem Regained.* Tel Aviv: Steimatzky, 1985.

Bergamini, David. *Japan's Imperial Conspiracy.* London: Granada, 1972.

Best, Gary Dean. "Financing a Foreign War: Jacob Schiff and Japan, 1904-05." *American Jewish Historical Quarterly* 61 (1972).

———. "Jacob Schiff's Early Interest in Japan." *American Jewish History* 69 (1980): 355-359.

Betta, Chiara. "From Orientals to Imagined Britons: Baghdadi Jews in Shanghai." *Modern Asian Studies* 37 (2003): 999-1023.

Bickers, Robert, and Christian Henriot, eds. *New Frontiers: Imperialism's New Communities in East Asia 1882-1953.* Manchester: Manchester University Press, 2000.

Bieder, Joan, and Eileen Lau, *The Jews of Singapore.* Singapore: Suntree Media, 2007.

Blackburn, Kevin, and Karl Hack, eds. *Forgotten Captives in Japanese Occupied Asia.* London: Routledge, 2008.

Bloch, Kurt. *German Interests and Policies in the Far East.* New York: Institute of Pacific Relations, 1940.

Bloch, M. *Ribbentrop.* New York: Crown Publishers, 1992.

Borg, Dorothy. *Pearl Harbor as History: Japan-American Relations 1931-1941.* New York: Columbia University Press, 1973.

Boyd, Carl. "The Berlin-Tokyo Axis and Japanese Military Initiative." *Modern Japanese Studies* 15 (1981): 321-345.

Brandt, Albert A. "Banzai Anti-Semitism: Hitler's Gift to Japan." *The Menorah Journal* (1944): 113-121.

Bressler, B. "Harbin's Jewish Community, 1898-1958, Politics, Prosperity and Adversity." In *The Jews of China: Historical and Comparative Perspectives*, edited by Jonathan Goldstein, Armonk, NY: Sharpe, 1999:200-215.

Bronner, Stephen E. *A Rumor about the Jews: Reflections on Anti-Semitism and the Protocols of the Learned Elders of Zion.* New York: St. Martin's Press, 2000.

Brooker, Paul. *The Three Faces of Fraternalism: Nazi Germany, Fascist Italy and Imperial Japan.* Oxford: Clarendon Press, 1991.

Brown, Delmer. *Nationalism in Japan.* Berkeley: University of California Press, 1955.

Burkhard, Hugo. *Tanz mal Jude: Von Dachau bis Shanghai.* Nuremberg: Richard Reichenbach, 1967.

Buruma, Ian. *The Wages of Guilt: Memories of the War in Germany and Japan.* New York: Farrar, Strauss, and Giroux, 1994.

Butow, Robert. *Tojo and the Coming of the War.* Princeton: Princeton University Press, 1961.

Chapman, J.W.M. "The Polish Connection: Japan, Poland and the Axis Alliance." *Proceedings of the British Association for Japanese Studies*, edited by Gordon Daniels and Peter Lowe, Sheffield: University of Sheffield, Centre of Japanese Studies, 1977: 57-78.

Carpi, Daniel. "The Mufti of Jerusalem, Amin el-Husseini, and his Diplomatic Activity during World War II (October 1041-July1943)." *Studies in Zionism* 7 (1983): 101-131.

Cecil, Robert. *The Myth of the Master Race: Alfred Rosenberg and the Nazi Ideology.* New York: Dodd, Mead & Co. 1972.

Cesarani, David. *Port Jews: Jewish Communities in Maritime Trading Centers 1550-1950.* London: Cass, 2002.

Chandler, Albert. *Rosenberg's Nazi Myth.* London: Greenwood Press, 1945.

Cohen, Israel. *Journal of a Jewish Traveler.* London: Bodley Head, 1925.

Cornfield, Justine and Robin, eds. *Encyclopaedia of Singapore.* Singapore: Scarecrow Press, 2006.

Cowan, Ida G. *The Jews in the Remote Parts of the World.* Englewood Cliffs, NJ: Prentice Hall, 1971.

Crowley, James. *Japan's Quest for Autonomy: National Security and Foreign Policy 1930-1938.* Princeton: Princeton University Press, 1966.

Davidowitz, Lucy. *The War against the Jews, 1933-1945.* New York: Holt, Reinhart, and Winston, 1986.

Dicker, Herman. *Wanderers and Settlers in the Far East: A Century of Jewish Life in China and Japan.* New York: Twayne, 1962.

Dirksen, Herbert, Von. *Moscow, Tokyo, London: Twenty Years of German Foreign Policy.* Norman, OK: University of Oklahoma Press, 1952.

Dikotter, Frank. *The Discourse of Race in Modern China.* Stanford: Stanford University Press, 1992.

———. *The Construction of Racial Identities in China and Japan.* London: C. Hurst & Co., 1977.

Dobson, Hugo. "The Failure of the Tripartite Pact: Familiarity Breeding Contempt between Japan and Germany, 1940-1945." *Japan Forum* 2 (1999): 179-190.

Dobson, Hugo, and Nobuko Kosuge. *Japan and Britain at War and Peace.* London: Routledge, 2009.

Dower, John. *War Without Mercy.* New York: Pantheon, 1986.

Duus, Peter, Ramon H. Myers, and Mark R. Peattie. *The Japanese Wartime Empire, 1931-1945*. Princeton: Princeton University Press, 1989.

Duus, Peter, ed. *Cambridge History of Japan, Vol. 6*. Cambridge: Cambridge University Press, 1988.

—— and Daniel Okimoto. "Fascism and History of Prewar Japan: The Failure of a Concept." *Journal of Asian Studies* 39 (1979).

Eber, Irene. *Chinese and Jews: Encounters between Cultures*. London: Valentine Mitchell, 2008.

——, ed. *Voices from Shanghai: Jewish Exiles in Wartime China*. Chicago: University of Chicago Press, 2008.

——. *Wartime Shanghai and the Jewish Refugees from Central Europe: Survival, Existence, and Identity in a Multi-Ethnic City*. Berlin: De Gruyter, 2012.

Egorova, Yulia. *Jews and India: Perceptions and Image*. London: Routledge, 2006.

Ehrlich, Avrum M., Ed. *The Jewish-Chinese Nexus: A Meeting of Civilizations*. London: Routledge, 2008.

——. *Encyclopedia of the Jewish Diaspora: Origins, Experiences, and Culture*. Santa Barbara: ABC-CLIO, 2009.

Ephraim, Frank. *Escape to Manila: From Nazi Germany to Japanese Terror*. Urbana, IL: University of Illinois Press, 2003.

Ezra, Esmond David. *Turning back the Pages: A Chronicle of Calcutta Jewry*. London: Brookside Press, 1986.

Feingold, Henry. *The Politics of Rescue: The Roosevelt Administration and the Holocaust, 1938-1945*. New Brunswick, NJ: Rutgers University Press, 1970.

Ferguson, Joseph. *Japanese–Russian Relations, 1907-2007*. London: Routledge, 2008.

Fletcher, Miles. *The Search for a New Order: Intellectuals and Fascism in Prewar Japan*. Chapel Hill, NC: University of North Carolina Press, 1982.

Fogel, Joshua. "The Japanese and the Jews in Harbin 1898-1930." In *New Frontiers: Imperialisms, New Communities in East Asia 1892-1953*, edited by Robert Bickers, et al, Manchester: University of Manchester Press, 2000: 88-108.

Fogelman, Eva. *Conscience and Courage: Rescuers of Jews during the Holocaust*. New York: Anchor, 1994.

Fox, John P. "Japanese Reactions to Nazi Germany's Racial Legislation." *The Wiener Library Bulletin* 23/2-3 (1969).

Fox, John P. *Germany and the Far Eastern Crisis 1931-1938: A Study in Diplomacy and Ideology*. Oxford: Oxford University Press, 1982.

Fredman-Cernea, Ruth. *Almost Englishmen: Baghdadi Jews in British Burma*. Lanham, MD: Lexington Books, 2007.

Freyesen, A. *Shanghai und die Politik des Dritten Reiches*. Wurzburg: Konigshausen und Neumann, 2000.

Furuya, H.S. "Nazi racism toward the Japanese: ideology vs. realpolitik." *Nachrichten der Gesselschaft fur Natur und Volkerkunde Ostasiens* 157-158 (1995): 17-75.

Galliano, Luciana. "Manfred Gurlitt and the Japanese Operatic Scene 1939-1972." *Japan Review* 18 (2006): 215-248.

Gao Bei. *Shanghai Sanctuary: Chinese and Japanese Policy Toward European Jewish Refugees in World War II*. Oxford: Oxford University Press, 2013.

Gerson, Ruth, and Makinger, Stephen. *Jews in Thailand*. Bangkok: River Books, 2011.

Gilboa, Violet. *China and the Jews*. Cambridge, MA: Harvard University Press, 1992.

Goldstein, Jonathan, ed. *The Jews of China: Historical and Comparative Perspectives*. Armonk, NY: Sharpe, 1999.

Goldstein, Jonathan. "Japan and Israel: From Erratic Contacts to Recognition to Boycott to Normalization." In *Israel and the World Powers*, edited by Colin Schindler, London: I.B. Tauris, 2014: 234-283.

———. "Shaping Zionist Identity: The Jews of Manila as a Case Study." *Israel Affairs* 15/3 (2009): 296-304.

———. "Across the Indian Ocean: The Trade, Memory and Transnational Identity of Singapore's Baghdadi Jews, 1995-2013." *The Journal of Indo-Judaic Studies* 13 (2013): 97-117.

———. "Shanghai as a Model and Microcosm of Eurasian Jewish Identities, 1850-1950." *Religions and Christianity in Today's China* 3 (2013): 18-45.

———. "Memory, Place and Displacement in the Formation of Jewish Identity in Rangoon and Surabaya." In *Zachor v'Makor: Place and Displacement in Jewish History and Memory*, edited by David Cesarani, Tony Kushner, and Milton Shain, London: Valentine Mitchell, 2009: 88-98.

———. "Secular, Jewish, Filipino and Zionistic: From Marranos to Bagel Boys." in *Mizrekh: Jewish Studies in the Far East*, edited by Ber Boris Kotlerman. Frankfurt: Peter Lang, 2010.

——— and Dean Kotlowsky. "The Jews of Manila: Manuel Quezon, Paul McNutt and the Politics and Consequences of Holocaust Rescue." in *Between Mumbai and Manila*, edited by Manfred Huter, Bonn: Bonn University Press, 2013: 123-138.

Golub, Jennifer. "Japanese Attitude toward Jews." Pamphlet, American Jewish Committee, Los Angeles, 1992.

Goodman, David G., and Masanori Miyazawa. *Jews in the Japanese Mind*. Lanham, MD: Lexington Books, 1995.

———. "Anti-Semitism in Japan, History and Current Implications." In *The Construction of Racial Identities in China and Japan*, edited by Frank Dikotter, Honolulu, HI: University of Hawaii Press, 1977: 177-198.

———, ed. *Japanese Cultural Policies in Southeast Asia during World War II*. New York: St. Martin's Press, 1991.

———. *The Protocols of the Elders of Zion, Aum, and Antisemitism in Japan*. Jerusalem: Vidal Sassoon International Center for the Study of Anti-Semitism, 2005.

———. "Current Japanese Attitude toward the Jews and their Implications for US-Japan Relations." *Occasional Papers, Program in Arms Control, Disarmament and International Security* (September 1989). University of Illinois.

Gordon, Andrew. *A Modern History of Japan from Tokugawa Times to the Present*. Oxford: Oxford University Press, 2003.

Gutwein, Daniel. "Realpolitik or Jewish Solidarity: Jacob Schiff's Financial Support for Japan Revisited." in *Rethinking the Russo-Japanese War: Centennial Perspectives*, edited by Rotem Kowner, Leiden: Brill, 2007: 123-138.

Hadler, J. "Translations of Antisemitism: Jews, the Chinese, and Violence in Colonial and Post-Colonial Indonesia." *Indonesia and the Malay World* 32 (2004): 291-313.

Haroutunian, Harry. "Japanese Revolt against the West: Political and Cultural Criticism in the 20th Century." in *Cambridge History of Japan*, Vol. 6, Peter Duus, ed. Cambridge: Cambridge University Press, 1989: 711-774.

Hauser, Ernest. *Shangahi: City for Sale*. New York: Harcourt Brace, 1940.

Havens, Thomas R. *Valley of Darkness: The Japanese People and World War II*. New York: Norton, 1978.

Ho Feng-Shan. *My Forty Years as a Diplomat*. Hong Kong: Chinese University Press, 1990.

Hennot, Christian, ed. *In The Shadow of the Rising Sun: Shanghai under Japanese Occupation*. Cambridge: Cambridge University Press, 2004.

Heppner, Ernest G. *Shanghai Refuge: A Memoir of the World War II Jewish Ghetto*. Lincoln, NE: University of Nebraska Press, 1993.

Hilberg, Raul. *The Destruction of European Jews*. New York: Holmes and Meyer, 1985.

His-Huey Liang. *The Sino-German Connection*. Assen: Van Gorcum, 1978.

Hochstadt, Steve. *Exodus to Shanghai: Stories of Escape from the Third Reich*. New York: Palgrave MacMillan, 2012.

Hutter, Manfred, ed. *Between Mumbai and Manila*. Bonn: Bonn University Press, 2013.

Hyman, Mavis. *The Jews of the Raj*. London: Hyman Publishers, 1997.
Ienaga, Saburo. *The Pacific War 1931-1945*. New York: Pantheon Books, 1978.
Ike, Nobutaka. *Japan's Decision for War*. Stanford: Stanford University Press, 1967.
Ikeda, Afikumi. "Japan's Relations with Israel." in *Japan in the Contemporary Middle East*, edited by J.A. Allen and Kaoru Sugihara, London: RoutledgeCurzon/SOAS, 1993: 150-161.
Ikeda, Afikumi. "Japan's Perception of Jews and Israel." *Forum* 59 (1986): 73-84.
Ikle, Frank. *German-Japanese Relations, 1936-1940*. New York: Bookman, 1957.
———. "Japan's Policy towards Germany." in *Japan's Foreign Policy 1868-1941*, edited by James Morley, New York: Columbia University Press, 1974:.2 65-339.
Inuzuka Kiyoko. *Yudaya Mondai to Nihon no Kosaku: Kaigun Inizuka Kikan no Kiroku* (The Jewish Question and Japan's Maneuvering of the Jews: The Records of the Navy and the Inuzuka Organ). Tokyo: Nihon Kogyo Shinbunsha, 1982.
Iriya, Akira. *The Origins of the Second World War in Asia and the Pacific*. London: Routledge, 1987.
Jackson, Stanley. *The Sassoons*. New York: Dutton, 1968.
Jewish Community of Japan, 50th Anniversary Yearbook, Tokyo, Jewish Community of Japan, 2004.
Japan Directory. Listing of Foreign Companies and Individuals in Japan, 1879-1904.
Jong, L. de. *The Collapse of a Colonial Society: The Dutch in Indonesia during the Second World War*. Leiden: KITLV Press, 2002.
Jose, Ricardo, and Ikehata Setsuo, eds. *The Philippines under Japan*. Manila: Ataneo de Manila University Press, 1999.
Kamenetz, Roger. *The Jews of the Lotus*. San Francisco: Harper and Sons, 1994.
Kamsma, Theo. *The Jewish Diasporascape in the Straits: An Ethnographi Study of Jewish Businesses across Borders*. Dissertation, Vrije Universiteit, Amsterdam, 2010.
———. "The Artful Deletion of Israeli/Jewish Presence in the Straits." In *Between Mumbai and Manila*, edited by Manfred Hutter, Bonn: Bonn University Press, 2013: 163-188.
Kaneko, Martin. *Kobe: Yudayajin nanmin 1940-1941* (Kobe, Jewish refugees 1940-1941). Tokyo: Mizunowa Shuppan, 2003.
———. *Die Judenpolitik der Japanischen Kriegsregierung*. Berlin: Metropol Verlag, 2008.
Kasza, George. *The State and Mass Media in Japan 1918-1945*. Berkeley: University of California Press, 1988.

———. "Fascism from Above? Kakushin Right in Comparative Perspective." In, *Fascism outside Europe*, Stein Ugelvik Larsen, *ed.* Boulder, CO: Social Science Monographs, 2001.

Katz, Nathan. "Jewish Communities in Asia." in *The Oxford Handbook of Global Religions*, edited by Marc Juergensmeyer, Oxford: Oxford University Press, 2006: 231-241.

Keraney, Gerald. "Jews under Japanese Domination 1939-1945." *Shofar* 21/3 (1993): 54-59.

Kitade, Akira. "How the Sugihara Survivors Reached Japan." *Kokusai Kankou Jouhou* (June 2011).

Kirby, William. *Germany and Republican China*. Stanford: Stanford University Press, 1984.

Kohno Tetsu. "Debates on the Jewish Question in Japan." in *Bulletin of the Faculty of Liberal Arts* 46 (1983): 1-33.

———. "The Jewish Question in Japan." *Jewish Journal of Sociology* 29 (1987): 37-54.

Kotlerman, Boris, ed. *Mizrekh: Jewish Studies in the Far East*. Frankfurt: Peter Lang, 2010.

Kotlowsky, Dean. "Breaching the Paper Walls. Paul V. McNutt and Jewish Refugees to the Philippines 1938-1939." *Diplomatic History* 23 (2009): 865-896.

Kotsuji, Abraham. *From Tokyo to Jerusalem*. New York: Geis, 1964.

Kovalio, Jacob. *The Russian Protocols of Zion in Japan: Yudayaka, Jewish Peril, Propaganda and Debates in the 1920's*. New York: Peter Lang, 2009.

Kowner, Rotem. *On Ignorance, Respect and Suspicion: Current Japanese Attitudes Towards Jews*. Jerusalem: Vidal Sassoon Center, 1997.

———. "Tokyo Recognizes Auschwitz: The Rise and Fall of Holocaust Denial in Japan, 1989-1999." *Journal of Genocide Studies* 2/3 (2001): 257-272.

———. "The 'Protocols' in a Land without Jews: A Reconsideration." *Anti-Semitism International* 3-4 (2006): 66-77.

———. *On Symbolic Anti-Semitism: Motives for the Success of the Protocols in Japan and Its Consequences*. Jerusalem: Vidal Sassoon Center/Posen Papers in Contemporary Anti-Semitism. Jerusalem: Vidal Sassoon Center, 2006.

———, ed. *Rethinking the Russo-Japanese War: Centennial Perspectives*. Leiden: Brill, 2007.

———. "The Japanese Internment of Jews in Wartime Indonesia and its Causes." *Indonesia and the Malay World* 38 /112 (2010): 349-371.

———. "The Strange Case of Japanese Revisionism." in *Holocaust Denial: The Politics of Perfidy*, Robert Wistrich. Ed. Berlin: De Gruyter, 2012: 181-194.

———. "An Obscure History: The Prewar History of the Jews in Indonesia." *Indonesia Today* 104 (2011).

———, and W. Demel, eds. *Race and Racism in Modern East Asia: Western and Eastern Constructions*. Leiden: Brill, 2013.

———. *Race and Racism in East Asia: Interactions, Nationalism, Gender and Lineage*. Leiden: Brill, 2015.

Kranzler, David. "Women in the Shanghai Jewish Refugee Community." in *Between Sorrow and Strength: Women Refugees of the Nazi Period*, Sibylle Quack.ed. Washington: German Historical Institute, 1955.

———. *Japanese, Nazis and Jews: The Jewish Refugee Community in Shanghai, 1938-1945*. New York: Yeshiva University Press, 1976.

———. "Japanese Policy towards the Jews 1938-1941." *Japan* Interpreter 2/ 4 (1977): 493-527.

———. "Japan Before and During the Holocaust." in *The World Reacts to the Holocaust*, David Wyman, ed. Baltimore: Johns Hopkins Press, 1996.

———. "The Japanese Ideology of Anti-Semitism and the Holocaust." in *Contemporary Views on the Holocaust*, Randolph Braham, ed. Boston: Kluwer-Nijhoff, 1983: 79-107.

Krasno, Rena. *Strangers Always: A Jewish Family in Wartime Shanghai*. Berkeley: Pacific View Press, 1992.

———. "History of Russian Jews in Shanghai," in Roman Malekh, ed. *The Jews in China*. Sankt Augustin: Monumenta Serica Institute, 2000, 331-344.

———. *The Last Glorious Summer, 1939: Shanghai-Japan*. Hong Kong: Old China Hand Press, 2001.

———. *Once Upon a Time in Shanghai: A Jewish Woman's Journey through 20th century China*. Beijing: China Intercontinental Press, 2008.

Krebs, Gerhard. *Japan's Deutschland Politik 1935-1941*. Hamburg: 1984.

———. "Antisemitismus und Judenpolitik der Japaner." in *Exil Shanghai*, George Armbruster, et al, eds. Berlin: Hentrich und Hentrich, 2000: 58-76.

———. "The Jewish Problem in Japanese German Relations, 1933-1945." in *Japan in the Fascist Era*, E. Bruce Reynolds, ed. New York: Palgrave MacMillan, 2004: 107-132.

———. "Die Juden und der Ferne Osten. Ein Literaturbericht." *Nachrichten der Gesselschaft fur Natur und Vokerkunde Ostasiens* 175-176 (2004): 229-270.

Kreiner, Joseph, and Regine Mathias. *Deutschland: Japan in der Zwischen Kriegszeit*. Bonn: University of Bonn Press, 1990.

Kreissler, Francoise. "Japan's Judenpolitik 1931-1945." In *Formierung und Fall der Achse Berlin-Tokyo*, Gerhard Krebs and Bernd Martin, eds. Munich: Lidicum, 1984: 187-210.

Krug, Hans-Joachim, Yoichi Hirama, Berthold Sander-Nagashima, and Axel Niestle. *Reluctant Allies: German-Japanese Relations in World War II*. Annapolis: Naval Institute Press, 2001.

Kubata, Taro. "Sugihara Chiune, dei Juden retter aus Japan." *Zeitschrift fur Geschischtst Wissenschaf* 55 (2007): 645-660.

Kublin, Hyman. "Star of David and the Rising Sun." *Jewish Frontier* 25 (1958): 19.

———. Entries on Japan and Kobe. *Encyclopaedia Judaica* Vol. 9, 1280 and Vol. 10, 1118-9. New York: Macmillan, 1972.

Kudo Akira, Tajima Nobuo, and Erich Pauer, eds. *Japan and Germany: Two Latecomers to the World Stage, 1890-1945.* Folkestone: Global Oriental, 2009.

Kuppa, Peter, ed. *Youtai: Presence and Perceptions of Jews and Judaism in China.* Frankfurt: Peter Lang, 2008.

Larsen, Stein Ugelvik. "Was There Fascism Outside Europe? Diffusion from Europe and Domestic Impulses." in *Fascism outside Europe*, Stein Ugelvik Larsen, ed. Boulder: Social Science Monographs, 2001: 705-818.

Lebra, Joyce. *Japan's Greater East Asia Co-Prosperity Sphere in World War II, Selected Readings and Documents.* Oxford: Oxford University Press, 1975.

Leininger, Vera. "Jews in Singapore: Tradition and Transformation." in *Between Mumbai and Manila*, Manfred Hutter, ed. Bonn: Bonn University Press, 2013: 53-64.

Leitner, Yecheskel. *Operation Torah Rescue: the Escape of the Mirrer Yeshiva from Wartorn Poland to Shangahi in China.* New York: Feldheim, 1987.

Leo Baeck Institute. *Destination Shanghai: Refugees or Stateless Jews.* New York: Leo Baeck Institute, 1996.

Leventhal, Dennis. *The Jewish Community of Hong Kong: An Introduction.* Hong Kong: Jewish Historical Society of Hong Kong, 1988.

———, and Mary Leventhal, eds. *Faces of the Jewish Experience in China.* Hong Kong: Hong Kong Jewish Chronicle, 1990.

Levine, Hillel. *In Search of Sugihara: The Elusive Japanese Diplomat who Risked His Life to Rescue 10,000 Jews from the Holocaust.* New York: The Free Press, 1996.

Liberman, Yaakov. *My China.* Jerusalem: Geffen Publications, 1997.

Livni, Itamar. "The German Jewish Immigrant Press in Shanghai." in *At Home in Many Worlds*, Raoul D. Findeisen et al, eds. Wiesbaden: Harrassowitz Verlag, 2009: 273-283.

Lincoln, Anna. *Escape to China 1939-1948.* New York: Maryland Books, 1982.

Malek, R, ed. *From Kaifeng to Shanghai: Jews in China.* Sankt Augustin: Monumenta Serica Monograph, Series XLVI, Nettetal, Steyer Verlag, 2000.

Maltarich, W.G. *Samurai and Superman: National Socialist Views of Japan.* Bern: Peter Lang, 2005.

Martin, Bernd. *Deutschland und Japan in Zweiten Weltkrieg: Von Angriff auf Peral Harbor bis Deutschen Kapitulation.* Gottingen: Musterschmidt Verlag, 1969.

———. *Japan and Germany in the Modern World*. New York: Oxford University Press, 1995.

———. "The Axis in the Face of Defeat. Military and Diplomatic German-Japanese Relations." in *The Closing of the Second World War: Twilight of a Totalitarianism*, David Pike, ed. New York: Peter Lang, 2001: 69-81.

Martinet, Isabella. *Les Juifs de Shanghai: XIX-XX siecles*. Paris: Roillat, 2008.

Maruyama, Naoki. "Japan's Response to the Zionist Movement in the 1920's." in *The Buelltin of the Graduate School of International Relations*, Tokyo: International University of Japan, 1984: 27-40.

———. "Japan's Anti-Semitism and U.S.-Japan Relations." Paper presented at the Southern Japan Seminar. Atlanta, GA: 23 April, 1994.

———. "The Shanghai Zionist Association and the International Politics of East Asia until 1936." in *The Jews of China: Historical and Comparative Perspectives*, Goldstein, J. ed. Armonk, NY: Sharpe, 1999: 251-266.

———. *Taiheiyo senso to Shanhai no Yudaya nanmin* (The Pacific War and the Jewish Refugees in Shanghai). Tokyo: Hosei Daigaku, 2005.

———. "Facing a Dilemma: Japan's Jewish Policy in the late 1930's." in *War and Militarism in Modern Japan: Issues of History and Identity*, edited by Guy Podoler, ed. Folkestone: Global Oriental, 2009: 22-38.

Matsusaka, Y.T. *The Making of Modern Manchuria, 1904-1932*. Cambridge, MA: Harvard University Press, 2001.

Maul, Heinz E. *Why did Japan Not Persecute the Jews?* Tokyo: Fuyo Shobo Shuppan, 2004.

Maxon, Yale. *Control of Japanese Foreign Policy: A Study of Civil-Military Rivalry 1930-1945*. Westport, CT: Greenwood Press, 1973.

McKale, Donald. *The Swastika outside Germany*. Kent: Kent State University Press, 1977.

———. "The Nazi Party in the Far East." In *Journal of Contemporary History* 12 (1977): 291-311.

Medzini, Meron. "Jewish Nationalist in a Japanese Prison Camp." in *Studies in Japanese Culture*, Tokyo: Pen Club, 1973: 299-303.

———. "China, the Holocaust and the Birth of the Jewish State." *Israel Journal of Foreign Affairs* 7:1 (2013): 112-124.

Meskill, Johanna. *Hitler and Japan: The Hollow Alliance*. New York: Atherton Press, 1966.

Meyer, Maisie J. *From the Rivers of Babylon to the Whangpoo: A Century of Sephardi Jewish Life in Shanghai*. Lanham: University Press of America, 2003.

Mitchell, Richard H. *Thought Control in Prewar Japan*. Ithaca: Cornell University Press, 1976.

Mitter, Rana. *China's War with Japan, 1937-1945.* London: Allen Lane, 2013.

Mizuuchi, Ryuta. *Sugihara Visas: Unknown Facts and Hidden Intentions.* Paper presented in Jerusalem, April 13, 1987.

Morley, James. *The Japanese Thrust into Siberia 1918.* New York: Columbia University Press, 1957.

———. *Japan's Foreign Policy: A Resarch Guide.* New York: Columbia University Press, 1974.

———, ed. *Deterrent Diplomacy, Japan, Germany and the USSR 1935-1940.* New York: Columbia University Press, 1976.

———, ed. *The China Quagmire: Japan's Expansion on the Asian Continent 1933-1941.* New York: Columbia University Press, 1983.

Morris, Ivan. *Japan 1931-1945: Militarism, Fascism, Japanism.* Boston: Heath, 1967.

Murphy, Rhoads. *Shanghai: Key to Modern China.* Cambridge, MA: Harvard University Press, 1953.

Nagasaki, Kenritsu. *Survey of the Foreign Households in the Nagasaki Concession 1880-1900.* Nagasaki.

Najita, Tetsuo and Harry D. Harootunian. "Japanese Revolt against the West: Political and Cultural Criticism in the 20th Century." in *Cambridge History of Japan Vol. 6*, Peter Duus, ed. Cambridge University Press, 1988: 711-774.

Nathan, Ezekiel. *The History of the Jews in Singapore, 1830-1945.* Singapore: Herbilu, 1986.

Nish, Ian. *Japan's Foreign Policy, 1869-1942: Kasumigaseki to Miyakezaka.* London: Routledge, 1977.

Nova, Fritz. *Alfred Rosenberg: Nazi Theorist of the Holocaust.* New York: Buccaneer Books, 1986.

Nozaki, Yoshiko. *War Memory, Nationalism and Education in Postwar Japan, 1945-2007.* London: Routledge, 2008.

Nussbaum, Chaim. *Chaplain on the River Kwai: Story of a Prisoner of War.* New York: Shapolsky, 1988.

Ogata, Sadako. *Defiance in Manchuria, the Making of Japanese Foreign Policy, 1931-1932.* Berkeley: University of California Press, 1964.

Oka, Yoshitaka. *Konoe Fumimaro – A Political Biography.* Tokyo, 1983.

Oyama, T. *Toa to Yudaijin Mondai* (East Asia and the Jewish Problem). Tokyo: Chuo Koron Sha, 1941.

Palusz-Rutkowska, Ewa, and Andrej Romer. "Polish-Japanese Secret Cooperation during World War II: Sugihara Chiune and Polish Intelligence." In *Japan Forum* 2 (1995): 285-316.

Pan Guang. *The Jews of Shanghai.* Shanghai: Shanghai Pictorial Publishing House, 1995.

——. *Jews in China*. Beijing: China International Press, 2001.
——, ed. *The Jews in Asia: Comparative Perspectives*. Shanghai: Shanghai Joint Publishing Co., 2007.
Pansa, Birgit. *Juden unter japanischer Herrschaft: Judische Exilerfahrungen der Sonderfall Karl Lowith*. Munich: Lidicum, 1999.
Parfitt, Tudor. *The Jews of Africa and Asia: Contemporary Anti-Semitism and other Pressures*. Singapore: Minority Rights Group, 1987.
Peattie, Mark. *Ishiwara Kanji and Japan's Confrontation with the West*. Princeton: Princeton University Press, 1975.
Pereira, N.G.O. *White Siberia*. Montreal: McGill-Queens University Press, 1996.
Podoler, Guy, ed. *War and Militarism in Modern Japan: Issues of History and Identity*. Folkestone: Global Oriental, 2009.
Presseissen, Ernest. *Germany and Japan: A Study in Totalitarian Diplomacy, 1933-1941*. The Hague: Nijhoff, 1958.
Presser, J. *The Destruction of Dutch Jews*. New York: Dutton, 1968.
Rescue Attempts during the Holocaust. Jerusalem: Yad Vashem, 1977.
Reynolds, E. Bruce, ed. *Japan in the Fascist Era*. New York: Palgrave MacMillan, 2004.
Ricklefs, Merle. *A History of Modern Indonesia since c. 1200*. Stanford: Stanford University Press, 2008.
RIJ, Jan Van. *Some of Them. The Story of a Russian Jewish Family and its Worldwide Peregrinations in Times of War and Revolution*. Paris: L'Harmatten, 2011.
Ristaino, Macia R. *Port of Last Resort: The Diaspora Communities of Shanghai*. Stanford: Stanford University Press, 2001.
Rittner, C., ed. *Anne Frank in the World, Essay and Reflections*. Armonk, NY: Sharpe, 1998.
Roland, Joan G. *The Jewish Communities of India*. New Brunswick: N.J. Transaction Publishers, 1989.
Rosenman, Stanley. "Japanese Anti-Semitism: Conjuring up Conspiratorial Jews in a Land without Jews." *The Journal of Psychology* 25 (1997): 2-32.
Ross, James R. *Escape to Shanghai: A Jewish Community in China*. New York: Free Press, 1994.
Roth, Cecil. *The Sassoon Dynasty*. London: Hale, 1941.
Rubin, Evelyn Pike. *Ghetto Shanghai*. New York: Shengold, 1993.
Rubenstein, Richard L. "Religion and the Uniqueness of the Holocaust." In *Remembering the Future: The Holocaust in an Age of Genocide*, John K. Roth and Elizabeth Maxwell, eds. London: Palgrave MacMillan, 2001: 13-14.
Russel, Edward. *The Knights of Bushido*. London: Cassel, 1958.
Sakai, Shogun. *Yudaya minzoku no da-iinbo*. Tokyo: Naigai Shobo, 1924.

Sakamoto, Pamela Rotner. *Japanese Diplomats and Jewish Refugees: A World War II Dilemma.* New York: Praeger, 1998.

Sato Izumi. *History of the Kobe Jewish Community.* Paper presented at the 96th annual meeting of the American Anthropological Association, Washington, DC, November 21, 1997.

Schmidt, Gilya G. "Why the Chinese People are Interested in Judaism, the Holocaust and Israel." in *Between Mumbai and Manila*, Manfred Hutter, ed. Bonn: Bonn University Press, 2013: 259-268.

Schroeder, Paul. *The Axis Alliance and Japanese American Relations.* Ithaca: Cornell University Press, 1958.

Seaton, Philip. *Japan's Contested War Memories: The 'Memory Rifts' in Historical Consciousness of World War II.* London: Routledge, 2007.

Sekine Maho. *Nihon senryoko no Shanghai Yudayajin Getto: "Hinan"to "kanshi" hazama de* (Shanghai Ghetto under the Japanese Occupation). Kyoto: Showado, 2010.

Shatzkes, Pamela. "Kobe: A Japanese Haven for Jewish Refugees 1940-1941." *Japan Forum* 3 (1991): 257-273.

Shaoul, Raquel. "Japan and Israel: An Evaluation of Relationship- Building in the Context of Japan's Middle East Policy." In *Israel: The First Hundred Years*, Efraim Karsh. Ed. London: Cass, 2004.

Shapiro, Isaac. *Edokko: Growing Up a Foreigner in Wartime Japan.* New York: Universe, 2009.

Shickman-Bowman, Z. "The Construction of the Chinese Eastern Railway and the Origin of the Harbin Jewish Community, 1898-1931." in *The Jews of China: Historical and Comparative Perspectives*, Goldstein, J. ed Armonk, NY: Sharpe, 1999.

Shillony, Ben-Ami. "Japan and Israel: The Relationship that Withstood Pressure." in *Middle East Review 18 (1985).*

———. "Japan and Israel: The Special Relationship." in *Japan and the Middle East in Alliance Politics*, Ronald Morse. Ed. Washington, DC: The Woodrow Wilson Center, 1985.

———. *Politics and Culture in Wartime Japan.* Oxford: The Clarendon Press, 1991.

———. *The Successful Outsiders: The Jews and the Japanese.* Rutland, VT: Tuttle, 1991.

———. "The Flourishing Demon: Japan in the Role of the Jews?" in *Demonizing the Other: Antisemitism, Racism and Xenophobia*, Robert Wistrich. Ed. Amsterdam: Harwood Academic, 1999.

———. "Auschwitz and Hiroshima: What can the Jews and the Japanese do for World Peace.", in *Bulletin of the International House of Japan* 27 (2007): 1-18.

---. "Jews against Japanese or Jews with Japanese in the War, Jewish Response to the War." in *Rethinking the Russo-Japanese War: Centennial Perspectives*, Rotem Kowner, ed. Leiden: Brill, 2007: 393-400.

Shioden, Nobutaka. *Yudaya Shiso Oyobi Undo*. Tokyo: Naigai Shobo, 1941.

---. *Kaikoroku*. Tokyo: Misuzu Shobo, 1964.

Sirota-Gordon, Beate. *The Only Woman in the Room: A Memoir of Japan, Human Rights and the Arts*. Chicago: Chicago University Press, 2014.

Skya, Walter. *Japan's Holy War: The Ideology of Radical Shinto Ultranationalism*. Raleigh, NC: Duke University Press, 2008.

Smele, Jonathan. *Civil War in Siberia: The Anti-Bolshevik Government of Admiral Kolchak*. London: Cambridge University Press, 1996.

Smethhurst, Richard. *From Foot Soldier to Finance Minister, Takahashi Korekiyo, Japan's Keynes*. Cambridge, MA: Harvard East Asia Center, 2007.

Sommer, Theo. *Deutschland und Japan zwischen den Machten 1935-1940*. Tubingen: Mohr, 1962.

Steinberg, John, and David Wolff, eds. *The Russo-Japanese War in Global Perspective*. Leiden: Brill, 2005 and 2007.

Sugihara, Seishiro. *Chiune Sugihara and Japan's Foreign Ministry*. Lanham: University Press of America, 2001.

Sugihara, Yukiko. *6000 min no Inochi no Visa* (Visas for 6000 Lives: One Japanese Diplomat Aided the Jews). South San Francisco: Edu-Comm Plus, 1995.

Szpilman, Christopher. "Fascist and Quasi Fascist Ideas in Interwar Japan 1918-1941." in E. Bruce Reynolds, ed. *Japan in the Fascist Era*, New York: Palgrave McMillan, 2004.

Taniuchi Yutaka. *The Miracle Visas*. Jerusalem: Geffen, 2001.

Tarling, N., ed. *Cambridge History of Southeast Asia: Vol. 2, the 19th and 20th Centuries*. Cambridge: Cambridge University Press, 1992.

Teshima, Ikuro. *The Ancient Jewish Diaspora in Japan: The Tribes of Hada, their Religious and Cultural Influences*. Tokyo: Tokyo Bible Seminary, 1973.

Tobias, Sigmund. *Strange Haven: A Jewish Childhood in Wartime Shanghai*. Urbana, IL: University of Illinois Press, 1999.

Tokayer, Marvin and Mary Swartz. *The Fugu Plan: The Untold Story of the Japanese and Jews during World War II*. New York: Paddington Press, 1979.

---. *Ancient History of the Jewish and Japanese Mystery*. Tokyo: Sannondoi Publications, 2009.

---, and Ellen Rodman. *Pepper, Silk and Ivory: Amazing Stories about Jews and the Far East*. Jerusalem: Geffen, 2014.

Toland, John. *The Rising Sun: The Decline and Fall of the Japanese Empire, 1936-1945*. New York: Modern Library, 1970.

Toyama, Kiyohiko. *War and Responsibility in Japan*. London: Routledge, 2018.

Tsurumi, Yoshi. "Anti-Semitism in Japan: The Ghost that has returned to Haunt." *Pacific Basin Quarterly* (1990).

Ullman, Richard. *Intervention and the War*. Princeton: Princeton University Press, 1961.

Warhaftig, Zerach. *Refugee and Survivor: Rescue Efforts during the Holocaust*. Jerusalem: Yad Vashem, 1988.

Wasserstrom, Jeffrey N. *Global Shanghai, 1850-2010*. London: Routledge, 2008.

Wei, Qu and Shuxiao Li, eds. *The Jews in Harbin*. Harbin: Social Sciences Documentation Publishing House, 2003.

Weinberg, Gerhard. "German Recognition of Manchoukuo.", in *World Affairs Quarterly* 28 (1957): 149-164.

Weiner, Michael. *Race and Migration in Imperial Japan*. London: Routledge, 1994.

Werblowsky, Zvi. "The Japanese and the Jews." in *The Jewish Journal of Sociology* 20 (1978): 75-81.

Wilson, George M. *Radical Nationalist in Japan: Kitta Ikki 1883-1937*. Cambridge: Harvard University Press, 1969.

Wippich- Rolf, Harold, ed. *Japan-German Relations 1895-2006*. London: Routledge, 2006.

Wischnitzder, Mark. *Visas to Freedom: The History of HIAS*. New York: World Publishing, 1956.

Xu, Xin. "Jewish Diaspora in China." in *Bulletin of the Association of Former Residents of China* 45 (2012): 32-41.

Yamamuro, Shin'ichi. *Manchuria under Japanese Domination*. Philadelphia: University of Pennsylvania Press, 2006.

Yasue, Norihiro. *Kakumei undo wo abaku: Yudaya no chi wo fumite* (Unmasking a Revolutionary Movement: Setting Foot on Jewish Soil). Tokyo: Shokasha, 1931.

_____. *Sekai Kakumei no Rimeru* (The Seamy Side of The World Revolution). Tokyo: Niseisha, 1924.

_____. *Yudaya no Hitobito*. Tokyo: Gunjin Kaikan Jigyobu, 1934.

Yeh Wen Hsin. *Wartime Shanghai*. London: Routledge, 1998.

_____ and Christian Henriot, eds. *In the Shadow of the Rising Sun: Shanghai under Japanese Occupation*. Cambridge: Cambridge University Press, 2004.

Yegar, Moshe. "Thailand: The Four Corners, Jewish Communties in the Far East." in *Forum* 38 (1980).

Yoshida, Toshio. "Yudayaijin to Tokumukikancho: Yudaya Minzoku wo sukutta Yasue Taisa no shogai" (The Jews and the Office of Special Military Forces: The Career of Colonel Yasue who Saved the Jewish People). *Bungei Shunju* 41 (1963): 156-164.

Young, L. *Japan's Total Empire: Manchuria and the Culture of Imperialism*. Berkeley, CA: University of California Press, 1998.

Ziaohong Cheng, Sawadi Noriko, and Judy Meschel. *The Last Refuge: The Story of Jewish refugees in Shanghai*. Teaneck, NJ: Ergo Media, 2004.

Zuroff, Ephraim. *The Response of Orthodox Jewry in the United States to the Holocaust: The Activities of the Vaad Hahatsala Rescue Committee, 1939-1945*. New York: Ktav, 2000.

Works in Hebrew

Aluph, Nathan. *Singapore Jewry on the Threshold of Paradise*. Tel Aviv: Golan, 1996.

Assia, Yehuda. *Bridges of My Life*. Tel Aviv: Maariv, 2005.

Avichai, Eliyahu. *The Tribes of Israel: The Lost and the Dispersed*. Jerusalem: Amishav, 1990.

Ben Yaacov, Avraham. *Chapters in the History of Babylonian Jews: The History of the Baghdadi Sassoon Family*. Jerusalem: Religious World Books, 1999.

Bernstein, Avraham, et al. *Sunrise in the East*. Jerusalem: Prager Center, 1998.

Birnbaum, Eliyahu. *Jews of the World*. Tel Aviv: Makor Rishon, 2010.

Eber, Irene. *Way of the Land: The Jewish Communities in Harbin, Tianjin, and Shanghai*. Tel Aviv: Beit Hatfutsot, 1986.

———. *China and Jews: Jewish Refugees in Shanghai during World War II*. Jerusalem: 2002.

———, and Abraham Altman. "The Flight to Shanghai, 1938-1940: The Larger Setting." in *Yad Vashem Studies* 28 (2000): 42-71.

Edelstein, Jacob. "The Mir Yeshiva in Shanghai during the Second World War." in *Kivunim* 19 (1983): 127-134.

Eidelberg, Yosef, Bambra. *New Approach to Solving the Riddle of the Exodus from Egypt and the Mystery of the Ten Tribes*. Jerusalem: Hamatmid, 1972.

Fliss, Lily. *Story of My Life: Berlin, Shanghai, Kfar Saba*. Kfar Saba: Kfar Saba, Private Edition, 2011.

Fradkin, Avraham. *Periods in the Circle*. Tel Aviv: A. Fradkin, 1990.

Gutman, Israel, ed. *Encyclopaedia of the Holocaust*. Tel Aviv: Sifriat Hapoalim-Yad Vashem, 1990.

Hirschberg, Ziegmund and Gertrude. *From Berlin to Shanghai: Letters to Eretz Israel*. Jerusalem: Yad Vashem, 2013.

Kashani, Reuven. *Jewish Communities in the Far East*. Jerusalem: Va'ad Adat HaSefaradim, 1982.

———. "New Jewish Communities in the Map of the Wandering of our Nation in the Far East, Chapter VIII: A Jewish Community in Japan." *Bamaracha* 254 (1982): 10-11.

Kaufman, Avraham. *Rofe Hamachane* (The Camp's Doctor). Tel Aviv: Am Oved, 1971.

Kaufman, Teddy. *The Jews of Harbin Live on in My Heart*. Tel Aviv: Association of Former Jewish Residents in China, 2004.

Kissin, Avraham. *Imprisoned by the Mikado's Soldiers: The Story of an Israeli Prisoner in Japan*. Tel Aviv: Ma'arachot, 1970.

Klemperer-Cooperman, Ayelet. "Only God Will Protect Me: Jews in Japanese Concentration Camps in Indonesia." in *Zmanim* 127 (2014): 72-79.

Kowner, Rotem. "End of a Colonial Community: Indonesian Jewry during World War II." in *Zmanim* 127 (2014): 60-71.

Leitner, Yechezkel. *Rescuing the Torah: The Flight of the Mirrer Yeshiva Students from War-torn Poland to Shanghai, China*. Jerusalem: Leitner, 1990.

Levine, Hillel. *The Sugihara List: The Search for the Good*. Tel Aviv: Yedioth Achronot, 1996.

Medzini, Meron. "Introduction to the Characteristics of Japanese Racism in the 20th Century." In *Genocide: between Racism and Genocide in the Modern Era*, Yair Auron and Isaac Lubelsky, eds. Raanana: Open University Press, 2011: 146-160.

———. *Under the Shadow of the Rising Sun: Japan and the Jews during the Holocaust Era*. Ben Shemen: Modan, 2012.

Pan Guang. "Antisemitism and Zionism through Chinese Eyes." in *Kivunim* 3 (1994): 111-115.

Rosenhouse, Judith, and Rotem Kowner. "Hebrew and Japanese are Not Related: A Comparative Linguistic Study." in *Chelkat Lashon* 35 (2004): 43-64.

Shillony, Ben-Ami. "Hatred of Jews without Jews: The Antisemitic Ideology of Japan during World War II." in *Zion* 46 (1981): 125-145.

———. "Japanese Views of Jews and Judaism." *Publication of the Harman Center for Contemporary Judaism*, the Hebrew University of Jerusalem and the Shazar Center, 1993.

———. *Traditional Japan: Culture and History*. Tel Aviv: Schocken, 1995.

———. *Modern Japan: Culture and History*. Tel Aviv: Schocken, 1997.

———. *Japan from a Personal Perspective*. Tel Aviv: Schocken, 2011.

Sharett, Moshe. *A Voyage in Asia*. Tel Aviv: Davar, 1957.

The Hebrew Encyclopaedia. Tel Aviv: Encyclopaedia Publishing Co., 1949.

Weiman, Gabriel, and Baruch Nevo. *The Singapore Riddle*. Jerusalem: Tsivonim, 2001.

Yegar, Moshe. "The Jewish Community in Penang, Malaya, Travel Impressions." in *Gesher* 3-4 (1973): 156-158.

———. "History of the Jewish Community of Singapore." In *Gesher* 1 (1974): 50-65.

———. *The Long Journey to Asia: A Chapter in the Diplomatic History of Israel.* Haifa: Haifa University Press, 2004.

Yehezkel-Shaked, Ezra. *The Jews, Opium, and Kimono: The Story of the Jews in the Far East.* Jerusalem: Rubin Mass, 1997.

Zariz, Ruth. *Flight before the Holocaust.* Tel Aviv: Hakibbutz Hameuchad, 1990.

Zuroff, Ephraim. "The Rescue of Polish Yeshiva Students Via the Far East During the Holocaust." in *From Generation to Generation*, 49-76.

Zuroff, Ephraim. "The Issue of Entry Permits to Shanghai in 1941: The Problem of Preference in Saving Lives." in *Yad Vashem Studies* 13 (1983): 237-256.

Endnotes

Introduction

1 Ben-Ami Shillony, *The Successful Outsiders: The Jews and the Japanese* (Rutland, VT: Tuttle, 1991).

2 Rotem Kowner's work includes the following: *On Ignorance, Respect and Suspicion: Current Japanese Attitude towards Jews* (Jerusalem: Vidal Sassoon Center, 1997);. "Tokyo Recognizes Auschwitz: The Rise and Fall of Holocaust Denial in Japan 1989-1999," *Journal of Genocide Studies* 3 (2001): 257-272; "The Protocols in a Land Without Jews: A Reconsideration," *Anti-Semitism International* 3-4 (2006): 66-77; and "On Symbolic Anti-Semitism: Motives for the Success of the Protocols in Japan and its Consequences," in *Posen Papers in Contemporary Anti-Semitism* (Jerusalem: Vidal Sassoon Center, 2006); and "The Japanese Internment of Jews in Wartime Indonesia and its Causes," *Indonesia and Malay World* 38 (2010): 349-371. He is also the editor of *Rethinking the Russo-Japanese War: Centennial Perspectives* (Leiden: Brill, 2007).

Among Ben-Ami Shillony's pertinent works are: "Japan and Israel: The Relationship that Withstood Pressure," *Middle East Review* 18 (1985); *The Successful Outsiders: The Jews and the Japanese* (Rutland: Tuttle, 1992); "Auschwitz and Hiroshima: What We the Jews and the Japanese do for World Peace," *Bulletin of the International House of Japan* 27 (2007): 1-18; "The Flourishing Demon: Japan in the Role of the Jews," in Robert Wistrich, ed., *Demonizing the Other: Anti-Semitism, Racism and Xenophobia* (Amsterdam: Harwood Academic, 1999); "Jews Against Japanese or Jews with Japanese in the War, Jewish Response to the War," in Rotem Kowner, ed., *Rethinking the Russo-Japanese War, Centennial Perspectives*, 393-400; "Hatred of the Jews without Jews: The Anti-Semitic Ideology of Japan during World War II," *Zion* 46 (1981): 125-145; *Japanese Views of Jews and Judaism* (Jerusalem: Hartman Center for Contemporary Judaism, The Hebrew University of Jerusalem, and the Shazar Center, 1993); and *Japan from a Personal Perspective* (Tel Aviv: Schocken, 2011).

3 Among works by German scholars on Japan and the Jews see Martin Kaneko, *Die Judenpolitik der Japanischen Kriegsregirierubg* (Berlin: Metropol Verlag, 2008); Gerhard Krebs, *Japan's Deutschland Politik 1935-1941* (Hamburg: 1984); ibid, "Die Juden und der Ferne Osten. Ein Literaturbericht," *Nachrichten der*

Gesselschaft fur Natur und Volkerkunde Ostasiens 175-176 (2004): 229-270; Francoise Kreissler, "Japan's Judenpolitik 1931-1945," in Gerhard Krebs and Bernd Martin, eds., *Fornierung und Fall der Achse Berlin-Tokyo* (Munich: Lidicum Verlag, 1984), 187-210; Bernd Martin, *Deutschland und Japan in Zweiten Weltkrieg: Von Angriff auf Pearl Harbor bis Deutschen Kapitulation* (Gottingen: Museterschmidt Verlag, 1969); Heinz Maul, *Why did Japan not Persecute the Jews?* (Tokyo: Fuyo Shobo Shippan, 2004); Birgit Pansa, *Juden unter Japanischer Exilfahrungen der Sonderefal Karl Lowith*(Munich: Lidicum, 1999).

4   For a list of major works dealing with the Shanghai Jewish Community, see note 63.

5   See, for example, Ikeda Afikumi, "Japan's Perception of Jews and Israel," *Forum* 59 (1986): 73-84; Inuzuka Kiyoko *Yudaya Mondai to Nihon no Kosaku: Kaigun Znuzuka Kikan no Kiroku* (The Jewish Question and Japan's Strategy: The Records of the Navy and Inuzuka) (Tokyo: Nihon Kogyyo Shinbunsha), 1982; Kohno Tetsu, "Debates on the Jewish Question in Japan," *Bulletin of the Faculty of Liberal Arts Hosei University, Tokyo* (1983): 1-33; ibid, "The Jewish Question in Japan," *Jewish Journal of Sociology* 29 (1987): 37-54; Kobayashi Masayuki, *Yudayajin* (The Jews) (Tokyo: 1977); Abraham Kotsuji, *From Tokyo to Jerusalem* (New York: Geis, 1964); and Kubata Taro, "Sugihara Chiune, dei Juden retter aus Japan," *Zeitschrift fur Geschischts Wissenschaft* 55 (2007): 645-600.

One of the more prolific Japanese scholars on Jewish issues is Maruyama Naoki. Among his works are "Japan's Response to the Zionist Movement in the 1920's," *Bulletin of the Graduate School of International Relations, Tokyo*, 2 (1984): 27-40; "The Shanghai Zionist Association and the International politics of East Asia until 1936," in Jonathan Goldstein, ed., *The Jews of China: Historical and Comparative Perspectives* (Armonk, NY: Sharpe, 1999), 251-266; "Facing a Dilemma: Japan's Jewish Policy in the late 1930's," in Guy Podoler, ed., *War and Militarism in Modern Japan: Issues of History and Identity* (Folkestone: Global Oriental, 2009), 22-38; "Japan's Anti-Semitism and U.S.-Japan Relations," paper presented at the Southern Japan Seminar, Atlanta, April 23 1994; and *Taiheiyo senso to shanhai Yudaya nanmin* (The Pacific war and the Jewish Refugees in Shanghai) (Tokyo: Hosei Daigaku, 2005). Other books of interest on this topic include Miyazawa Masanori, *Yudayajin Ronko* (Tokyo: 1973); Ryuuta Mizuuchi, "Sugihara Visas, Unknown Facts and Hidden Intentions," paper presented in Jerusalem, April 13, 1987; Sakai Shogun,. *Yudaya Minzoku no dai-imbo* (Tokyo: Naigai Shobo, 1924); Sato Izumi, "History of the Kobe Jewish Community," paper presented at the 96th Annual Meeting of the American Anthropological Association, Washington

DC, November 21, 1997; Sekine Maho, *Nihon senryoko no Shanghai Yudayajin Getto* (Shangahi Ghetto under the Japanese Occupation) (Kyoto: Showado, 2010); Sugita Rokuichi, *Higashi Ajia e kita Yudayajin* (Tokyo: 1967); Teshima Ikuro, *The Ancient Jewish Diaspora in Japan: The Tribe of Haka, Their religious and Cultural Influences* (Tokyo: Tokyo Bible Seminary, 1973); Yamamuro Shinichi, *Manchuria Under Japanese Domination* (Philadelphia: University of Pennsylvania Press, 2006); and Yasue Norihiro, *Kakumei undo wo abaku: Yudaya no chi wo fumite* (Unmasking a Revolutionary Movement: Setting foot on Jewish Soil) (Tokyo: Shokasha, 1931).
6   Shillony, *The Successful Outsiders*.

Chapter 1: Early Jewish Settlers in Japan

1. For the history of the Nagasaki community, see its entry in *Encyclopaedia Judaica* vol. 12, 758; Herman Dicker, *Wanderers and Settlers in the Far East: A Century of Jewish Life in China and Japan* (New York: Twaine, 1962); Reuven Kashani, *Jewish Communities in the Far East* (Jerusalem: 1982); And Ezra Yehezkel-Shaked, *The Jews, Opium and the Kimono: The Story of the Jews in the Far East* (Jerusalem: Rubin Press, 1997). On the Ginsburg family history see Jan Van Rij, *Some of Them* (Paris: L'Harmattan, 2011). See also *The Nagasaki Kenritsu Survey of Foreign Households in the Nagasaki Concession, 1880-1900*, and *The Japan Directory: Listings of Foreign Companies and Individuals in Japan, 1879-1904*.

2. There are a number of studies that include information on the Kadoories, among them Dennis Leventhal, *The Jewish Community of Hong Kong* (Hong-Kong: Hong Kong Historical Society, 1988) and Mavis Meyer, *From the Rivers of Babylon to the Whampoo: A Century of Sephardi JewishLife in Shanghai* (Lanham, MD: University Press of America, 2003).

3. On the Sassoon family see Cecil Roth, *The Sassoon Dynasty* (London: Hale, 1941).

4. On the Yokohama community, see Herman Dicker, *Wanderers and Settlers in the Far East* (New York: Twayne, 1962); Reuven Kashani, *The Jewish Community in Japan* (Jerusalem: 1982); Israel Cohen, *The Journal of a Jewish Traveler* (London: Bodley Head, 1925); and Ezra Yehezkel-Shaked, *The Jews, Opium and the Kimono* (Jerusalem: Rubin Mass, 1997). See also *The Jewish Community of Japan, 50th Anniversary Yearbook* (Tokyo: Jewish Community of Japan, 2004).

5. On Trumpeldor's imprisonment in Japan see my article "Jewish Nationalist in a Japanese Prison Camp," in *Studies in Japanese Culture* (Tokyo: Pen Club, 1973), 299-303. See also N. Benari, and A. Kenaani, *Yosef Trumpeldor:*

His Deeds and Era (Tel Aviv: 1950); Y.S. Kanner, *Yosef Trumpeldor: A Hero Among His People* (Tel Aviv: Sinai, 1940); Shulamit Laskov, *Trumpeldor: A Biography* (Haifa: Shikmona, 1972); Menachem Poznanski, ed., *The Life of Yosef Trumpeldor* (Tel Aviv: Am Oved, 1945); and Pessach Lipovitsky, *Yosef Trumpeldor: His Life, Personality and Deeds* (Tel Aviv: Culture and Education, 1967).

6. For Jacob Schiff's involvement in financing Japan's war effort see: Cyrus Adler, *Jacob Schiff: His Life and Letters* (New York: Doubleday, 1928); Gary D. Best, "Financial Diplomacy: The Takahashi Korekiyo Mission 1904-1905," *Asian Studies* 12 (1974); ibid, "Financing a Foreign War: Jacob Schiff and Japan, 1904-05," *American Jewish Historical Quarterly* 61 (1972); ibid, "Jacob Schiff's Early Interest in Japan," *American Jewish History* 69 (1980): 355-359; A.J. Sherman, "German-Jewish Bankers in World Politics: The Financing of the Russo-Japanese War," *Leo Baeck Institute Yearbook* 1983: 59-73; Daniel Gutwein, "Realpolitik or Jewish Solidarity: Jacob Schiff's Financial Support for Japan Revisited," in Rotem Kowner, ed., *Rethinking the Russo-Japanese War*, 123-138; and Richard Smethurst, *From Foot Soldier to Finance Minister: Takahashi Korekiyo, Japan's Keynes* (Cambridge, MA: Harvard East Asia Center, 2007).

7. For a broad perspective of the Russo-Japanese War, see: Rotem Kowner, ed., *Rethinking the Russo-Japanese War*; K. Asakawa, *The Russo-Conflict* (London: Kennikat Press, 1970); Richard Connaughton, *The War of the Rising Sun and the Tumbling Bear* (London: Routledge, 1988); and John Stephen, *The Russian Far East: A History* (Stanford: Stanford University Press, 1994).

8. Chaim Weizmann, *Trial and Error* (London: 1948).

Chapter 2: Jewish Settlers in Japan at the Beginning of the Twentieth Century

1 See the documentary collection of the Hebrew Immigrant Aid Association in New York.

2 On the Kobe community, see *Encyclopaedia Judaica* 10, 118-1119; Herman Dicker, *Wanderers and Settlers*; Ezra Yehezkel-Shaked, *The Jews, Opium, and the Kimono*; Israel Cohen, *The Journals of a Jewish Traveler*; and Martin Kaneko, *Yudayajin nanmin, 1940-1941*(Kobe Jewish Refugees, 1940-1941) (Tokyo: Mizunowa Shuppan, 2003). See also Sato Izumi, "History of the Kobe Jewish Community," paper presented at the 96th annual meeting of the American Anthropological Association, Washington, DC, Nov. 21, 1997, and Pamela Shatzkes, "Kobe: A Japanese Haven for Jewish Refugees 1940-1941," *Japan Forum* 3 (1991): 257-273.

3   See David Goodman and Masanori Miyazawa, *Jews in the Japanese Mind* (Lanham, MD: Lexington Books, 1995) and Shillony, *The Successful Outsiders*.
4   On early Japanese interest in Judaism, see: Shillony, *The Successful Outsiders*; Goodman and Miyazawa, *Jews in the Japanese Mind*; Benite Ben Dor, *The Ten Lost Tribes: A World History* (Oxford: Oxford University Press, 2009); and Marvin Tokayer, *Ancient History of the Jewish and Japanese Mystery* (Tokyo: Sanmondoi Publications, 2009).

Chapter 3: Japanese Images of the Jews: Myths, Canards and Fears

1   On McLeod, see his books *Korea and the Lost Ten Tribes of Israel* (Yokohama, 1879) and *Japan and the Lost Tribes of Israel* (Nagasaki, 1879).
2   For material on Sakai see Sakai Shogun, *Yudaya Minzoku no dai-imbo* (Tokyo: Naigai Shobo, 1924). On Sakai and Oyaba see also Shillony, *The Successful Outsiders*, and Goodman and Miyazawa, *Jews in the Japanese Mind*.
3   On Eidelberg see Rotem Kowner and Judith Rosenhouse, "Hebrew and Japanese are Not-Related: A Comparative Linguistic Study," in *Chelkat Lashon* 35 (2004): 43-64.
4   *Chuo Koron* (Tokyo: June 1905).
5   For the definition of Kokutai see Ben-Ami Shillony, *Modern Japan: Culture and History* (Tel Aviv: Schocken, 1997), 174-175.
6   On Japan's intervention in Siberia see: David Dallin, *The Rise of Russia in Asia* (Hamden: Archon Press, 1971); Joseph Ferguson, *Japanese-Russian Relations, 1907-2007* (London: Routledge, 2008); John J. Stephen, *The Russian Far East: A History* (Stanford: Stanford University Press, 1994); James Morley, *The Japanese Thrust into Siberia, 1918* (New York: Columbia University Press, 1957); Henry Norton, *The Far Eastern Republic of Siberia* (London: Allen and Unwin, 1923); and Jonathan Smele, *Civil War in Siberia: The Anti-Bolshevik Government of Admiral Kolchak* (Cambridge: Cambridge University Press, 1996); N.G. Pereira, *White Siberia* (Montreal: McGill-Queens University Press.
7   There is a vast literature on the *Protocols of the Elders of Zion*. See, for example, the entry on themin the *Encyclopedia Judaica*. See also: Norman Cohn, *Warrant for Genocide* (London: Eyre and Spottiswoode, 1967); David Goodman, "The Protocols of the Elders of Zion: Aum and Anti-Semitism in Japan, (Jerusalem, Vidal Sassoon International Center for the Study of Anti-Semitism, no. 2, 2005); Jacob Kovalio, *The Protocols of Zion in Japan: Yudayaka/Jewish Peril, Propaganda and Debates in the 1920's* (New York: Peter Lang, 2009); Rotem Kowner, "The Protocols in a Land without Jews:A Reconsideration," *Anti-Semitism International* 3-4 (2006): 66-77; ibid, "On Symbolic Anti-Semitism: Motives for the Success of

the Protocols in Japan and its Consequences," Posen Papers; David Kranzler, "The Japanese Ideology of Anti-Semitism and the Holocaust," in Randolph Braham, ed., *Contemporary Views of the Holocaust* (Boston: Kluwer-Nijhoff, 1983), 79-107, and Stanley Rosenman, "Japanese Anti-Semitism: Conjuring up Conspiratorial Jews in a Land without Jews," *The Journal of Psychology* 25 (1997): 2-32.

8   For the circulation of the *Protocols* in Japan in the 1920's, see Yasue Norihiro, *Sekai Kakumei no Rimen* (The Seamy Side of the World Revolution) (Tokyo: Niseisha, 1924).

9   For a biography of Konoye, see Oka Yoshitaka, *Konoye Fumimaro: A Political Biography* (Tokyo: 1983).

10 See Sakuzo Yoshino, "Iwayara sekai-teki himitsu no kessha no Shotai," in *Chuo Koron* (June 1921): 2-42.

11 For material on Yasue Norihiro, see Avraham Altman, "Controlling the Jews, Manchukuo Style," in Malek Roman, ed., *Jews in China*, 300-305. See also Yasue Hiro, *The Dairen Special Services Agency and the Visionary Jewish State* (in Japanese)(Tokyo: 1989).

12 See Inuzaka Kiyoko, *Yudaya Mondai to Nihon no Kosaku: Kaigun Inuzuka Likan no Kiroku* (The Jewish Question and Japan's Strategy: The Records of the Navy and Inuzuka) (Tokyo: Nihon Kogyo Shinbunsha, 1982).

13 See Shioden Nobutaka, *Yudaya shiso oyobi undo* (Tokyo: Naigai Shobo, 1941). See also his *Kaikoroku* (Tokyo: Misuzu Shobo, 1964).

14 On Kitta Ikki, see George Wilson, *Radical Nationalist in Japan: Kitta Ikki, 1883-1937* (Cambridge, MA: Harvard University Press, 1969.)

15 For information on Ludwig Reiss, see Shillony, *The Successful Outsiders*, 131.

16 For material on Kanzo Uchimure and Hasegawa Nizkan, see Shillony, *The Successful Outsiders*.

Chapter 4: Nazi Antisemitism and its Influence on Japan in the 1920's and 1930's

1   There is a vast literature on Japanese-German relations. See, for example: Kurt Bloch, *German Interests and Policies in the Far East* (New York: Institute of Pacific Relations, 1940); Carl Boyd, "The Berlin-Tokyo Axis and Japanese Military Initiative," *Modern Japanese Studies* 15 (1981): 321-345; Herbert Von Dirksen, *Moscow, Tokyo, London: Twenty Years of German Foreign Policy* (Norman, OK: University of Oklahoma Press, 1952); Hugo Dobson, "The Failure of the Tripartite Pact: Familiarity Breeding Contempt between Japan and Germany," *Japan Forum* II (1999): 179-190; H.S. Furuya, "Nazi Racism toward the Japanese: Ideology vs. Realpolitik," *achrichten der Gesselschaft fur Natur und Volkerkunder Ostasiens* 157-158 (1995): 17-75; Ienaga Saburo,

The Pacific War, 1931-1945 (New York: Pantheon Books, 1978); Frank Ikle, *German-Japanese Relations, 1936-1940* (New York: Bookman, 1957; Gerhard Krebs, *Japan's Deutschland Politik, 1935-1941* (Hamburg: 1984); Hirama Krug and B. Nagashima, *Reluctant Allies: German-Japanese Naval Relations in World War II* (Annapolis, MD: Naval Institute Press, 2001); Kudo Akira, Tajima Noburo, and Pauer Erich, eds., *Japan and Germany: Two Latecomers to the World Stage, 1890-1945* (Folkestone: Global Oriental Press, 2009); W.G. Malatrich, *Samurai and Superman: National Socialist Views of Japan* (Bern: Peter Lang, 2005); Bernd Martin, *Deutschland und Japan in Zweiten Weltkrieg: Von Angriff auf Pearl Harbor bis zur Deutschen Kapitulation* (Gottingen: Musterschmidt Verlag, 1969); ibid, *Japan and Germany in the Modern World* (New York: Oxford University Press, 1995); Johanna Meskill, *Hitler and Japan: The Hollow Alliance* (New York: Atherton Press, 1966); James Morley, *Deterrent Diplomacy: Japan, Germany and the USSR, 1935-1940* (New York: Columbia University Press, 1976); Ian Nish, *Japan's Foreign Policy, 1868-1945* (London: Routledge, 1977); Ernest Presseissen, *Germany and Japan: A Study in Totalitarian Diplomacy, 1933-1941* (The Hague: Nijhoff, 1958); Paul Schroder, *The Axis Alliance and Japanese-American Relations* (Ithaca, NY: Cornell University Press, 1958); and Paul Wippich, ed., *Japan-German Relations, 1895-1945* (London: Routledge, 2006).

2   See David Goodman and Masanori Miyazawa, *Jews in the Japanese Mind* (Lanham, MD: Lexington Books, 1995).

3   For quotes on Jewish influence in the United States and the Jews' supposed aim of destroying America, see Ben-Ami Shillony, "Hatred of Jews without Jews: Japan's Anti-Semitic Ideology during World War II," *Zion* 46 (1981): 125-145.

4   On Alfred Rosenberg see: Robert Cecil, *The Myth of the Master Race: Alfred Rosenberg and the Nazi Ideology* (New York: Dodd & Mead, 1972); Albert Chandler, *Rosenberg's Nazi Myth* (New York: Greenwood Press, 1945); Fritz Nova, *Alfred Rosenberg: Nazi Theorist of the Holocaust* (New York: Buccaneer Books, 1986); and James Whisher, *The Philisophy of Alfred Rosenberg* (New York: Noontide Press, 1996).

5   For books on German-Japanese relations, see reference 34.

6   See Marvin Tokayer and Mary Swartz, *The Fugu Plan: The Untold Story of the Japanese and the Jews during World War II* (New York: Paddington Press, 1979).

7   Some Japanese writers thought that Hitler was a passing fad. See John Fox, "Japanese Reactions to Nazi Germany's Racial Legislation," *The Wiener Library Bulletin* 23 (1969); H. Furuya, "Nazi Racism Toward the Japanese: Ideology vs.

Realpolitik," *Nachrichten der Gesselschaft for Natrur und Volkerkunde Osasiens* 157 (1995): 17-75.

Chapter 5: Japanese Experts on Jews, Judaism, and Zionism

1   On Yasue and Inuzuka see Yoshia Toshio, "Yudaijin to Tokumukikancho: Yudaya Minzoku wo sukutta Yasue Taisa no shogai (The Jews and the Office of Social Military Forces: The Career of Colonel Yasue, Who Saved the Jewish People)," *Bungei Shinju* 41 (1963): 156-164; and Inuzuka Kiyoku, *Yudaya Mondai to Nihon no Kosaku: Kaigun Inuzuka Kikan no Kiroku* (The Jewish Question and Japan's Strategy: The Records of the Navy and Inuzuka) (Tokyo: Nihon Kogyo Shinbunsha, 1982).
2   On the Jewish community in Harbin, see B. Bressler, "Harbin's Jewish Community 1898-1958, Politics, Prosperity and Adversity," in Jonathan Goldstein, ed., *The Jews of China*, 200-215; Herman Dicker, *Wanderers and Settlers in the Far East*; Joshua Fogel, "The Japanese and the Jews in Harbin 1898-1930," in Robert Bickers, et al, eds., *New Frontiers: Imperialists, New Communities in East Asia, 1892-1953* (Manchester: University of Manchester Press, 2000), 88-108; Hayasaka Takashi, "Shikan no ketsudan: Minshu to Attsu no shogun Huguchi Kiichiro," *Bungei Shinju* (2010); Teddy Kaufman, *The Jews of Harbin Live On in My Heart* (Tel Aviv: Association of Former Jewish Residents of China, 2004);. Pan Guang, *Jews in China* (Beijing: China International Press, 2001); Z. Shickman-Bowman, "The Construction of the Chinese Eastern Railway and the Origins of the Harbin Jewish Community, 1898-1931," in Goldstein, *The Jews of China*; Irene Eber, *Way of the Land: The Jewish Communities of Harbin, Tianjin, and Shanghai, An Introduction* (Tel Aviv: Beit Hatfutsot, 1986); R. Malek, ed., *From Kaifeng to Shanghai: Jews in China* (Sankt Augustin: Monumenta Serica Monograph Series XLVI, 2000); Xu Xin, "Jewish Diaspora in China," *Bulletin of the Association of Former Jewish Residents of China* 45 (2012): 32-41; and Wei Qu and Shuxiao Li, eds., *The Jews of Harbin* (Harbin: Social Sciences Documentation Publishing House, 2003).
3   See: Maruyama Naoki, "Japan's Response to the Zionist Movement in the 1920's," *Bulletin of the Graduate School of International Relations* 2 (1984); Shillony, *The Successful Outsiders, 151-163*; Goodman and Miyazawa, *Jews in the Japanese Mind*.
4   Maruyama, "Japan's Response to the Zionist Movement."
5   On the Kadoorie family, see Mavis Meyer, "The Sephardi Jewish Community of Shanghai and the Question of Identity," in Roman Malek, ed., *Jews in China*, 345-373 and Mavis Meyer, *From the Rivers of Babylon to the Whangpoo:*

A Century of Sephardi Life in Shanghai (Lanham MD: University Press of America, 2003).
6 Israel Cohen, *The Journal of a Jewish Traveler* (London: Bodley Head, 1925).
7 Maruyama.
8 On Japan-Arab ties, see Frank Shulman, "The Nature of Japanese Activity in the Middle East: Japanese Middle Eastern Economic and Political Relations Since World War II," unpublished MA thesis, Ann Arbor, University of Michigan Center for Japanese Studies, 1968.

Chapter 6: Japan and the Jews of Manchuria Beginning in 1931
1 On Japan and the Jews of Manchuria see: Avraham Altman, "Controlling the Jews, Manchukuo Style," in R. Malek, ed., *From Kaifeng to Shanghai*, 279-317; Jonathan Goldstein, *The Jews of China*; Gerald Keraney, "Jews Under Japanese Domination, 1939-1945," *Shofar* 21 (1993): 54-59; Y. Matsusaka, *The Making of Modern Machuria, 1904-1932* (Cambridge: Harvard University Press, 2001). Ogata Sadako, *Defiance in Manchuria: The Making of Japanese Foreign Policy, 1931-1932* (Berkeley: University of California Press, 1964); Pamela Rotner Sakamoto, *Japanese Diplomats and Jewish Refugees: A World War II Dilemma* (New York: Praeger, 1998); Yamamuro Shiníchi, *Manchuria under Japanese Domination* (Philadelphia: University of Pennsylvania Press, 2006); L. Young, *Japan's Total Empire: Manchuria and the Culture of Wartime Imperialism* (Berkeley: University of California Press, 1998).
2 On Japan's New Order, see Francis C. Jones, *Japan's New Order in East Asia: Its Rise and Fall, 1937-1945* (London: Oxford University Press, 1954).
3 On the Kaspe Affair, see D. Ben-Canaan, *The Kaspe File: A Case Study of Harbin as an Intersection of Cultural and Ethnical Communities in Conflict* (Harbin: Heilongjang People's Publishing House, 2009) and David Bergamini, *Japan's Imperial Conspiracy* (London: Panther Books, 1971), 562-566.
4 Altman, *Controlling the Jews, Manchukuo Style*.
5 Kaufman, Teddy, *The Jews of Harbin*.
6 On the Far East Congress see Altman, *Controlling the Jews, Manchukuo Style*, and Maruyama Naoki, "Facing a Dilemma: Japan's Jewish Policy in the late 1930's," in Guy Podoler, ed., *War and Militarism in Modern Japan: Issues of History and Identity* (Folkestone: Global Oriental, 2009), 22-38.
7 On the Birobijan Plan see Tokayer, *The Fugu Plan*.
8 Arita's response in the Diet quoted in Goodman and Masanori, *The Jews in the Japanese Mind*.
9 Kaufman, *The Jews of Harbin*.
10 Xu Xin, "Jewish Diasporas in China."

Chapter 7: Passports, Entry Visas, and Transit Visas: Japan's policy toward Jewish Refugees (1935-1941)
1　Pamela Sakamoto, *Japanese Diplomats and Jewish Refugees*.
2　Maruyama Naoki, "Facing a Dilemma."
3　On the Five Ministers Conference see Maruyama.
4　Shillony, *The Successful Outsiders*, and Goodman and Miyazawa, *Jews in the Japanese Mind*.

Chapter 8: The Jews of Shanghai under Japanese Rule
1　There is an extensive literature on the Shanghai Jewish community. It includes: Avraham Altman and Irene Eber, "Flight to Shanghai, 1938-1940: The Larger Setting," *Yad Vashem Studies* 28 (2000): 42-71; Bernice Archer, *The Internment of Western Civilians under the Japanese 1941-1945: A Patchwork of Internment* (Hong Kong: Hong Kong University Press, 2008); Bei Gao, *Shanghai Sanctuary: Chinese and Japanese Policy Towards European Jewish Refugees in World War II* (New York: Oxford University Press, 2013); Irene Eber, *Chinese and Jews: Encounters between Cultures* (Middlesex, Mitchell Valentine, 2008); Irene Eber, *Voices from Shanghai: Jewish Exile in Wartime China* (Chicago: Chicago University Press, 2008); Irene Eber, *Wartime Shanghai and the Jewish Refugees from Central Europe: Survival, Existence and Identity in a Multi-Ethnic City* (Berlin. De Gruyter, 2012); Jacob Edelstein, "The Mir Yeshiva in Shanghai During the Second World War," *Kivunim* 19 (1983): 127-134; A. Freyesen, *Shanghai und fie Politik des Dritten Reiches* (Wurzburg: Koningshausen and Neumann, 2000); Violet Gilboa, *China and the Jews* (Cambridge, MA: Harvard University Press, 1993); Jonathan Goldstein, *The Jews of China*; Jonathan Goldstein, "Shanghai as a Mosaic and Microcosm of Eurasian Jewish Identities, 1850-1859," *Religions and Christianity in Today's China* 3 (2013): 18-45; Ernst Heppner, *Shanghai Refugee: A Memoir of the World War II Jewish Ghetto* (Lincoln: University of Nebraska Press, 1993); His-Huey Liang, *The Sino-German Connection* (Assen: Van Gorcum, 1978); Steve Hochstadt, *Exodus to Shanghai: Stories of Escape from the Third Reich* (New York: Palgrave MacMillan, 2012); William Kirby, *Germany and Republican China* (Stanford: Stanford University Press, 1984); David Kranzler, *Japanese, Nazis and Jews: The Jewish Refugees in Shanghai, 1938-1945* (New York: Yeshiva University Press, 1976); Rena Krasno, *Strangers Always: A Jewish Family in Wartime Shanghai* (Berkeley: Pacific View Press, 1992); Rena Krasno, *The Last Glorious Summer 1939: Shanghai-Japan* (Hong Kong: Old China Press, 2001); Yecheskel Leitner, *Operation Torah Rescue: The Escape of the Mirrer Yeshiva from Wartorn Poland to Shanghai in China* (New York: Feldheim, 1987); Leo

Baeck Institute, *Destination Shanghai: Refugees or Stateless Jews* (New York: Leo Baeck Institute, 1996); Itamar Livni, "The German Jewish Immigrant Press in Shanghai," in Raoul Findeisen, et al, eds., *At Home in Many Worlds* (Wiesbaden: Harrasowitz Verlag, 2009), 273-283; Anna Lincoln, *Escape to China, 1939-1948* (New York: Maryland Books, 1982); Isabella Martinet, *Les Juifs de Shanghai:xix-xx siecles* (Paris: Roillat, 2008); Maruyama Naoki, "The Shanghai Zionist Association and the International Politics of the Far East until 1936," in Goldstein, *The Jews of China*; Maruyama Naoki, *Taiheiyo senso to Shanhai no Yudaya nanmin* (The Pacific War and the Jewish Refugees in Shangahi) (Tokyo: Hosei Daigaku, 2005); Maisie Meyer, *From the Rivers of Babylon*; Rana Mitter, *na's War with Japan* (London: Allen Lane, 2013); Rhoads Murphey, *Shanghai: Key to Modern China* (Cambridge MA: Harvard University Press, 1953); Pan Guang, *The Jews of Shanghai* (Shanghai: The Shanghai Pictorial Publishing House, 1995); Pan Guang, *The Jews of China* (Shanghai: China International Press, 2001); Marcia Ristaino, *Port of Last Resort: The Diaspora Communities of Shanghai* (Stanford: Stanford University Press, 2001); James Ross, *Escape to Shanghai: A Jewish Community in China* (New York: The Free Press, 1994); Evelyn Pike Rubin, *Ghetto Shanghai* (New York: Shengold, 1993); Pamela Sakamoto, *Japanese Diplomats and Jewish Refugees*; Maho Sekine, *Nihon Senryoku no Shanhai Yudayajin Getto* (The Shanghai Ghetto under the Japanese Occupation) (Kyoto: Showado, 2010); Marvin Tokayerand Mary Swartz, *The Fugu Plan*; Cheng Ziaohong, Noriko Sawadi, and Judy Meschel, *TheLast Refuge: The Story of the Jewish Refugees in Shanghai* (Teaneck, NJ: Ergo Media, 2004); Ephraim Zuroff, "The Issue of Entry Permits to Shanghai in 1941: The Problem of Preference in Saving Lives," *Yad Vashem Studies* 13 (1973): 237-256; And Ephraim Zuroff, *The Response of Orthodox Jewry in the United States to the Holocaust* (New York: Ktav, 2000).

2   On Yozef Meisinger, see Heinz Maul, *Why Has Japan Not Persecuted the Jews* (Tokyo, Fuyo Shobo Shuppan, 2004).
3   See Yosef Tekoah, "Memoirs," in Jonathan Goldstein, ed., *The Jews of China*.
4   On antisemitism in China, see Meron Medzini, "China, the Holocaust, and the Birth of Israel," *Israel Journal of Foreign Affairs* 7 (2013): 135-145.
5   Donald McKale, "The Nazi Party in the Far East," *The Journal of Contemporary History* 12 (1997): 291-311. See also Donald McKale, *The Swastika Outside Germany* (Kent: Kent State University Press, 1997).

Chapter 9: Jews in the Japanese-Occupied Territories during the War Years

1   For the March 1942 decisions, see Kranzler, *Japanese, Nazis and Jews.*

2   On the Singapore Jewish community in war and peace, see: Nathan Aluph, *Singapore Jewry on the Threshold of Paradise* (Tel Aviv: Golan, 1996); Joan Bieder and Eileen Lau, *The Jews of Singapore* (Singapore: Suntree Media, 2007); Justin and Robin Corfield, eds. *Encycloaedia of Singapore* (Singapore: Scarecrow Press, 2006); Peter Duus and R. Myers, *The Japanese Wartime Empire* (Princeton: Princeton University Press, 1996); Nathan Eze, *The History of the Jews of Singapore, 1830-1945* (Singapore: Herbilu, 1986); Reuven Kashani, *Jewish Communities in the Far East* (Jerusalem: 1982); R. Myers and M. Peattie, eds., *The Japanese Colonial Empire, 1895-1945* (Princeton: Princeton University Press, 1984); Gabriel Weiman and Baruch Navo, *The Singapore Riddle* (Jerusalem: Tsivonim, 2001); and Moshe Yegar, "History of the Jewish Community of Singapore," *Gesher* 1 (1974): 50-65.

3   On the Jews of Burma: see Ida Cowan, *The Jews in Remote Parts of the World* (Englewood Cliffs, NJ: Prentice Hall, 1971); Ruth Fredman-Cernea, *Almost Englishmen: Baghdadi Jews in British Burma* (Lanham, MD: Lexington Books, 2000); Jonathan Goldstein, "Memory, Place and Displacement in the Formation of Jewish Identity in Rangoon and Surabaya," in David Cesarani, Tony Kushner, and Milton Shain, eds., *Zakor v'Makor: Place and Displacement in Jewish History and Memory* (London, Valentine Mitchell, 2009), 88-98; Mavis Hyman, *The Jews of the Raj* (London: Hyman Publishers, 1997); and Gerald Keraney, "Jews Under Japanese Domination, 1939-1945," *Shofar* (1993): 54-59.

4   For the fate of the Jews in the Philippines during the war, see: Frank Ephraim, *Escape to Manila: From Nazi Tyranny to Japanese Terror* (Urbana: University of Illinois Press, 2003); Lewis Gleeck, *History of the Jewish Community in Manila*, n.d.; Jonathan Goldstein, "1942: A Year of Survival for Philippine Jews at the Edge of the Diaspora," *Australian Journal of Jewish Studies* (2014): 66-84; Jonathan Goldstein, "Secular, Jewish, Filipino and Zionistic: From Marranos to 'Bagel Boys,'" in Ber Boris Kotlerman, ed., *Mizrekh: Jewish Studies in the Far East Vol. 2* (Frankfurt: Peter Lang, 2010); Jonathan Goldstein, "Shaping Zionist Identity: The Jews of Manila as a Case Study," *Israel Affairs* 15 (2009): 296-304; and Dean Kotlowsky, "Breaching the Paper Walls: Paul McNutt and Jewish Refugees to the Philippines, 1938-1939," *Diplomatic History* 23 (2009): 865-896.

5   On the fate of the Jews in Indonesia, see: Henry Benda, J. Irikura, and K. Kishi, *Japanese Military Administration in Indonesia: Selected Documents* (New Haven: Yale University Press, 1965); Duus, Myers, and Peattie, eds., *The Japanese Wartime Empire*; J. Hadler, "Translations of Anti-Semitism: Jews, the Chinese and Violence in Colonial and Post Colonial Indonesia," *Indonesia and Malay World* 32 (2004):: 291-313; Jonathan Goldstein, "Memory, Place

and Displacement in the Formation of Jewish Identity in Rangoon and Surabaya," in David Cesarani, Tony Kushner, and Milton Shain, eds., *Zakor v'Makor*, 88-98; L. de Jong, *The Collpase of a Colonial Society: The Dutch in Indonesia During the Second World War* (Leiden, KITLV Press, 2002); and Rotem Kowner, Rotem, "An Obscure History: The Prewar History of the Jews in Indonesia," in *Indonesia Today* 104 (2011). The key articles on the fate of Indonesia's Jews under the Japanese are Rotem Kowner, "The Japanese Internment of Jews in Wartime Indonesia and its Causes," *Indonesia and the Malay World* 38 (2010): 349-371 and Rotem Kowner, "End of a Colonial Community: Indonesian Jewry in World War II," *Zmanin* 127 (2014): 60-71. See also: Ayelet Klemperer-Cooperman, "Only God will Protect Me: Jews in Japanese Concentration Camps in Indonesia," *Zmanim* 127 (2014): 72-79; Chaim Nussbaum, *Chaplain of the River Kwai: Story of a Prisoner of War* (New York: Shapolsky, 1988); J. Presser, *The Destruction of Dutch Jews* (New York: Dutton, 1968); and Merle Ricklefs, *A History of Modern Indonesia since c. 1200* (Stanford: Stanford University Press, 2008).

6   On the Hong Kong community, see Stanley Jackson, *The Sassoons*. See also: Tony Banham, *We Shall Suffer There: Hong Kong's Defenders Imprisoned, 1942-1945* (Hong Kong: Hong Kong University Press, 2009); Dennis Leventhal, *The Jewish Community of Hong Kong: An Introdcution* (Hong Kong: Jewish Historical Society of Hong Kong, rev. ed. 1988); and Dennis and Mary Leventhal, eds., *Faces of the Jewish Experience in China* (Hong Kong, Hong Kong Jewish Chronicle, 1990).

7   For the history of the Jews in French Indo-China, see: Pierre Birnbaum, *The Jews of the Republic: A Political History of the State of the Jews in France from Gambetta to Vichy* (Stanford: Stanford University Press, 1996); *The Universal Jewish Encyclopaedia* (New York: The Universal Jewish Encyclopedia Inc., 1942); and Eric Jennings, *Vichy in the Tropics: Petain's National Revolution in Madagascar, Guadeloupe and Indo-China, 1940-1944* (Stanford: Stanford University Press, 2004).

8   On the Jews of Penang, see Eliyahu Birnbaum, *Jews of the World* (Tel Aviv: Makor Rishon, 2010), 222-226.

9   The main source for the Thailand Jewish community is Ruth Gerson and Stephen Mallinger, *Jews of Thaland* (Bangkok: River Books, 2011). See also Yehuda Assia, *Bridges in My Life* (Tel Aviv: Maariv, 2005).

10 On the absorption of the Jews from South East Asia into the native Jewish communities of India, see Joan G. Roland, *The Jewish Communities of India* (New Brunswick, NJ: Transaction Publishers, 1989) and Esmond David Ezra, *Turning Back the Pages: A Chronicle of Calcutta Jewry* (London: 1986).

Chapter 10: A Japanese Righteous Gentile: The Sugihara Case

1. There exists a vast literature on Sugihara. Some of the more important works are: Ann Akabori Hoshinko, *The Gift: A Biographical Account of Japanese Diplomat Sugihara* (Sacramento: Edu-Comm Plus, 2005); Akira Kitade, "How the Sugihara Survivors reached Japan," in *Kokusai Kankou Jouhon* (International Tourism Center of Japan) (Tokyo: June 2011); J.W.M. Chapman, "The Polish Connection: Japan, Poland and the Axis Alliance," in Gordon Daniels and Peter Lowe, eds., *Proceedings of the British Association for Japanese Studies* (Sheffield: University of Sheffield Center for Japanese Studies, 1977), 57-78; EvaFogelman, *Conscience and Courage: Rescuers of Jews During the Holocaaust* (New York: 1994); Kubata Taro, "Sugihara Chiune, dei Juden retter aus Japan," *Zeitschrift fur Geschischts Wissenschaft* 55 (2007); 645-660; Yechezkel Leitner, *Operation Orah Rescue*; and Hillel Levine, *In Search of Sugihara: The Elusive Japanese Diplomat Who Risked his Life to Rescue 10,000 Jews from the Holocaust* (New York: The Free Press, 1996); Eva Palasz-Rutkowska, "Polish-Japanese Secret Cooperation During World War II: Sugihara Chiune and Polish Intelligence," *Japan Forum* 2 (1995); Mizuuchi Ryuta, "Sugihara's Visas: Unknown Facts and Hidden Memories," presented in Jerusalem, The Hebrew University, April 13, 1987; Sugihara Yukiko, *Rokusen min no Inochi no visa* (Visas for 6000 Lives: One Japanese Diplomat Aided the Jews) (Tokyo: Asahi Sonorama, 1990, and South San Francisco: Edu-Comm Plus, 1995); Sugihara Seishiro, *Chiune Sugihara and Japan's Foreign Ministry* (Lanham, MD: University Press of America, 2001); Tainuchi Yutaka, *The Miracle Visas* (Jerusalem: Geffen, 2001); Zorach Warhaftig, *Refugees and Survivors: Rescue Efforts During the Holocaust* (Jerusalem: Yad Vashem, 1988); *Rescue Attempts During the Holocaust* (Jerusalem: Yad Vashem, 1977); and Ephraim Zuroff, "The Rescue of Polish Yeshiva Students Via the Far East During the Holocaust," in *From Generation to Generation*, 49-76.

Chapter 11: The Japanese Policy toward the Jews in Japan's Home Islands

1. On Jewish musicians in Tokyo during the war, see Luciana Galliano, "Manfred Gurlitt and the Japanese Operatic Scene 1939-1972," *Japan Review* 18 (2006): 215-248.
2. Shillony, *The Successful Outsiders*, 178-189.
3. On popular antisemitism in Japan after the war, see: Jennifer Golub, "The Japanese Attitude Towards Jews," American Jewish Committee, Los Angeles, 1992; David Goodman, and Masanori Miyazawa, *Jews in the Japanese Mind*;David Goodman, "Anti-Semitism in Japan: History and Current

Implications," in Frank Dikoter, ed., *The Construction of Racial Identities in China and Japan* (London, 1977); David Goodman, "The Protocols of the Elders of Zion: Aum and Anti-Semitism in Japan," Jerusalem, Vidal Sassoon Center for the Study of Anti-Semitism, no. 2 (2005); Ikeda Afikumi, "Japan's Perception of Jews and Israel," *Forum* 59 (1986): 73-84; Rotem Kowner, "On Ignorance, Respect and Suspicion: Current Japanese Attitude towards Jews," Jerusalem, Vidal Sassoon Center for the Study of anti-Semitism, 1997; Rotem Kowner, "Tokyo Recognizes Auschwitz: The Rise and Fall of Holocaust Denial in Japan 1989-1999," *Journal of Genocide Studies* 3 (2001): 257-272; Rotem Kowner, "On Symbolic Anti-Semitism: Motives for the Success of the Protocols in Japan and its Consequences," Posen Papers in Contemporary anti-Semitism, Jerusalem; Stanley Rosenman, "Japanese Anti-Semitism: Conjuring up Conspiratorial Jews in a Land without Jews," *The Journal of Psychology* 25 (1997): 2-32; Zvi Werblowsky, "The Japanese and the Jews," *Jewish Journal of Sociology* 20 (1978): 75-81; and Ben-Ami Shillony, "Japanese Views of Jews and Judaism" (Jerusalem, Harriman Center for Contemporary Judaism, 1993).

Chapter 12: "The Jewish Question" in Japanese-German relations, 1936-1945

1   On the Jewish issue in Japan-German relations, see: Gerhard Krebs, "The Jewish Problem in Japanese-German Relations, 1933-1945," in Bruce E. Reynolds, ed., *Japan in the Fascist Era* (New York: Palgrave MacMillan, 2004), 107-132; and Francoise Kreissler, "Japan's Judenpolitik, 1931-1945," in Gerhard Krebs, and Bernd Martin, eds., *Formierung und Fall der Achse berlin-Tokyo* (Munich: Ludicum, 1984), 187-210.

Chapter 13: The Japanese, the Holocaust of European Jewry, and Israel

1   See: Ian Buruma, *The Wages of Guilt: Memories of War in Germany and Japan* (New York: Farrar, Strauss, and Giroux, 1994); Goodman and Miyazawa, *Jews in the Japanese Mind*; Thomas R. Havens, *Valley of Darkness: The Japanese People and World War II* (New York: Norton, 1978); Rotem Kowner, "Tokyo Recognizes Auschwitz".; Tetsu Kohno, "The Jewsish Question in Japan," *Jewish Journal, of Sociology* 29 (1987): 37-54; TetsuKohno, "Debates on the Jewish Question in Japan," *Bulletin of the Faculty of Liberal Arts* 46 (1983), 1-33; C. Rittner, ed., *Anne Frank in the World: Essays and Reflections* (Armonk, NY: Sharpe, 1998); Philip Seaton, *Japan's Contested War Memoirs* (London: Routledge, 2007); Shillony, *The Successful Outsiders*; Shillony, "Auschwitz and

Hiroshima: What Can the Jews and Japanese Do for World Peace," *Bulletin of the International House* 27 (2007): 1-18; Shillony, "The Flourishing Demon: Japan in the Role of the Jews," in Robert Wistrich, ed., *Demonizing the Other: Anti-Semitism, Racism and Xenophobia* (Amsterdam: Harwood Academic, 1999); and Toyama Kiyhiko, *War and Responsdibility in Japan* (London, 2008).

2   Shulman.

3   On Holocaust denial in Japan, see Kowner, "Japan Recognizes Auschwitz," and Yashiko Nozaki, *War Memory, Nationalism and Education in Postwar Japan* (London, 2008).

4   On Israel-Japan relations, see the following works in Hebrew: Elyashiv Ben-Horin, "Basic Outline of Israel's Position in Asia," *New Middle East* 4 (1957): 245-252; Yosef Haddas, "The Peace Process: The Multilateral Track," in Moshe Yegar, et al, eds., *The Foreign Ministy: The First Fifty Years* (Jerusalem: Keter, 2002), 211-226; Moshe Yegar, *The Long Journey to Asia:A Chapter in the History of Israeli Diplomacy* (Haifa: Haifa University Press, 2004); Yaacov Cohen, "Israel-Japan: 50 Years of Relationships, Past and Future," in Moshe Yegar, et al, eds., *The Foreign Ministry: The First Fifty Years*, 550-564; Meron Medzini, "Asia in Israel's Foreign Policy," *State and Government* 1 (1971): 110-121; Ben-Ami Shillony, "Japan and Israel: Continuing and Developing Relations," in Benjamin Neuberger, ed., *Selected Issues in Israel's Foreign Relations* (Tel Aviv: Open University, 1992), 441-452; Ben-Ami Shillony, "Japan and Israel: The Relationship that Withstood Pressure," *Middle East Review* 18 (1985); Moshe Sharett, *A Voyage in Asia* (Tel Aviv: Davar, 1957), and Raquel Shaoul, "Japan and Israel: An Evaluation of Relationship Building in the Context of Japan's Middle East Policy," in Ephraim Karsh, ed., *Israel: The First Hundred Years* (London: Cass, 2004).

5   Jonathan Goldstein, "Japan and Israel: From Erratic Contacts to Recognition to Boycott to Normalization," in Colin Schindler, ed., *Israel and the World Powers* (London: IB Tauris, 2013), 234-283.

Index

A
Adler, Cyrus, 7
Akira, Kitade, 121
Akira, Yamaji, 65
Akirev family, 107
Alaungpaya, King, 94
Allon, Yigal, 2
Almeida, Dr. Luis, 1
American Columbia Records, 131
American immigration law of 1924, 25
American-Jewish capitalists, 6–8
American Jewish Congress, 53, 58
American Jews, 33, 36, 46, 54, 57–59, 67, 69, 74–75, 80, 96, 104–105, 129, 148
American Joint Distribution Committee, 60, 94, 96, 121, 123
American occupation of Japan, 157–162
American Union of Orthodox Rabbis, 127
Anglo-Japanese Alliance in 1902, 44
Anti-Comintern Pact of 1936, 48, 53, 55, 67, 139
antisemitic publications, 24, 134. *see also* *The Protocols of the Elders of Zion*
antisemitism, 20–21, 68, 81–83, 103, 105–106. *see also* Japanese antisemitism; Russian antisemitism
Arab- Israel War, 168
Arab world, Japan's attitude, 156–157
Arafat, Yasser, 173
Arens, Moshe, 173
Asahi Shimbun, 134
Ashkenazi, Rabbi Meir, 72
Ashkenazi community, 99
Aso, Taro, 175
Axis Alliance, 88, 169, ix
Axis Pact of 1940, 59, 113, 124, 141–143, 149

B
Babel, Isaac, 40
Bachrach, Emil, 95
Baghdadi Jews, 94, 107
Balfour Declaration, 43–44, 109, 167

Bangkok Jews, 109–110
Barak, Ehud, 175
Baruch family, 107
Bataan Death March, 81
Begin, Menachem, 119
Beijing Jewish community, 62–63
Beitar Youth Movement, 52, 57
B'nai B'rith Anti-Defamation League, 164, 170
Bolshevik Revolution of 1917, 4, 9, 15, 18, 33, 40, 49, 72, 95
Borodin-Gruzenberg, Michail, 23
bubble economy, 173
Buddhism, 24
Bulgarian Jews, ix
Burmese Jews, 93–95
Bush, George W., 162

C
Camp Changi, 111
Camp Kanchanburi, 111
Caribbean Island of Curacao, ix
Catholicism, 105
Chang Tso Lin, 50
Checkbook Diplomacy, 174
Chiang Kai-Shek, 23, 29, 48, 82, 135
Chicherin, Grigori, 20
Chinese nationalism, 23, 30
    Chiune, Sugihara, 21, 70, 75, ix
    actions in saving Jews, 117–128
Christianity in Japan, 11–12, 14
Chuo Koron, 21
A Citizen's Guide to Assured Victory, 133
Clinton, Bill, 174
Cohen, Dr. Abraham, 76, 78
Columbus, Christopher, 41
comfort women, 161, 165
Committee for International Refugees (Nansen passports), 96
Committee for the Assistance of Jewish refugees in Shanghai, 74
Converso Portuguese Jew, 108

Cremieux Decree of 1870, 105
Czech Jews, 66, 74
Czech Legion, 16

D
Daoud, Pasha, 107
David, Sigmund, 3
David family, 107
David Sassoon and Sons Co., 2
Decoux, Jean, 105–106
de Decker, L.P.J, 123
Der Sturmer, 133
Deshima, 1
The Diary of Anne Frank, 162
Disputed Points over Auschwitz, 165
Dower, John, 133
Dutch East Indies Company, 1
Dutch Learning School (*Rangakusha*), 2

E
Ecole francaise d'Éxtreme Orient, 104
Egypt, 47
Ehrenburg, Ilie, 40
Eichmann, Adolph, 73, 146, 162
Eichmann trial, 169
Eidelberg, Joseph, 14
Einstein, Albert, 47
Eizenstein, Sergei, 40
Elman, Mischa, 131
European Jewry, ix
Ezra, Nissim Benjamin, 4, 46
Ezra family, 2

F
Far Eastern Jewish National Congress, 55–60
Fleisher, Benjamin, 5
Flinters family, 107
Ford, Henry, 22
Fourisson, Robert, 164
French Indo-China Jews, 104–107
"friendly enemy" territory, 87
Fugu Plan, 52–55
The Fugu Plan, 53
Fukuyama Holocaust Education Center, 166
Fumimaro, Konoe, 19, 69

G
Gabirol, Solomon, 94
Gemeinde, Judische, 76
General Structure for the Reconstruction of Japan (Kitta Ikki), 24

German-Japanese relations, 138–148
German Weimar Constitution, 138
Giichi, Tanaka, 16, 44
Ginzburg & Co., 3
Ginzburg family, 3–4
Globacki, Pius, 123
Goering, Herman, 100
Goldberg, Szimon, 131
Goodman, David, 11
Gorlitt, Manfred, 131
Grand family, 107
Great Depression, 33, 51, 54, 139
Greater East Asia Co-Prosperity Sphere, 74, 85, 89
The Great in the Small: The Coming of Anti-Christ and the Rule of Satan on Earth (Sergei Nilus), 18
Gulf War, 161–162
Guri, Chaim, 2

H
Hachiro, Arita, 60, 69, 124, 135
Hajime, Sugiyama, 88
Hamadera prisoner-of-war camp, 42
Harbin Jewish community, 8–9, 22, 25, 40, 42, 45–50, 52, 54–55, 57–58, 60–62, 81, 118
Hardoon, Aaron, 72
Hardoon family, 2, 72
Hebrew Immigrant Aid Association (HIAS), 9
He Feng Shan, 73
Heifetz, Yasha, 131
Herzog, Chaim, 173
Hideki, Tojo, 56
Himmler, Heinrich, 145
Hirobumi, Ito, Prince, 10
Hirohito, Emperor, 46, 166
Hiroshi, Oshima, 118, 136
Hitler, Adolph, 31, 36–37, 73, 82, 96, 164
  ideas about the Jews, 31–32
  racial doctrines, 31
Hochman, Joseph, 109
Holocaust, Japanese understanding of, 149–156, 162–163
  denial, 163–166, 176
Hongkew ghetto, 78–82
Hong Kong-Shanghai Banking Corporation, 102
Hong Kong's Jewish community, 102–104
Hong Kong Volunteer Defence Corps, 103
Horvat, Piotr, 16

Huberman, Bronislav, 131
Hull, Cordell, 67, 145
Hussein, Saddam, 161
Husseini, Haj Amin el, 146

I
Ichiro, Tokutomi, 133
Ikki, Kitta, 24
Imber, Naftali Herz, 8
Inazo, Nitobe, 42
India, Jewish refugees in, 111–112
Indonesian Jews, 98–102
Indonesia's declaration of independence, 101
Institute of Islamic Areas, 66
The International Jew (Henry Ford), 22
The International Secret Force, 68
Irving, David, 164
Islamic Area, 66
Israel-Egypt peace treaty, 161
Israel-Egypt Peace Treaty of 1979, 173
Israel-Jordan peace treaty, 161
Israel Messenger, 46–47
Israel-Palestine Declaration of Principles, 174
Iwakura Mission (1871-1872), 10

J
Jabotinsky, Zeév, 60
Japan, ix
    attitude to the Jews. *see* Japanese antisemitism
    diplomatic relations with Israel, x
    economic and industrial development of, 11
    economic crisis of 1990, 173
    economy, 1920s, 30
    foreign policy, 29
Japan Advertizer-Japan Times, 5
Japan and the Lost Tribes of Israel (Norman McCleod), 13
Japan Biographical Encyclopedia, 6
Japanese-American relations, 172
Japanese-American treaty, 1854, 3
The Japanese and the Ten Lost Tribes of Israel (Joseph Eidelberg), 14
Japanese anti-foreignism, 33
Japanese antisemitism, 10, 12, 21–23, 57, 69–70, 82–83, x–xi
    1941-1945, 133–137
    American immigration law of 1924 and, 25
    anti-cosmopolitanism and, 26
    anti-modern Western culture, 23–25
    in China, 82–83. *see also* Shanghai Jewish community
    domestic developments and, 23–28
    Hitler's influence, 31–32
    ideas from Nazi Germany, 33–34
    "Jewish Question" and, 27, 32–33, 35, 38, 46, 68, 78, 115
    Jews as bearers of Anglo-American self-centered individualism and materialism, 26
Japanese as descendants of the ten lost tribes, 13–15
Japanese Communist Party, 41
Japanese-occupied territory Jewry
    Bangkok community, 108–111
    Burma community, 93–95
    Dutch East Indies (Indonesia) community, 98–102
    "Eight Roofs" policy, 88
    French Indo-China community, 104–107
    general observations, 84–90
    Hong Kong community, 102–104
    Penang community, 107–108
    Philippino community, 95–98
    policy regarding, 112–116
    Singapore community, 90–93
    as "tolerated" or "protected" minority, 89
Japanese racism, 34–38
Japan Express, 5
Japan-Israel relations, 166–168
    central issue in, 169–170
    Israel-Egypt Peace Treaty of 1979, 173–176
    political and economic problems, 168–172
    warming relationship, 175
Japan-Palestine Friendship, 172
Japan's immigration laws (1935-1941)
    Five Ministers Committee, 67–70
    "Jewish and Muslim Affairs Committee," establishment of, 65–67
    "Open Door" policy, 67, 140
    toward American Jews, 67
    toward German Jews, 64–65
Japan-Soviet Union Non-Aggression Pact, 1941, 113
Jewish influence on Japanese, 13

Jewish musicians in Japan, 130–133
Jewish Problem, 23, 37, 133–134, 150, 156
"Jewish Question" in Japan, 27, 32–33, 35, 38, 46, 68, 78, 115
1936-1945, 138–148
Jewish Refugee Committee of Manila, 96
Jewish settlers in Japan, 9. *see also specific communities*
  early Japanese port cities, 2
  German-Jewish refugees, 138–148
  Jewish seamen and merchants, 1
  Nagasaki community, 2–4
  Portuguese Conversos, 1
  during Tokugawa regime, 1–2
  Yokohama community, 4–6
Jewish Studies, 68
Judaism, 2, 6, 11–14, 18, 26–27, 32, 41–42, 54, 82, 118
Judische Gemeinde, 72

K
Kadoorie, Sir Eli, 74, 103
Kadoorie family, 2
Kadourie, Elie, 45
Kaganovich, Lazar, 39
Kalvarisky-Margaliot, Chaim, 46
Kamenev, Lev, 19, 39
Kanji, Ishihara, 51
Kanzo, Uchimura, 42
Karachan, Lev (Leo), 23
Katsutoki, Sakai, 14
Kaufman, Abraham, 52, 58–60
Kaunas, Jewish refugees in, 70, 75, 117–120, 124–126
Keeler, Solomon, 3
Kellog-Briand Treaty, 1928, 29
Kenjiro, Tokutomi, 42
Kiichiro, Higuchi, 22, 35, 39, 60, 140
Kijuro, Shidehara, 29
Kingoro, Hashimoto, 118
Kinoye Tora, 14
Kisch, Frederick, 46
Kissinger, Henry, 172
Kiyoshi, Hiraizumi, 27
Kobe Jewish community, 4, 10–12, 75, 121–122, 132–133, 136
  Ashkenazim families, 10
  Sephardim families, 10
Koki, Hirota, 65
Kokutai, 19
Kolchak, Alexander Vasilyevich, 17

Komichi, Harada, 101
Korekiyo, Takahashi, 7
Koreshige, Inuzuka, 21, 35, 40–41, 53, 66, 75, 101, 127
Kowner, Rotem, xi
Kozo, Okamoto, 171
Kranzler, David, 46
Kreisler, Fritz, 131
Kristallnacht, 65
Kuhn, Bela, 19
Kuomintang, 23
Kwantung Army, 27, 32, 39, 50, 141

L
The Land of Israel, 99
Lassner, Sigmund David, 4
Lassner family, 3
League of Nations, 23, 29–30, 33, 44–45, 47–48, 139
Lenin, 16
Liebknecht, Karl, 19
Lowenthal, Rudolf, 62
Luxemburg, Rosa, 19
Lytton Commission, 32

M
MacArthur, Douglas, 22, 98
Machlis, Lev, 39
Madrid Peace Conference, 1991, 174
Magen Avot (Shield of the Fathers), 90
Mahler, Gustav, 131
Mainichi Shimbun, 134
Malayan Jews, 91
Mamoru, Shigemitsu, 124
Manchukuo, 33, 52, 54
Manchuria, 6, 9, 16, 22–23, 27–28, 32, 37, 39, 42, 45, 47–48, 69, 81, 96, 101, 118, 127–128, 130, 135, 140–142, 144, 152, 155, 165
  occupation of, 32–33, 50–52
Manchuria Faction, 51
Manchurian Jews, 37–39, 41–42, 47–50, 63
  after Japan's occupation, 50–52
  Fugu plan to settle European Jews in Manchukuo, 52–55
  mobilization of, 55–56
  during Pacific War, 60–61
Mann, Thomas, 131
Marco Polo, 164–165
Margolis, Laura, 75
Marks, Alexander, 4

Marshal, David, 91, 93
Marshall, David, 113
Marx, Karl, 19
Masaharu, Homma, 96
Masami, Uno, 173
Masanori, Miazawa, 11
Matsmiah Yeshua
    (Nurturing Redemption), 94
McCleod, Norman, 13
McNuttt, Paul, 96
Medzini, Moshe, 46
Meiji Restoration, 5, 10, 19
Mein Kampf ("My Struggle"), 31, 37, 82
Meisinger, Josef, 76–77
Menasseh family, 107
Menuhin, Yehudi, 131
The Merchant of Venice (Shakespeare), 10–11
Mitsugu, Shibata, 78
Mitsumasa, Yonai, 69
Mitsuo, Murase, 100
Molotov, Vyacheslav, 40
Molotov-Ribbentrop Pact, 119
Mordechai family, 107
Morito, Morishima, 54
Mosse, Albert, 5, 10
Mussolini, Benito, 38
The Myth of the 20th Century, 34, 37

N
Nagakage, Okabe, 135
Nagasaki Jewish community, 2–4
Nanyang Chinese, 86
Napoleon III, 17
Nash Pot, 56
Nathan, Sir Matthew, 102
National Socialist Workers Party, 31
Nazi Germany, 21, 23, 27–28, 33–34, 53, 55, 57, 59, 62, 64, 66–70, 73, 77–79, 88, 90, 99, 109–110, 112–113, 120, 124, 127, 131, 136, 139, 142, 160–161, 166, ix, xi
    Japanese media and, 139
Nazi racism, 34–38
Nazism in Germany, 33–38
Neiman, Hans, 77
Netanyahu, Benjamin, 175
Newman, Frank, Rabbi, 127
Nicholas II, 17
Nilus, Sergei, 18
Nippon-Columbia Records Company, 130
Nobosuke, Kishi, 53

Nobutaka, Shioden, 21, 135
Non-Aggression Pact, 1941, 144
Norihiro, Yasue, 21–22, 35, 40–41, 46, 55–56, 66, 101
Nuremberg Laws, 139
Nussbaum, Chaim, Rabbi, 101, 110

O
Okhrana, 17
Olmert, Ehud, 50, 175
Opium War (1839-1842), 2
Oslo Peace Process, 174

P
Palestinian Jewish community, 167
Pearl Harbor attack, 63, 75, 91, 99, 103, 110, 129, 143
Peel's Commission, 47
Peres, Shimon, 175
Perry, Mathew C., 2
Petain, Philippe, 105
Philippines' immigration laws, 96
Philippine Jews, 95–98
Pinto, Fernando Mendes, 108
Pleve, Viacheslav, 7
Plumer, Lord, 46
Portsmouth Peace Treaty of 1905, 7
Potsdam Ultimatum, 171–172
Pringsheim, Klaus, 131
The Protocols of the Elders of Zion, 17–23, 41, 54, 128, 164, xii

Q
Qingdao Jewish community, 62
Quezon, Manuel, 96

R
Rabin, Yitzhak, 2, 174–175
Radek, Karl, 19
Rama V, 109
Ranke, Leopold, von, 24
Rapallo Friendship Treaty, 1922, 20
rape of Nanjing, 57
Rathenau, Walther, 20
"Rice Riots" of 1919, 18–19
Riess, Ludwig, 6, 24
River Kwai, bridge on, 86, 101, 110
Romer, Tadeusz, 122
Roosevelt, Franklin D., 69
Roosevelt, Theodore, 7
Rosenberg, Alfred, 33, 89, 140

Russian antisemitism, 15–17
Russian-Jewish soldiers, 6–8
Russian Jews, 62, 72, 80, 95, 97, 109, 113, 115–116, 121, 145
Russian Revolution
    1905, 4, 9
    1917, 15, 62, 72, 109, xi
Russo-German pact of 1939, 119
Russo-Japanese War of 1905, 6, 20, 49

S
Saburo, Kurusu, 125
Sakuzo, Yoshino, 21
Sassoon, Sir Victor, 74
Sassoon family, 2
Schiff, Jacob, 7–8, 20
Schoyer, Raphael, 5
Seamy Side of the World Revolution, The, 21
Seishiro, Itagaki, 51, 69
Sekigunha (the Japanese Red Army), 171
Semyonov, Grigori, 17, 21
Sentaro, Kamuyama, 15
Sephardic Jews, 72–73, 78, 96, 109, 111
Shamir, Yitzhak, 175
Shanghai Ashkenazi Relief Association (SACRA), 72, 76
Shanghai Jewish community, 71, 136
    after Pearl Harbor attack, 75–76
    after Shanghai's occupation by Japan, 73–75
    German extermination plans, 76–78
    Hongkew ghetto, creation of, 78–82
Shanghai's occupation by Japan, 1937, 73–75
Shanghai Zionist Association, 4, 43
Sharon, Ariel, 175
Shigeaki, Ikeda, 69
Shigenori, Togo, 124
Shillony, Ben-Ami, 131, 134, xi
Shintoism, 24
Shinto temples, 13
Shiro, Ishiguro, 59, 74
Shukan Kinyobi, 165
Siberia, 17–18, 39, 49, 128
Singapore Jewish community, 90–93
Sino-Japanese war (1937-1945), 48, 67, 96, xii
Sirotta, Leo, 132
Six-Day War, 170–171
slave labor, 86, 101, 110
Sneh, Moshe, 119
Soka Gakkai, 165

Sorge, Richard, 77
Soviet Bolshevism, 23
Spanish-American War of 1898, 95
Stahmer, Heinrich, von, 97
"statute des Juifs," 105
Stimson, Henry, 33
Stimson Doctrine, 54
Sutemi, Chinda, 43
Swartz, Mary, 53
synagogues, 1, 4–5, 10, 13–14, 50, 61–62, 76, 78, 107, 109, 122
    Beit Aharon (The House of Aaron), 72
    Beit Israel (The House of Israel), 4
    Beth El (House of God), 95
    Magen Avot (Shield of the Fathers), 90
    Manila synagogue, 95, 97
    Ohel Leah (Leah's Tent) synagogue, 102
    Ohel Rachel (Rachel's Tent) synagogue, 71
    Ohel Shlomo, 122
Szigeti, Joseph, 131

T
Tadao, Yanaihara, 42
Taisho democracy, 29
Tekoa, Yosef, 80
Tetsuzo, Kotsuji, 122
Thai prisoner-of-war camps, 110
Theodore, 58
Tianjin Jewish community, 61, 76, 81, 116
Tientsin Hebrew Association, 61
Tokayer, Marvin, 53
Tokyo Electric, 131
Tokyo Symphony Orchestra, 131
Tomiichi, Muruyama, 174
Traces of Jews over the Generations, The, 33
Trans-Siberian Railway, 6, 16, 73, 114, 121, 143
treaty of Brest-Litovsk, 16
Treaty of Nanjing, 2
Trotsky, Leon, 19–20, 39
Trumpeldor, Yosef, 6
Tsuyanosuke, Higuchi, 21
Twenty-One Demands, 1915, 15

V
Vichy anti-Jewish laws, 107
Victor Record Company, 131
Volkischer Beobachter, 34

W
Warburg, Felix, 20
Warhaftig, Zerach, 119

War Without Mercy, 133
Weizmann, Chaim, 8, 44
White Nights of Love: Visas for 6,000 Jewish Refugees (Ichiyanagi Toshi), 126
White Russians, 17, 39, 41–42, 49–50, 52, 54–55, 57, 63, 72, 88, 114
Wiedemann, Fritz, 76
Wise, Stephen, Rabbi, 58
Witte, Sergey, 7
Wohlthat, Helmuth, 100
World Jewish Congress, 53, 57, 152, 164
World Zionist Organization, 43, 46, 53, 90

Y
Yaacov family, 107
Yagoda, Genrich, 39
Yamato people of Japan, 35
Yasuya, Uchida, 43–44
Yehezkel, M., 3

Yehuda family, 2
"Yellow" races, 31, 68
Yoffe, Adolph, 23
Yokohama Jewish community, 4–6, 45
Yomiuri Shimbun, 134
Yom Kippur War, 1973, 172
Yoshinori, Shirakawa, 45
Yoshisuke, Oikawa, 52
Yosuke, Matsuoka, 52, 135
Yotaro, Sugimura, 47

Z
Zenichiro, Oyabe, 14
Zimbalist, Efrem, 131
Zinoviev, Grigory, 19, 39
Zionism, 15, 42–45, 47, 49, 156–157, 167
Zionist movement, 42–48
Zwartendijk, Jan, 123
Zykman, Lev, 58–59, 124, 135

www.ingramcontent.com/pod-product-compliance
Lightning Source LLC
Chambersburg PA
CBHW061938220426
43662CB00012B/1950